THE
HOPI WAY

BY

LAURA THOMPSON

AND

ALICE JOSEPH

with a foreword by John Collier,
Commissioner of Indian Affairs

NEW YORK
RUSSELL & RUSSELL · INC
1965

FIRST PUBLISHED IN 1944 BY THE U. S. INDIAN SERVICE

REISSUED, 1965, BY RUSSELL & RUSSELL, INC.

L.C. CATALOG CARD NO: 65-18836

PRINTED IN THE UNITED STATES OF AMERICA

To
the Hopi Indians
who for centuries have known and
cultivated the Peaceful Way

CONTENTS

ILLUSTRATIONS

Walpi pueblo, First Mesa,
looking west from Sichomovi

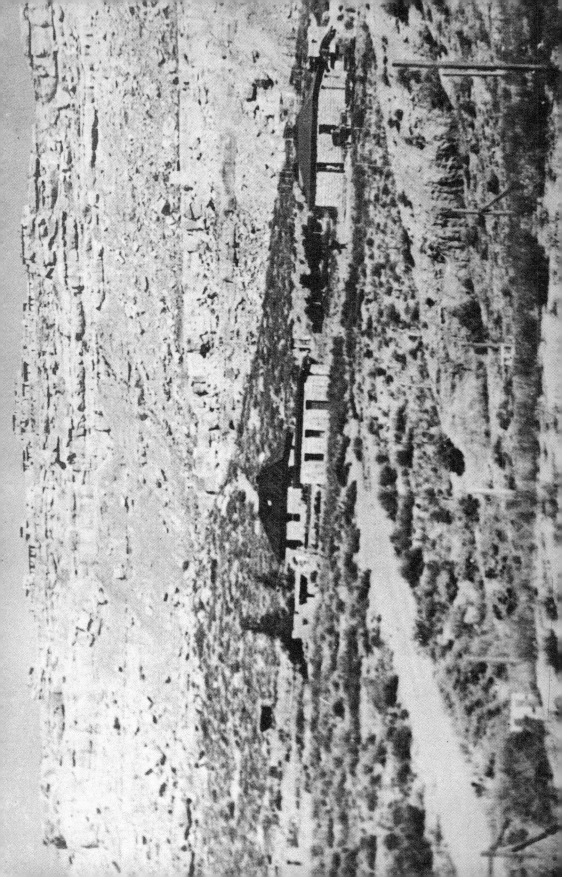

FOREWORD

BY JOHN COLLIER

COMMISSIONER OF INDIAN AFFAIRS

"The Hopi Way" is Volume One of a series to be published during 1944. These volumes result from a three-years' collaboration between the Indian Service and the Committee on Human Development of the University of Chicago; and members of other institutions have made substantial contributions.

I.

I endeavor to state briefly, from the standpoint of an administrator not technically versed in any of the specialized disciplines entering into these volumes, the considerations which influenced Indian Service to seek the research enterprise whose fruits the volumes will partly contain, and which influenced Indian Service to seek, on its own part, to be a creative co-worker in the research.

Every purposive effort, Herbert Spencer used to insist, produces (or may produce) the effect which is intended, but in addition it produces other effects. The "law of the multiplication of effects" necessitates this fact. The effects not sought for, and not taken into account, may be harmonious with the sought-for effect and may reinforce it, or they may divert, overwhelm, obliterate, cancel out or reverse the sought-for effect. The universal working of this "law of the multiplication of effects" is one of the prime reasons why men and societies cling to institutions and to fixed procedures, and resist social change. Institutions of all kinds and at all levels—from languages to stock exchanges, churches and states—have as one of their uses an effect of isolating the sought-for effects of effort—of keeping the sought-for effects within reach, as it were—and of shunting aside (or often, merely pushing outside of the field of awareness) the unsought-for effects.

Spencer, in his "The Study of Sociology," which is an ever-young classic, advised that biology should be the preferred discipline leading into the social sciences. This, because the countlessly complex organism is yet one, and the multiplying consequences of any organic event are not disregarded by the organism and cannot be disregarded by the scientist; and because, too, in dealing with organisms we are trained to deal with a self-activity from within.

In the same years when Herbert Spencer wrote "The Study of Sociology," Charles Darwin and Alfred Russel Wallace were establishing *natural ecology* as a branch of science which both depended upon and utilized, and was necessary to, many branches of science (and not only of biology). The multiplying effects which are countless within the organism, extend and still multiply beyond the organism, to other organisms and species and to the inorganic "environment," and they flood back in reciprocal action upon and into the organism. The "web of life" (many interpenetrating webs of life) is so much a reality that no separate life can be lived except as part of its web.

Now be it noted, as essential to what this foreword is trying to convey: sci-

First Mesa, looking west from Polacca

5

ence goes ahead by specializing its areas, and by the making of hypotheses and instruments ever more precisely useful and applicable. But science does not sunder the web of life, and the web sways, sustains, molds each particular life. The whole makes the parts, as truly as the parts make the whole. Multiplied consequences, sifted and assimilated and organized through time—through endless ages— are conserved and are converged inward upon the organism by the web of life or the total life-field; really, by the web of earth and the earth-field.

And in seeking to know this *wholeness* of the organism—its give-and-take within the web of life and within the life-field and earth-field—each one of the many hundreds of special hypotheses and instruments has to be employed with severe, technical fealty to its limited, special task or problem treated in isolation from the web of life and the earth-field. *But in addition*, not the specialized results only (discoveries or inventions), but the specialized processes, too, require all the time, or in repeated spiraling cycles, to take into account, to yield their own product into, to make of themselves vehicles of, the greater whole—the synergy of the organism, the synergy of the interrelated organisms, the synergy of the web of life and of the earth-field. Nay, more. The specialized enterprises are rewarded and justified, in the long run, just and only by their being joined in the symphony of understanding and of control, of which they are but musical notes or special instruments.

Lest some reader think that the thought here set down is poetical or mystical, rather than practical, I point to the single, quite unmystical example of soil conservation as practised in recent years. Soil conservation is *applied ecology*. The democratically organized Soil Conservation District is an applied ecology into which social organization has been incorporated. More significantly, it is human life and social organization finding their place in the web of life and the earth-field—refinding their previously lost place. Nothing merely mystical, is that which saves the soil by doubling the crop yield on the lands previously depleted by men who ignored the law of the multiplication of effects and the law that when wholes are wrecked, each several part is degraded in its turn.

Now, to pass straight into Indian Service and its aims and perplexities. Indian Service in the United States deals in total ways with whole societies. It does this for ill or for good. Through generations that look gray and cold now in retrospect, Indian Service pursued one and another special and decreed aim: to Christianize Indians, to substitute the individual Indian for the societal Indian, to make Indians into land individualists, to obliterate Indian superstition, to make go-getters of Indians. And policy was dominated by preconceptions as to the nature of Indian society. I cite two of these, from annual reports of Indian Commissioners in the 80's of the last century. The second quotation, dated 1886, reflects a usual view as to the types of emotion evoked in Indians by their own societies.

"To assist in the great work of redeeming these benighted children of nature from the darkness of their superstition and ignorance...."

"When they (Indian young people) return to their homes at night, and on Saturdays and Sundays, and are among their old surroundings, they relapse more or less into their former moral and mental stupor."

The presumption was one of administrative omnipotence. What was willed by authority, and put into action by authority—that was the thing which would be. The obscure complexes of personality and of group influence and ancient, present physical environment were ignored; good intention was deemed to be enough, without the need to measure results; and the law of the multiplication of effects was taken into account not at all. It followed, that not even the sense of reality of the Indian Service men and women out on the ground among the Indians was used in the making of headquarters policy. But I move into the immediate past, and the present.

We believe that some new factors have been put into the situation, which now are working against unrealism. Chief of these, of course, is tribal participation and self government. Important among the factors is the policy of bringing the schools close to the whole local population of Indians, and of varying the school curricula through incorporating local subject-matter in them, and of enabling Indian children to master the tool subjects through using the tools in the solving of whole and practical problems. A factor, again, is the service-wide orientation toward scientific, ecological land-use. Certainly one of the factors which "innoculate" against any auto-intoxication of willful ideas at headquarters, is the programming of reservation work through the "area project" method. In brief, Indian Service in these years has been brought measurably within the web of life and the world-field of the Indian. So far, so good.

There is, however, a different fact to take into account. Reforms tend to intellectually expend themselves. The half-dozen or dozen ideas that move men when new orders are taking the place of old orders, tend to become stereotyped in their turn. Actually they are mere beginnings, no more; but in a few years they often are found to have become conventionalized into ends. They start as hypotheses of exploration, they end as sufficient images of a fixed and finished world and of a task reduced to rote and ritual. Such is the usual human way. Can Indian Service know and insure that the usual human way is not or will not become *its* way?

Indian life profoundly registers a past which lives on. How little, as yet, we know of that past as it works dynamically in the Indian's soul! And Indian life is a zone of exceptional tensions, where pasts, presents and anxiously apprehended futures are working. And the sharp, unpractical mutations of Indian policy across a hundred years may have built a peculiar skepticism or resistantness into the Indian's unconscious mind. And the Indian individual is part of a group, and the individual and the group are part of the ecological environment, each group within its particular world-field. Change, at varying speeds, inhabits all of Indian life; change, at varying speeds, inhabits each group, each personality of the Indians. Is there any way to understand more surely, to predict more reliably, to act with knowledge more precise, so that we can know, genuinely, what worth our Indian effort has and how it may be made significantly more realistic, and so that our good (which we presume) may not become the enemy of a better?

The answer, if indeed there were one, must rest, it seemed to us, in the use of no one but of many techniques of observation and measurement *integratively*. Our hypothesis—a truism, which yet leads to discovery when deeply meditated—was that the web of life and the world-field are effective realities within the individual—factors in emotion, in behavior, in health and sickness, and weakness and power. And that the web of life and the world-field operate beneath as well as above the conscious threshold. And that the group and the individual are dynamically inseparable. And that the past, in the web of life and in the unconsciousness, is far more potent than can easily be known. And that trends of action and tensions of the body-soul are stubborn and imperious in men, though men may not know this fact at the conscious level.

From this hypothesis, there followed the method which we sought to have applied. Social history and the social present must be studied in relation to each other. The group structure, the group imperatives must be known, and the individual must be known as that personality-formation where the group forces clash and build (but not the group forces alone). Mind and performance in the individual must be measured, and through depth-psychology techniques, the types and trends of the individual unconsciousness must be explored. Bodily health must be examined. The physical environment, past as well as present, must be brought clearly, concretely into the picture. And finally, administration, in its subdivisions and as a whole, must be viewed afresh in the light of all of this data—data previously interrelated, so far as possible, within itself.

Into contact with the specialists— anthropologists, psychologists, physicians, and students of administration— the workers of Indian Service and, ideally, the Indians themselves, should be brought; and in the event, it has proved that important parts of the observational work of the project have been done by the lay members (White and Indian) of Indian Service.

With this object in view—the scientific evaluation of Indian Service, and scientific planning—and under the sway of the hypothesis stated, and by the correlative or integrative use of the methods implied, the several monographs of this series have been produced. Supplements dealing with administrative application will be presented at dates soon after the publication of each of the volumes, and it is hoped that there will be a final volume devoted to principles of Indian administration treated as a special case of universal democratic administration, and another devoted to the utilization of the whole body of the material for its light upon the science of society.

I have stated a view of life (and in so far, the view is merely my own), and an intended goal of investigation, and intended use of methods. None is likely to realize as acutely as those who have given themselves to the present enterprise, how incomplete is the accomplishment. If it should prove to have carried forward by one critical fraction of a degree (in the vast arc which will be explored through centuries) the integrative use of the special sciences in the knowing of man and the helpful control of his destiny, this result will have been enough. Certainly into our problem of Indian Service the enterprise has cast many beams of light that reach far. Areas immanently important, never clearly brought into the light before, are now in a clear and growing light. Will we administrators, who include all the field forces of Indian Service, use the light?

In a recent issue of INDIANS AT WORK, I wrote, and my thought took form from a reading of some of the materials of the present and the forthcoming monographs:

"Does one seek to influence an individual or a group? Let him discover what is central to the being of that individual or group. Let his effort at influence be near to, and not deviate sharply from, the line of force of that which is central to the being of the individual or group. Thus, he may influence profoundly and helpfully. Remember that deep and central preoccupations, devotions and views of life can be helped to apply themselves to new practical ends. Here is the secret of efficient and democratic administration. Indian policies in the last ten or twelve years have come much nearer to the things central in the Indian's being than they came in previous decades. Hence the marked increase in the social energy of Indians, and their great and persevering response to the various practical programs. But we need to keep on trying, with greater, not with diminishing, energy, and we need to press ever inward toward discovery of those attitudes, hopes, fears, patterns of functioning, and trends of the inner drive, which are central to the Indians. There is hardly any limit to the energy, the good-will, and the happiness which will meet us from within the Indian—if only we work with him at his own centers."

II.

"The Hopi Way" is Volume One of the tribal monograph series of this project which will include the Navaho, the Sioux, the Papago, and one or more pueblos of New Mexico. Each of the volumes will be followed by a supplement devoted to concrete administrative application. "The Hopi Way" speaks its own story. I here mention seven of the conclusions which I, as one reader, have found in "The Hopi Way."

1. The Hopi world-view is pre-Columbian and non-literate. It also is much nearer to the *emergent* world-view, symbolized by the word "field," the word "holistic," and the word "synergism": nearer to this emergent world-view of physics, of biology, of psychology and of sociology, than is our too-mechanistic "culture-lag" from the 18th and 19th centuries.

2. The nature world of the Hopi is one of the most perilous and severe of all nature worlds. The Hopi have met this changeless fact by building this difficult nature-world into the center of their psychic and social life. With the Elizabethan they could say

"Deep in that lion-haunted inland lies
 A mystic city, goal of high emprise,"

and their emprise of reaching into nature, to help and to move it at its profound center, goes forward in the individual's life and the communal life through the years and cycles.

3. The Hopi, thus making inner form and inner power of the limitations of their nature world, similarly have internalized their social limitations. These limitations are extremely severe. The Hopi have achieved peace, and not through policing but through the disciplines and the affirmations planted within each of their several souls. The achievement has been maintained across millennia and is maintained now. And the Hopi pay for their peace, severe payments.

4. The Hopi, without using a single one of the forms of democracy which distinguish (and limit) the European tradition, live in democracy. Within the limitations of Hopi existence which are simply incalculable (they are fully told in this monograph), the Hopi realize freedom. Though individual shortcoming may wreck the society and even the universe (so the Hopi believe), yet the individual's conduct and his thought, his emotion and his choices, are finally left to himself. They bear one another's burdens. They enter deeply into community responsibility and give to it their all. For the sake of the Race, the individual seeks ever to deepen and give form to his own consciousness. The Hopi have democracy, endure democracy, achieve democracy, with not one of those forms which, to too many minds, are the only tokens of the existence of democracy anywhere.

5. In so severe a world of nature and man that the Hopi, individual and group, seems like Nietzsche's rope-walker, these human beings, through creative action across many ages, have demonstrated a survival-capacity (spiritual and biological), compared to which the history of European groups and types appears like an
"Ever-breaking shore
     That tumbles in a godless deep."
This survival-capacity, as one of many aspects, is found now in the convergence of the results of performance tests and depth-psychology soundings. The Hopi rate mentally to a critical extent higher than other groups in the United States who have been thus tested and sounded.

6. These things are true. Yet reading the individual personality studies in

"The Hopi Way," one discovers the universal mechanisms of human nature at their almost changeless task. The Hopi is like to everybody else and unlike to everybody else. The whole suffuses and changes the refractory and constant parts.

7. Finally. Seen *whole*, the Hopi are a profoundly and intensely practical people. *Seen whole*. That nature-man constitution which they have built through their ages will incorporate any gain—any new tool or goal—which is contributive to Hopi destiny. Hopi destiny is not small or eccentric, but catholic and cosmic. The Hopi world-view and art of self-making are not less congenial to the world's future than to its less-recent past. The opportunity of pedagogy and of administration is immense and fascinating, in terms of the Hopi. But *in terms of the Hopi* this opportunity must be pursued. The mere intrusion of influence is mostly wasted effort; when successful, it is in that measure damaging. Only those who read this book thoughtfully will know how tragically damaging the unsophisticated intrusion of supposed benefits into Hopi life can be.

INTRODUCTION

In the remote highlands of northern Arizona, surrounded by a vast desert, live the Hopi Indians, the vigorous, modern descendants of pueblo or town dwelling peoples who settled in the vicinity many centuries ago. These Indians are unique in many ways. They are the westernmost representatives of the great Pueblo peoples, who today extend eastward to the Rio Grande River and who in prehistoric times covered a much larger area. The Pueblos, within the limits of their highly specialized environment, developed one of the most advanced non-metal-using cultures known to man, and the most complex of any Indians north of Mexico.

Of these remarkable people, the Hopi are the only surviving group of desert dwellers[1]. With inventive genius they have grappled with an exceedingly inhospitable environment and developed a way of life that has enabled them to survive for centuries as dry farmers living in desert towns and entirely surrounded by traditional predators—nomadic Indian marauders, militantly proselyting Spaniards, and more recently, land-hungry Navaho and Americans. Moreover, they have accomplished this mainly without the use of physical force. The Hopi call themselves the "Peaceful People"[2] and their culture is oriented toward peace. Today this group of about 3500 Indians, in the heart of the Navaho country, have retained the dynamic integrity of their native culture—their value-system and original outlook on life, their complex and absorbing ritual, their social structure, and much of their

technology—in spite of all the pressures of modern civilization. In fact, they have probably preserved more of their ancestral heritage than any other Indian tribe in the United States. Moreover, they show practically no admixture with Whites.

How is it that a mere handful of people with so few apparent resources have been able to accomplish this extraordinary feat? Undoubtedly the desert, in its isolating and contact-resisting functions, has been an important factor in the process, but obviously it has not been the only factor. Other desert tribes in the United States under similar pressures—the Papago, to cite an example of another peace-loving group included in this research project —have shown less stability and have in a relatively short time lost much of their old culture. What is the secret of Hopi vitality and resourcefulness? Is there not much that the modern world may learn from them?

In the following study we have approached these questions by attempting to analyze the development of Hopi personality in relation to the total environment viewed in historical perspective, and to present our results in such a way as to serve as a background for further research on the problem of how the Hopi, a cultural island in the stream of modern American life, may be assisted in continuing to develop their potentialities, and in making not only a creative adjustment to modern conditions, but also a unique and valuable contribution to the nation and the world.

Footnotes will be found in Appendix, page 134 ff.

11

The work is part of the results of the Indian Education Research Project, sponsored jointly by the Committee on Human Development of the University of Chicago and the United States Office of Indian Affairs. The object of the Indian Education Research is to attempt systematically to evaluate the Indian administrative program with special reference to the effect of the Indian New Deal policies on the Indians as individuals, to indicate the direction toward which these policies are leading and to suggest if possible how the effectiveness of Indian administration may be increased. In it an attempt has been made experimentally to bring to bear on this problem an integration of techniques from several disciplines, especially social anthropology, psychology, psychiatry, medicine, and ecology. Since the inauguration of the research in September 1941, investigations have proceeded in five tribes: Hopi, Navaho, Sioux, Papago and one or more of the New Mexico pueblos. Analyses and interpretations of the results of the research as well as detailed descriptions of the methods used and test results obtained, will be published in due course.

The Hopi live in 11 villages[3] on or below three adjoining mesas, which rise dramatically several hundred feet above the high northern Arizona desert floor. (See page 19). Since, for obvious reasons, we could not study all the Hopi villages for purposes of this analysis (even though this might have been considered desirable), we selected two communities which we hoped together would give us some understanding of the tribe.

The first selected community consists of three interrelated villages of the First or East Mesa: Walpi and its extension, Sichomovi, whose stone houses merge with the cliffs of the mesa top, and Polacca, a recent settlement located just below. This community includes all the villages of the First Mesa with the exception of

Hano, a Tewa-speaking[4] pueblo adjacent to Sichomovi. The Hanoans are reputed to be the descendants of a group of Pueblo people who migrated from the Rio Grande region around 1700. Although they have intermarried extensively with the Hopi, they remain, on account of traditional, sociological, ceremonial and linguistic ties, a distinct social unit.[5] The second selected community includes two villages of the Third or West Mesa: Oraibi[6] atop the cliffs and its modern colony, Kyakotsmovi[7] or New Oraibi, at the base. Although closely related through kinship and traditional bonds, these two villages form a striking contrast in that Oraibi is one of the most ancient and conservative of the Hopi pueblos, while New Oraibi is one of those most influenced by modern western civilization. In fact, Oraibi is probably the oldest continuously inhabited town in the United States.[8] According to surface potsherd finds, which show an unbroken record of ceramic development, it has been occupied since about 1150 or earlier. That is, 350 years before Columbus discovered America, Hopi were already living on this site.

The data concerning Hopi personality have been drawn partly from the literature but mainly from field investigations of 190 children aged 6 to 18 years,[9] 81 children from the First Mesa group and 109 children from the Oraibi group. The Oraibi figure includes all the children residing in Old and New Oraibi within the age range, with the exception of a few individuals whom it was not possible to test for various reasons.[10] The Oraibi sample is therefore representative of the age grades 6 to 18 years in these two communities. At First Mesa all the children of school age were selected except those whose residence or ceremonial affiliations were with the village of Hano, or who were considered to be Tewa[11] rather than Hopi. It should be noted that in this sample there are only six boys of 14 or over. The First Mesa

Sichomovi pueblo, First Mesa, looking southwest from Hano

AGE SEX	5-7 YEARS M	F	8-10 YEARS M	F	11-13 YEARS M	F	14-18 YEARS M	F	TOTAL M	F	GRAND TOTAL
FIRST MESA	11	7	9	16	8	13	6	11	34	47	81
ORAIBI	11	10	13	8	14	19	16	18	54	55	109

Age and sex distribution of children in study

sample may be considered fairly representative of the group. The age and sex distributions of the two samples of Hopi children studied are shown above.

The personalities and life histories of these children were studied by means of a battery of psychological tests, of both the projective and the performance types,[12] supplemented by interviews, observations and reports from parents, teachers, and other community members, and by medical examinations. The field work began in June 1942, and ended in August 1943. Much of the testing and interviewing was done by Indian Service teachers, trained by members of the Research Staff and supervised by the authors. Tests requiring a trained and experienced professional specialist for their administration—namely, the medical examinations, the Rorschach (Ink Blot), and Thematic Apperception (adapted) —were given by one of the authors, Alice Joseph, M. D., physician on the staff of the Indian Service, who spent four months on the Hopi Reservation.[13] The field data were analyzed by technicians on the Research Staff, and the final analysis and integration of the test results were the work of Dr. Joseph.

Whereas the data concerning personality have been obtained mainly from field work initiated and carried out by project personnel, those concerning the total social structure and the physical environment have been drawn chiefly from the voluminous Hopi literature, both published and unpublished. These data have been analyzed by the other author, Laura Thompson, anthropologist on the staff of the Committee on Human Development, University of Chicago, and Co-

ordinator of the Indian Education Research Project. They are somewhat less extensive, especially regarding recent historical developments, for the First Mesa group than for Oraibi. It should not be inferred on this account, however, that the Oraibi group is considered the more important or representative of the Hopi today. On the contrary, a knowledge of both groups is necessary for an understanding of present conditions in the tribe.

The following study of Hopi personality development in its interrelationship with the total environment, falls into five parts: namely, Part I, a brief description of Hopi society in its geographical and historical setting; Part II, the expected course of individual development through the life cycle; Part III, personality studies of selected children; Part IV, the actual developmental sequence as revealed in the attitudes and reactions of the sample of 190 children studied by means of tests and interviews; and Part V, some findings drawn from these data. Parts I, II and V have been written by Laura Thompson; parts III and IV by Alice Joseph.

As has been stated, this study has been designed to serve as a basis for further research on the problem of Hopi administration. Interpretation of the results of the analysis at the administrative level will constitute the second phase of the study, to be presented subsequently. The authors have tried to orient the study toward meeting the needs of administrative personnel (such as teachers, doctors, nurses and technicians) for a clear and concise yet accurate account of Hopi society and its dynamics, and at the same time to present the results of original research.

A street in Old Oraibi pueblo
Third Mesa

In attempting thus briefly and comprehensively to discuss problems which are highly complex and controversial, we are aware of the dangers of oversimplification, misrepresentation and omission. We offer the work humbly in the hope that it may throw more light on the important problem of the interrelationship between the individual and the total environment, and contribute toward the development of a scientific method of cooperative social analysis, which may serve as a basis for systematic planning toward humanity-liberating goals. We consider the results to be exploratory rather than definitive; nevertheless, we hope they may serve as a guide to more precise formulations in the future. Their full significance and comparative value will be apparent only in the context of the total results of the Indian Education Research Project.

ACKNOWLEDGMENTS

In a large cooperative research project it is difficult, if not impossible, to acknowledge adequately the many different kinds of effort which have fused into the whole and made possible the final result. The function of the authors has been somewhat in the nature of catalytic agents responsible for formulating, channelizing and crystallizing the problems and the data, but the study itself has grown out of the cooperative efforts of many individuals, each of whom has made a unique contribution by bringing to bear on the central problem his particular efforts, training and experience.

We wish to express our appreciation to all those individuals who have had any part in implementing the project, including the Hopi Indians themselves, particularly the selected children and their families, and the members of the Indian Service Staff who contributed so generously of their time and energy to aid in the research.

We thank especially John Collier, Commissioner of Indian Affairs and Chairman of the Research Committee on Indian Education of the Office of Indian Affairs, who initiated the project and gave to it his inspiration and active support at every stage of its development; W. Lloyd Warner, Professor of Anthropology and Sociology and Chairman of the Research Committee on Indian Education of the University of Chicago, who brought to bear on the problem his insight and experience in directing cooperative research enterprises and who helped in planning the project, training the field workers, and guiding the sociological aspects of the research; Robert J. Havighurst, Professor of Education, Secretary of the Committee on Human Development of the University of Chicago and a member of the Indian Education Research Committee, who helped to plan and guide the psychological research and to analyze the field data; Willard Beatty, Director of the Education Division of the Office of Indian Affairs, who opened up the resources of the Education Division of the Indian Service and directed the printing of the manuscript; and Ralph Tyler, Chairman of the Department of Education of the University of Chicago, who served on the Research Committee.

We are also very much indebted, for advice and assistance, to Clyde Kluckhohn, Associate Professor of Anthropology, Harvard University; Fred Eggan, Associate Professor of Anthropology, University of Chicago, and his wife, Dorothy Eggan; Bruno Klopfer, Director of the Rorschach Institute; Eugene Lerner, Professor of Psychology, Sarah Lawrence College; Grace Arthur, Psychologist; A. F. Whiting, Acting Assistant Professor of Anthropology, University of Oregon; and also to Mischa Titiev, Assistant Professor of Anthropology, University of Michigan, who kindly permitted us to use the proofs of his forthcoming monograph on "Old Oraibi."

Finally, we express our deep grati-
tude to all those who helped in carrying out the field work on the Hopi Reservation and without whose generous
assistance this project could not have
been completed, including Burton
Ladd, Superintendent of the Hopi Indian Agency; Dorothea C. Leighton,
M. D., Special Physician, Office of Indian Affairs; Edward Kennard, Anthropologist, Office of Indian Affairs; R.
M. Tisinger, Superintendent of Education, Phoenix Indian School; Wayne
Pratt, former Reservation Principal,
Hopi Agency; Dow Carnal, Reservation
Principal, Hopi Agency; Samuel Rosen-
berg, Principal of the Polacca Day
School; Joseph Brinkerhoff, Principal
of the Hopi High School, Oraibi; and
the following teachers   in   the   Hopi
Schools who gave long and tiring hours
outside their regular assignments to
the testing and interviewing program:
Ethel Burt, Fred Kabotie, Betty Lewis,
Mary Mitchell, Inez Pratt, Lila Rosen-
berg, Beryl Wagner, Cecille Wallace
and Elizabeth White. And we also
thank Carl V. Mt. Pleasant and Milton
Snow for the use of their excellent
photographs of the Hopi and Hopiland; William E. Henry for analysis of
the Thematic Apperception test (revised); Ray Birdwhistell for analysis of
the interviews; Brooke Mordy for content analysis of the Free Drawing test;
Iva Schmidt and Jean Hall for help in
the analysis of the Emotional Response
test; Jeanette Murstine for help in
the analysis of the Moral Ideology test;
Minna Korol and Inez Pratt for help in
the analysis of the Draw-A-Man test;
and Rhea R. Hilkevitch and Wayne
Pratt for help in the analysis of the
Grace Arthur Point Performance Scale.
                                        L. T.
                                        A. J.

I. THE HOPI WEB OF LIFE

1. THE STRUGGLE FOR SURVIVAL
IN HOPILAND

From the flat roof of the Bear clan house at Walpi we look out on a breathtaking panorama. This is the traditional post of the pueblo Sun Watcher, whose observations of the position of the rising sun against the jagged eastern horizon have for centuries set the Walpi-Sichomovi seasonal calendar of rites and work.[1] This skyline calendar is formed mainly by the Hopi Buttes and Antelope Mesa, in a deep crevice of which lies Keams Canyon, seat of the Hopi Agency 12 miles away.

We are perched atop the tip of the First Mesa which is only a few yards wide. It is a narrow tongue of rock, a sheer precipice on the flat summit of which rise the terraced stone houses of three adjacent pueblos, as though grown to the mesa. Walpi, which is really one long, honeycombed apartment house, rising two or three stories toward the sky, is separated by 100 yards from Sichomovi to the northeast, by a dizzying, razor-backed saddle. The houses of Sichomovi follow the mesa top and merge with those of Hano. Thus the three pueblos are geographically a single unit.

Directly below us, a sheer drop of about 800 feet, we can distinguish some modern and adobe houses, the Day School compound, the Baptist church and the store. This is the recent settlement of Polacca, clustered near the ancient Polacca Spring, which supplies water to it as well as to the mesa pueblos. Although piped to Polacca, the water from the spring must be hauled by truck or burro, or even carried by women, to the top of the mesa, for the people have not allowed the Government to have it pumped up. Before the recent increase in draft animals, all the water used in the Hopi pueblos was carried in earthenware jars up the steep mesa trails from springs in the cliffs below.

Twelve miles to the west looms the Second Mesa with its three villages, Mishongnovi, Shipaulovi and Shungopovi. And ten miles beyond is the Third Mesa with Oraibi and its offshoots— New Oraibi, Hotevilla and Bakabi.[2]

These three Hopi mesas are really the southern spurs of a single, tablelike formation called Black Mesa, which extends north and northwestward from our Walpi lookout for a distance of 60 miles. On it grow scattered juniper and pinyon, interspersed with sagebrush. This land mass makes possible the existence of the pueblos and distinguishes Hopiland from the surrounding Navaho desert. It acts as a sort of subterranean reservoir, in which a small but relatively permanent water supply is stored. Moisture, seeping through its permeable sandstone surface to the underlying bed rock, finally emerges in the cliffs of its southern escarpments, in the form of springs. Near these springs the Hopi have for centuries built their pueblos.

The mesa is also characterized by the presence of sand dunes which have a relatively high moisture holding capacity and hence tend to prevent a rapid run-off after rains and to provide good land for dry farming.

Black Mesa is drained by the

New Oraibi, village below Third Mesa, seen from the northeast

ephemeral streams of the Tusayan Washes. Eroding deep valleys in their southwestward flow toward the Little Colorado, they have carved out the Hopi mesas and cut arroyos in the desert floor below. On account of a natural erosion epicycle, which has occurred over the whole Southwest since 1880 and has been increased critically through overgrazing, these arroyos are deepening rapidly, the Oraibi Wash having cut to a depth of about 80 feet in the last 50 years.[3]

The great plain, stretching out before us, slopes gently southwestward toward the Painted Desert basin of the Little Colorado. It is really a vast plateau, 6000 feet above sea level, and on it grow grasses and desert shrubs. As we look over this beautiful but barren landscape we marvel that the ingenuity of man has made it support a sedentary population. But below us are orchards, here and there in the silt soil of the washes are green sweeps of corn, and almost invisible against the sand and rock are slow-moving flocks of sheep.

The nearest railroad town, Winslow, lies about 70 miles to the south. And far to the southwest the snowy peaks of the San Francisco Mountains, traditional home of the rain-bringing cloud gods, dominate the scene as the problem of rainmaking looms large in Hopi thought.

For the annual precipitation in Hopiland is only 10 to 13 inches, and this falls mainly in the form of torrential summer downpours, which suddenly flood the washes and frequently sweep away the crops. Every third or fourth year the corn crop fails fully to mature from lack of water. In some years there is no rain at all and occasionally a long drought occurs and the springs dry up. At such times even the providence of the Hopi, who store up food one to three years ahead, does not avail, and these self-sufficient people are forced to seek outside help or perish. Such droughts are rare, but are

not forgotten, and present a constant threat to Hopi existence. Under these circumstances it is easy to understand why much of the Hopi ceremonial is directed toward bringing rain.

Not only is the water supply in Hopiland extremely limited and unreliable, but the growing season is short[4] at best and likely to be cut at either end by killing frosts. The main planting season is from May to June and the main harvest, in September. Planting dates are so important that they are part of the sacred lore and are determined traditionally by the Sun Watcher on the basis of solar observations.[5] There is a marked seasonal as well as daily variation in temperature, the annual mean being about 51 degrees. To add to his difficulties, the Hopi farmer has to contend with strong winds, which blow almost constantly and often with such force as to stir up sand storms and to injure or kill the crops. Farming under these conditions is extremely precarious and possible only by great skill and diligence and by special methods which the Hopi have developed through the centuries.

Corn, the main crop, is cultivated chiefly by flood water farming. Successful maturation by this method requires considerable foresight and precision, for the fields are located on the flood plains and at the mouths of arroyos, where the crop is in danger of destruction through either floods or silt coverage. The Hopi select the fields, as well as the seed to be planted each year, with great care. A man chooses for planting several plots (about an acre apiece) of various types of soil, rather than a single field, so that even if the crop in one locality is destroyed, that in another may mature, and thus he protects himself as far as possible against the loss of his entire harvest. This selection of fields is possible because usually not more than half of the available fields are cultivated at any one time.[6] The success of Hopi agriculture, in fact, depends on

Hopi gardens

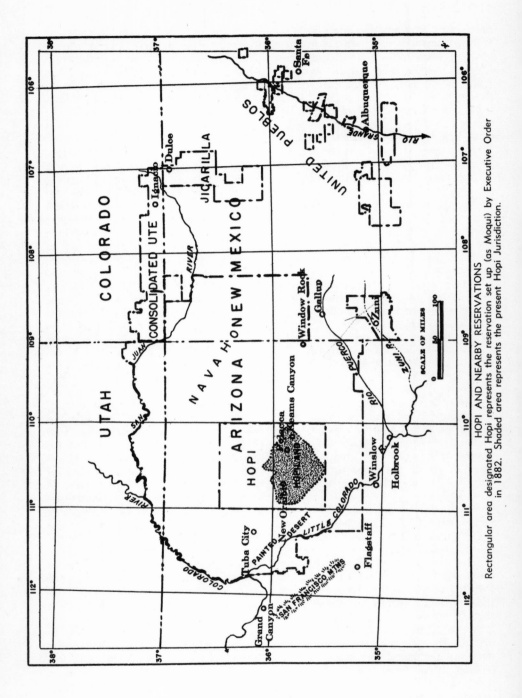

HOPI AND NEARBY RESERVATIONS

Rectangular area designated Hopi represents the reservation set up (as Moqui) by Executive Order in 1882. Shaded area represents the present Hopi Jurisdiction.

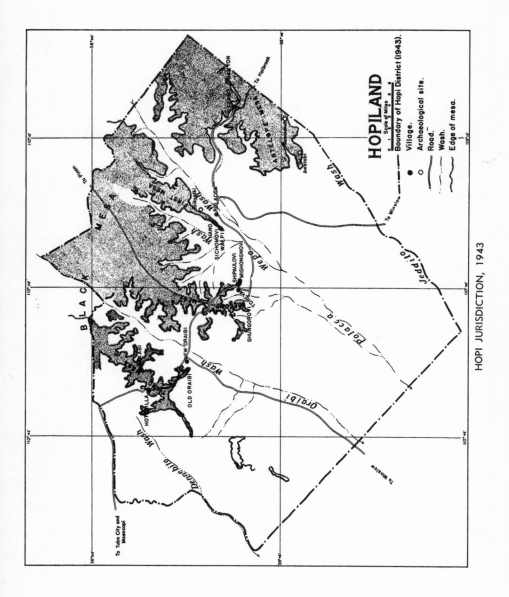

HOPILAND

Scale of Miles

Boundary of Hopi District (1943).
● Village.
○ Archaeological site.
Road.
Wash.
Edge of mesa.

HOPI JURISDICTION, 1943

19

this flexibility of individual boundaries and the use of several plots by each household, and hence any system of fixed allotments for each individual would be disastrous to traditional Hopi economy.[7]

Seeds for planting are considered the sacred property of the matrilineal household and are inherited through the female line.[8] Those seeds to be used for the next season's crops are selected by the women of each household after discussion with the men, except for those planted by a man in the first year of marriage. In this case, he uses seeds from his mother's household, a gift important in the reciprocal exchange which forms part of the wedding rites. In planting, holes 10 to 15 inches deep are dug in the ground and 10 to 20 seeds are dropped in each hole. As the corn matures some plants are destroyed by wind, field mice and cut worms, so that only about half the seeds bear fruit.

Corn and beans are also cultivated on sand dunes where the high moisture content of the soil enables them to grow without surface flooding or irrigation. About 20% of the land under cultivation by Hopi is of this type.[9] On the sand dune fields, however, each individual clump must be protected, during the early stages of growth at least, by some sort of windbreak, usually of brush held down by stones. Abandoned lines of stones indicating ancient windbreaks in use in the 13th century, according to the archaeological investigations, may still be seen in the Jeddito valley.[10] The modern Hopi also protect the young plants with tin cans and other available debris.

Seepage areas at the mesa bases are also cultivated, mainly as orchards, for since the introduction of fruit trees by the Spaniards, peaches and other fruit crops such as apricots, pears and apples, have become Hopi staples, and orchards cover about 813 acres[11] of Hopiland. Finally, the land around some of the springs is terraced, irrigat-ed and planted with vegetables such as beans, squash, chili, melons, pumpkins and onions. There are, however, only about 11 acres[12] of such vegetable gardens and, whereas the field crops are cultivated by the men, these gardens are women's work.[13]

By trial and error through the years, the Hopi is constantly improving his farming methods. He experiments with new techniques and new varieties of plants, accepting those that are useful, rejecting the impractical or obsolete. Most of the ancient varieties of corn and other food plants have been discarded in favor of new varieties that are easier to grow or prepare, have a greater yield, or are more palatable.[14] Modern agricultural implements are gradually replacing the ancient dibble, weed cutter and rake. This is most marked at New Oraibi, where it is estimated that three-quarters of the household groups have plows and scrapers and many of these also have teams and wagons.[15] The Government, through its agricultural extension work, is attempting to increase Hopi farming output by constructing flood irrigation projects, teaching the people irrigation farming, and improving the orchards by the introduction of new seedlings and trees suitable to the climate. Always, however, the desert environment plays a dominant role in Hopi acceptance of new traits and on this account, although constantly improving in detail, the basic agricultural technology of these people has changed but little since prehistoric times[16] and dry farming is still, as it was in the past, the main Hopi industry.[17]

The Hopi supplement their use of cultivated plants with a wide range of wild and semi-cultivated species.[18] A few of these, such as Indian millet, alkali sacaton, dropseed, wild potato and pinyon, are important as staple foods, while others are valued for seasoning, medicinal purposes and craftwork. The Hopi's knowledge and use of the floral environment is remarkable. About 200

A Hopi farmer at work

Chas. Loloma

wild species of flowering plants grow in the vicinity of their villages, and names and uses for all but a dozen are known to informants or recorded in the literature. They also collect plants at considerable distances from their mesas. Much of the supply of fuel has to be hauled from the forests of the Black Mesa, a journey of a day or more to the north, and occasionally they go as far as the San Francisco Peaks, about 80 miles away, for timber.

In the past the Hopi depended on natural products much more than they do today. The young men went on long collecting journeys, during which they were exposed to thirst, enemies and supernatural dangers. The most arduous of these was to the vicinity of the Grand Canyon to get salt and pigments.[19]

The Hopi also mined soft coal in prehistoric and early historic times from veins near their villages, by hand methods,[20] and used it to fire their pots and to heat the rooms where they wove cotton cloth and manufactured other craft articles, which were traded widely. Thus the presence of coal which the Hopi could mine by hand methods facilitated the building of a surplus of manufactured articles which in turn formed the basis of a network of trade relations throughout the Southwest.[21]

The Hopi have been skilled craftsmen and traders since prehistoric times. In fact, all the crafts noted by the first Spaniards who visited the pueblos in 1540 are still produced. The introduction of new materials and markets have brought about some deviation from ancient standards but the methods used are basically the same.[22] Whereas certain crafts, such as weaving, and the manufacture of household pottery and yucca twill baskets, are practiced on all the mesas (though not with equal intensity),[23] others are confined to one locality. For instance, coiled baskets are made only by the women of Second Mesa, wicker baskets by those of the Third, and

painted pottery only by those of the First. The localization of basketry probably persists from ancient times. The art of making decorated pottery, however, although widespread among the Hopi villages in the past, practically died out in the 19th century. It was revived in 1895 by Nampeyo, a Tewa woman from Hano, who, drawing inspiration from potsherds excavated at the abandoned pueblo of Sikyatki, founded a new school of Hopi pottery. The introduction of this medium of artistic expression among the women of First Mesa has released an upsurgence of creativity and has led to the production of quantities of pots for the commercial market. Although this ware, manufactured relatively rapidly by the old coiled method without a wheel, is somewhat inferior technically to the ancient, it is outstanding in originality, variety and mastery of design.[24] Great importance is attached to the aesthetic quality of the design, which is usually first conceived as a balanced whole in the artist's mind and then applied spontaneously without benefit of tracings or measuring devices. Although a "road line," broken to prevent bad luck, usually borders the inner edge of the design and certain conventions regarding spatial arrangements are observed, no two pots are ever alike and individuality among potters is so marked that the work of each can be distinguished without any signature or trademark.[25]

Few if any Hopi devote full time to craftswork, but practically all Hopi women are active craftworkers, making either pottery or basketry, and many men are engaged part-time in weaving and other craft industries, such as the making of moccasins, kachina dolls, and jewelry. The output of weaving varies with the villages, our two communities producing relatively small amounts compared with the Second Mesa villages and Hotevilla.[26] Moreover, there is a seasonal variation in craft production which apparently

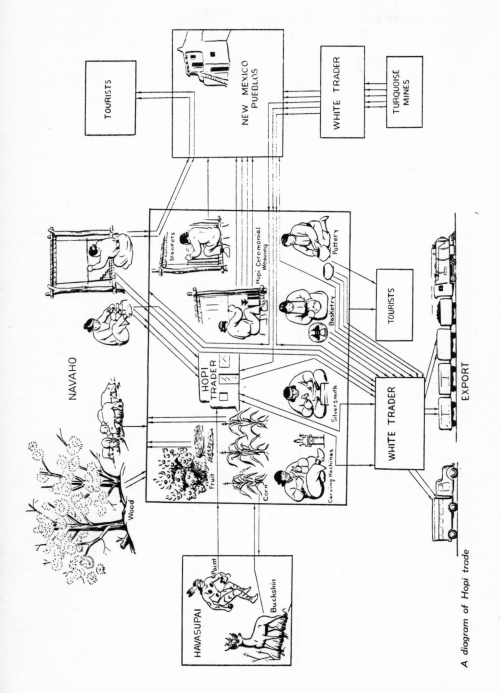

A diagram of Hopi trade

dovetails with other work, pottery being made chiefly from March to August, baskets from December to September, and woven goods from January to August.[27]

Although the home consumption of craft goods is very important in Hopi culture, actually the tribe retains only about one-fifth of the annual output. Of the remainder about three-fifths is sold to Whites and one-fifth traded or sold through a rather complicated system of inter-tribal exchange to other Indians, chiefly the pueblos of New Mexico or the Navaho.[28] In this system the Hopi act as sedentary middlemen as well as producers, receiving blankets, wood and mutton from the Navaho in exchange for silver and turquoise (which they have received from the Rio Grande), woven belts and garters, peaches, melons and corn. In exchange for jewelry, they give to the Rio Grande pueblos woven products, especially those of a ceremonial nature. Commercial traders also take an active part in this system. (See page 23).[29]

The policy of the Government is to encourage the production of Hopi arts and crafts and to increase and facilitate their marketing. For this purpose a survey of present conditions has been made.[30]

Hunting is another ancient Hopi activity which still persists, although it was formerly much more important in Hopi life than it is at present. Actually Hopi hunting today is confined chiefly to rabbits and other small game, but it still retains a good deal of the excitement, sporting flavor and ritual of the traditional chase when, within the memory of the living, antelope, deer and mountain sheep, as well as an occasional mountain lion, grizzly bear or gray wolf, were the quarry.[31] The Hopi is an exceedingly skillful hunter and trapper with what we might call a sportsmanlike attitude toward game. He prefers to outrun or stalk his prey on foot rather than to pursue it with horses or dogs, and to club or smother it rather than to use a gun or (formerly) a bow. And he daringly scales or descends the cliffs to rob a nest of its eaglets under fierce attack of the mother bird, or lures and captures the mature birds with his bare hands. These methods, as well as the ritual accompanying them, reveal his interest in the conservation of game which he believes must be protected, propitiated and entreated not to become angry when killed, so that it will increase and prosper.

Concomitant with the decrease and disappearance of the wild fauna on the Hopi ranges, there has been a gradual increase in sheep and cattle, which were introduced by the Spaniards. But although the work of tending the flocks and herds affords a break in the rather exacting and confining agricultural routine, it can hardly provide an adequate substitute for the thrill of the chase. Moreover, herding on the northern Arizona plateau imposes a certain degree of mobility on the herders, which is somewhat out of keeping with the traditional sedentary Hopi life, and apparently the Hopi have not yet mastered this new industry with their age old technical skill, nor have they vested in it such strong sanctions of myth and ritual as they have farming. In spite of this, livestock has in recent years become increasingly important to the Hopi, and in 1942 was the source of 34% of the annual income of about $279,800.[32] (See opposite page).

In contrast to the Navaho practice, Hopi herds are tended and usually also owned by men. Not all Hopi men are stockmen, however.[33] Among many herders, grazing is subsidiary to farming, the usual practice being for several owners to pool their small flocks, each man herding them in turn. With some families, especially on First Mesa, however, grazing is the main occupation, the men of the household spending much of their time in sheep camps at some distance from home.[34]

The Government, through its exten-

HOPI INCOME SOURCE

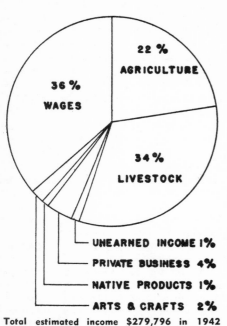

22 % AGRICULTURE

36 % WAGES

34% LIVESTOCK

UNEARNED INCOME 1%

PRIVATE BUSINESS 4%

NATIVE PRODUCTS 1%

ARTS & CRAFTS 2%

Total estimated income $279,796 in 1942

sion activities, has attempted to raise the standard of animal industry among the Hopi by introducing sound stock management policies. Springs have been improved and small streams have been dammed to supply stock with water, for at least part of the year and active encouragement has been given to the branding of stock, sheep dipping, the improvement of breeds by the introduction of purebred Rambouillet rams and registered Herefords, the segregation of rams in special pastures, the raising of fodder, the construction of corrals, the organization of stock cooperatives,[35] and the reduction of range stock. In spite of these efforts the 1942 lamb crop was only 54.6% of the total number of mature ewes.[36]

Unfortunately the increase in herds in Hopiland correlates with the present natural erosion epicycle and these factors have contributed to deteriorate the range to such an extent as to precipi-

tate a crisis. Although a livestock reduction program was introduced to the Hopi by the Government some time ago, it was not pushed until the summer of 1943 when, due to a severe drought, the range crisis became acute. At this time the Hopi ranges were heavily overstocked. Hopi pasturage, especially that of the Third Mesa, was so depleted that unless the stock was reduced quickly many of the sheep and cattle would die on the range. The program called for an average reduction of about 44% of the herd of each individual owner on Third Mesa, about 20% of the stock of each owner on First Mesa, and about 22% on Second.[37]

Naturally the program was extremely painful to Hopi stockmen, but while the First and Second Mesa groups accepted it, appointed committees to judge each individual case on the basis of household needs and successfully reduced their stock to carrying capacity, the stockmen of Third Mesa, incited by off-Reservation cattle interests which furnished legal advice, attempted to stir up the owners on the other mesas against it and created a considerable amount of disturbance. The Superintendent and his associates induced some leading citizens of Holbrook to take action in reducing off-Reservation pressure. By promising to aid the herders in process of reduction with loans, transportation and marketing, and to try to get them more land and thus help to reduce the pressure of the expanding population on the limited Reservation resources, they persuaded the Third Mesa group to accept the reduction program, which is reported to have been carried to completion.

We have tried very briefly to describe Hopiland and the use the Hopi have made of this land through the centuries. We have noted how the presence of relatively permanent springs and a relatively low run-off after rains have differentiated this region from the surrounding desert, attracted settlers and made possible the growth of a sedentary population. We have seen that these desert dwellers through the years developed a technology which, although severely limited by the environment, at the same time took full advantage of it; that they, in fact, showed a remarkable inventiveness and ingenuity in working out methods of exploitation and conservation of the natural resources available to them without the use of metal tools. Moreover, we have observed that this environment is constantly changing, not only in its geological base, but also in its fauna and flora; that through both natural and cultural factors, it is becoming progressively eroded and denuded of plant cover. Furthermore, some of the ways by which the Hopi have adjusted themselves to these changes through modification of old uses and incorporation of new ones (made available through their increasing contact with the outside world), have been pointed out and also an area (the livestock industry) in which recently they have had trouble in adjusting.

As we continue our study of the Hopi it may be well to bear in mind that, in this particular interrelationship of human beings to the non-human environment, the desert with its scant and erratic water supply plays the role of the main limiting and permitting agent in the acceptance of new material traits, and chiefly on this account the basic technology of the Hopi, although constantly improving in detail, really has not changed a great deal through the centuries.

As the analysis progresses, however, we shall see that every change in culture adopted by the Hopi must eventually pass two rigorous tests. Not only must it have survival value in the desert environment, but it must also be reconciled or rationalized, partially at least, in regard to the Hopi value system and world view.

Continuing our study of Hopi patterns of interaction with the external environment, we shall now discuss briefly some significant facts concerning Hopi history and population movements.

2. LOOKING BACK ACROSS A MILLENNIUM

At least a thousand years before Columbus discovered America, and probably much earlier, Hopiland was already inhabited by an agricultural people who dug themselves pit houses in the ground, made basketry and crude pottery, and cultivated corn, beans and cotton.[1] The culture of these people, called Basketmaker III, extended over much of the Southwest, and it is interesting to note that on and below First Mesa alone, at least six sites have been discovered near the two main springs—Polacca and Sikyatki, some distance to the northeast of it. A few of these sites also show, by their im-

proved type of pottery, evidence of continued occupation into what archaeologists call the Proto-Pueblo (Pueblo 1) period. These people also settled below the mesa northwest of the present site of Walpi at Kuchaptuvela, which we shall call Walpi No. 1. A little later, the pit houses developed into the small masonry dwellings of the Early Pueblo (Pueblo II) culture, found not only at First Mesa but also elsewhere, including sites near Oraibi on and below the Third Mesa.

Cultural development among the Pueblos reached a peak during the late Middle Ages (European calendar) with the growth of large pueblos and cliff dwellings of the Classic Pueblo Period (Pueblo III), centering in the basins of the San Juan and Little Colorado. In Hopiland pueblos grew up at Walpi No. 1 and Sikyatki, at Shungopovi below the present Second Mesa site, at Oraibi (which apparently has been occupied continuously ever since), as well as elsewhere.

In 1291-99 (a date fixed by studying tree rings of beams excavated from the pueblos) there occurred a great drought, which apparently was an important factor in bringing about a movement of various peoples and an end of the Classic Period. A sudden influx of people into Hopiland increased the size of the towns and changed the style of the pottery. The towns grew into cities covering a dozen or more acres. About this time the great pueblos of Sikyatki on the ancient Basketmaker site, and Awatobi and Kawaiokuh on Antelope Mesa, were founded.[2] Thus by the time America was discovered practically all the important Hopi groups, as we know them today, had been established, Oraibi being the only one to occupy its present site.

When the Spaniards of Coronado's expedition, traveling from Zuni, arrived in 1540 there were seven Hopi pueblos: Awatobi, the easternmost which remained for almost two centuries the gateway to the "Moqui" (as the Hopi were called), Sikyatki, Kawaiokuh, Walpi No. 1, Mishongnovi, Shungopovi, and Oraibi (the westernmost and most isolated).[3] But at once the number began to be reduced, for Coronado's men attacked and destroyed Kawaiokuh. Sikyatki was the next pueblo to be abandoned—destroyed, according to tradition, by the Walpians on account of a dispute of long standing over the use of First Mesa lands and water. As we shall see, Awatobi came third. For a time it looked as though Oraibi might be the fourth of the great Hopi pueblos to be abandoned, but since its population is now increasing the ancient pueblo may survive for some time to come.

After the first encounter, early contacts with the Spaniards (mainly explorers and seekers after gold) were sporadic and, except for the formal submission of the Hopi to Spain (1598), were relatively unimportant. In 1628, however, two Spanish Franciscan priests, accompanied by soldiers, arrived in Hopiland and soon three missions were established: San Bernardino at Awatobi, San Bartolome at Shungopovi with a chapel at Mishongnovi, and San Francisco at Oraibi with a chapel at Kisakovi (Walpi No. 2), just southwest of Walpi No. 1.

Not much is known about the Catholic mission period, which lasted for 52 years, because most of the Spanish records were destroyed in the Great Pueblo Revolt in 1680. At this time almost all the pueblos, including the Hopi, united and drove the missionaries and other Spaniards from their land. We know, however, that the Hopi acquired from the Spaniards many new traits which had a marked effect especially on their technology—including cultivated plants such as peaches and grapes, chili and watermelon; domestic animals such as sheep, cattle, mules and burros; herding and breeding practices; the tanning of leather; and farm tools such as the plowshare.[4] Certain changes, not altogether clear, occurred in their religious practices and beliefs, such as perhaps the introduction of aspects of Spanish witchcraft which supplemented old Indian lore. Moreover, new diseases began to appear, such as smallpox, trachoma, tuberculosis, measles, whooping cough, typhoid and probably syphilis.

The Revolt was followed by a movement of pueblos and Pueblo peoples. The Hopi pueblos of Walpi No. 2, Shungopovi and Mishongnovi moved for protection to their present sites on the mesa tops; part of the Shungopovi people settling Shipaulovi[5] and part of the Walpians moving later (before

1782) to Sichomovi.[6] Refugees against Spanish reprisals from the Rio Grande began to arrive in Hopiland, and they founded the town of Hano on First Mesa[7] and apparently also Payupki on the Second. The Spaniards made several attempts to reconquer the Hopi— physically a n d spiritually—which, though unsuccessful, were not without important repercussions. Awatobi, for receiving two Catholic priests, was attacked and destroyed by some of the other Hopi pueblos (about 1700), according to tradition, and Payupki was attacked by Spaniards and Catholic Zuni and later abandoned when its inhabitants returned to the Rio Grande (about 1742). Only Oraibi, the largest and most isolated Hopi pueblo, remained secure on her ancient foundations.

The Spanish officials also tried by methods other than the use of force to reduce the Hopi to submission. In 1780, for example, after a devastating drought[8] in Hopiland, they invited the tribe to settle on lands in the lower Rio Grande Valley, but many of the Hopi refused[9] and with the help of their inhospitable desert (the crossing of which was called "journey of death" by the Spaniards)[10] succeeded by subterfuge and passive resistance in outwitting their powerful adversaries and remained the only group of Pueblo peoples whom the Spanish soldiers and missionaries failed to recapture.

The Spaniards, however, were not the only disrupting factors with which the Hopi had to contend during these difficult years. Groups of Navaho, having acquired great mobility through the introduction of the horse, had been putting pressure on the Hopi since as early as the 18th century. Around the turn of the 19th century, other nomadic Indian tribes (chiefly Ute, Paiute and Apache), also began to move into the surrounding country and raid the Hopi fields and villages.[11] These raids increased as the power of Spain in the New World dwindled, and the Navaho

especially became a serious menace to the existence of the tribe in the period of lawlessness following the Mexican revolt (1823). A severe drought and an epidemic of smallpox in 1853-54[12] and a recurrence of both in still more severe forms some ten years later, brought the Hopi to one of the worst crises in their history. Having resisted attempts of Mormon missionaries to get them to move to Utah (1858-65), and of the American Indian Agent in Arizona to get them to move to the Tonto Basin south of Flagstaff (1866), finally in 1867 some Hopi were driven by accumulated misfortunes to seek refuge at Zuni and other pueblos. As soon as they had rallied their strength, however, most of these refugees returned to their mesas, and they brought with them several Zuni traits, including a new style of pottery decoration and certain ceremonials, the influence of which may be seen in Hopi culture to-day.[13] Also some Hopi learned the Spanish language.

From this time on the Hopi have felt increasingly the effects of the American regime, which began with the Treaty of Guadalupe Hidalgo (1848).[14] American troops, freed for service in the West after the Civil War, succeeded in checking and finally eliminating the Navaho raids. The trail across the desert to Hopiland, practically closed to traffic for 50 years, was thus reopened (1868) and influences from the outside began to multiply.

About 1870 the first traders and Protestant missionaries arrived at Keams Canyon and soon a mission school was established (1875).[15]

Moreover, the Government at Washington began to show an interest in the Hopi.[16] A Special Agent was appointed for the tribe (1870) and the "Moqui" Reservation of 3,920 square miles was set aside by Executive Order in 1882. The first Government school[17] was opened at Keams Canyon in 1887, a year after several leading men from the First and Second Mesas had formally requested a school. Most of the villages, however, were indifferent to the innovation, Oraibi refusing altogether to send any children away from home. Only the First Mesa pueblos welcomed the school, the majority of the children being drawn from them, especially Hano. As a result, compulsory quotas of children, to be filled by each village, were established.

The Oraibians, stating that they did not wish to have anything to do with the Government, continued to resist and also refused to have a census taken. Events in the pueblo reached a peak when, according to the provision of the Indian Allotment Act (1887), the subdivision of Hopi lands in severalty was ordered and surveyors were sent to the Reservation (1891).[18] This disturbed the Hopi, but whereas the chiefs of Walpi met the situation by sending a petition to Washington, bearing the symbol of every clan and requesting the Government to respect the ancient land ownership, those of Oraibi pulled up the surveyor's stakes and threatened to destroy the school. When a small party of officials and soldiers arrived under orders to arrest the chiefs, the Oraibians made a formal declaration of war, and order was not restored until two companies of cavalry, threatening the pueblo with guns, took five of the village chiefs to Fort Wingate as prisoners (1891).[19]

At this time Oraibi[20] was still the most populous Hopi village with an estimated population of 1200.[21] It was also the most hostile[22] pueblo with little contact with the outside world. On the other hand, First Mesa, which had been the buffer to White and Navaho influences since the destruction of Awatobi 200 years before, was friendly to visitors and less resistant to change. Its resident population, according to a house-to-house census by Stephen (1893) was 544, of whom 381 were from Walpi and Sichomovi.[23] Already a White trader, bringing his goods by solid-wheeled wagon from Santa Fe,

had established himself at Coyote Spring, some distance from the mesa, and two houses, below Hano, marked the beginning of the settlement of Polacca. The Hopi went occasionally about 75 miles south to the railroad to trade, and a dozen White visitors attended the Snake Dance.

During the next two decades outside influences among the Hopi increased rather rapidly. Whereas theretofore the activities of the Protestant mission and Government school had been considerably circumscribed by the remoteness of their headquarters at Kéams Canyon, missions and schools now began to be built on or near the mesas. A Mennonite mission was established at Oraibi in 1893 and a rival Baptist mission at Polacca the following year.[24] Government day schools were built within walking distance of all the pueblos: at Polacca and Oraibi in 1894 and at Toreva (below Mishongnovi) in 1897.[25] With the missions and schools came traders, and the present modern settlements below the mesas began to take form. Moreover progressive Hopi started to acquire horse-drawn farm implements from the Government.[26]

Although a slight attempt was made to improve the health of the people through activities of field matrons, with a few exceptions the Hopi were not vaccinated, and in 1898-99 the tribe was again decimated by another smallpox epidemic.[27]

These changes served to crystallize a feud which had been developing for some time at Oraibi.[28] The pueblo split into two rival factions, the "Hostiles" who refused to have anything to do with the Government, the schools or the missions, and the "Friendlies" who were willing to compromise.[29] Since the Hopi do not sanction physical violence in any form, this struggle expressed itself overtly mainly in the disruption of the pueblo's ceremonial life which, as we shall see in subsequent chapters, lies at the very heart of Hopi culture.

A crisis was precipitated when a group of conservatives from Shungopovi moved to Oraibi at the invitation of the "Hostiles" leader (1904). A severe drought followed and Tewaquaptewa, Village Chief and leader of the "Friendlies," insisted on the return of the Shungopovis in order, as he said, to ease the water situation. Since neither side would yield and open conflict was prohibited traditionally and also by the Government, in the summer of 1906 both sides agreed to settle the issue by means of a contest. The two parties faced each other on either side of a goal line just outside Oraibi, the "Friendlies" with their backs toward the pueblo, and each side pushed forward until the "Friendlies" finally triumphed by pushing over the line. The "Hostiles," thus forced out of the pueblo, founded the village of Hotevilla on the mesa eight miles northeast of Oraibi, and thereby reduced the population of the ancient pueblo to about 600. At this point the Government Agent stepped in and arrested the leaders of both sides, as well as most of the "Hostile" men. These "Hostiles" were sentenced to from three months to three years of hard labor, while Tewaquaptewa and his nephew were sent for four years to school in California.[30] Thus depleted, the Hotevilla band suffered considerably during the following winter and this strengthened their resistance to the Government. Subsequently the less conservative members of the group returned to Oraibi but were driven out again and founded the village of Bakabi (1907), on the mesa half a mile east of Hotevilla.

The population of Oraibi was still further reduced by migrations to Moencopi, Oraibi's summer colony 40 miles to the west, which now became a permanent Hopi village. Also people began to move to New Oraibi at the foot of the mesa, especially after the return of Tewaquaptewa (1910) who, having changed his attitude toward Whites considerably during his years at school, now insisted that all converts to Christianity must leave the pueblo.

Oraibi's population continued to dwindle for some years but, judging by the number of children in the pueblo today, it is apparently picking up again. However, the once great pueblo now has the appearance of a ruin amidst which live less than 200 souls.

Regarding the population of the tribe as a whole, the census figures are unreliable until the last decade or two. However, using them as indicative of trends, we find that the population apparently lost ground or remained practically stationary from the final decade in the 19th century until about the second decade of the 20th. It then began to increase, gaining about 12% from 1920 to 1932, and 25% from 1933 to 1943.[31] This is an average increase per annum of 2.5% across the last ten years, which is three and a half times the 1940 rate of increase for the United States population as a whole. In 1943 the population density per square mile in the Hopi Jurisdiction (see page 32) was 3.04, as against 1.81 in the original "Moqui" Reservation, 1.42 in the surrounding Navaho Reservation, and 1.00 in adjacent rural areas. The approximate death rate was 25 per 1000, as against 13.3 for the United States Indian population as a whole, 12 for the State of Arizona, and 10.5 for the United States as a whole.

DEATH RATE

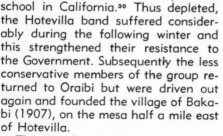

HOPI	25
U.S. INDIAN	13.3
ARIZONA	12
U.S.A.	10.5

Estimated rate per 1000 population, 1942

INFANT MORTALITY

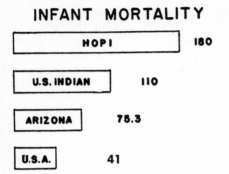

HOPI	180
U.S. INDIAN	110
ARIZONA	75.3
U.S.A.	41

Estimated rate per 1000 live births, 1942

The approximate birth rate was 40 per 1000, as against 25.3 for the Indian population as a whole, 25.9 for Arizona, and 19.5 for the United States. (See figure below). And infant mortality was estimated as 180 per 1000 live births for the Hopi, as contrasted to 110 for the Indians as a whole, 75.3 for Arizona, and 41 for the United States. The estimated population of the tribe on January 1, 1943 was 3558, (1831 males and 1727 females)[32] of whom 96% were living on the Reservation. There were in addition some 80 other Indians and 100 Whites.

The native population increase in the last ten years coincides with the most recent period of change among the Hopi, particularly regarding their relationship to the Government. Before this time the Federal Government had assumed an arbitrary role, the avowed purpose of which was to break up the traditional life of the Hopi and destroy

BIRTH RATE

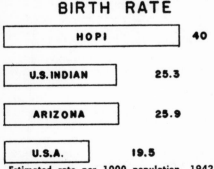

HOPI	40
U.S. INDIAN	25.3
ARIZONA	25.9
U.S.A.	19.5

Estimated rate per 1000 population, 1942

the power of their "priests" and "chiefs," at the same time encouraging the Indians to develop White industries and skills. This attitude was reflected in most Government policies and contacts; as for instance, the persistent attempts on the part of the Federal Government to allot the Hopi lands in severalty (the first of which extended from 1892 to 1894 and the second from 1907 to 1910);[33] the rule of compulsory attendance at schools, enforced by troops who compelled the people to give up their children during their formative years; and the encouragement of both Hopi and Navaho to increase their livestock as much as possible, regardless of range capacity. Moreover, when as a result of the growth of their herds the Navaho encroached on Hopi-occupied lands, the Government did nothing to protect the Hopi. These factors helped to create in the minds of the Hopi a lack of confidence and general negative attitude toward the Government and to increase their sense of insecurity.

Soon after 1933, however, the tribe began to feel the effects of the Indian New Deal. Under the Indian Reorganization Act (Wheeler-Howard), accepted by the Hopi in 1935, the Government helped the tribe to draw up a Constitution by which an attempt was made to give it the opportunity to develop self government through the formation of a Tribal Council, composed of representatives from each village.[34] This was an attempt to provide the tribe with a mechanism by which it could grow into a self governing unit, with legally established rights and responsibilities, under the protection of the Federal Government. The first Council met in 1937 and since then the Council has been struggling to establish itself in the face of the traditional lack of political unity between the villages, a point which will become clearer in subsequent chapters.

In conjunction with the new Government policy of allowing the Indians free cultural expression, the Hopi day schools were developed along progressive lines and carried through the secondary school level (at New Oraibi), attendance was made non-obligatory,[35] the ceremonial life was officially sanctioned, and native arts and crafts were encouraged. To improve the health of the tribe, the hospital at Keams (established in 1913 for both Hopi and Navaho) was modernized,[36] its staff was increased, a field physician was stationed at Oraibi and a field nurse at Polacca and one at Second Mesa, water facilities were developed and made sanitary for a number of the villages, and a course in hygiene was added to the school curriculum. Finally, in accordance with the new policy of helping Indians to develop and conserve their natural resources, an extensive program of land and resource improvement by means of soil and moisture conservation practices, and improved farming and range methods, was inaugurated. This was described in Chapter 1. And for the first time the Hopi were given a Superintendent charged with devoting himself exclusively to their interests.

On the other hand, whereas the land base of many Indian tribes has been increased under the new administration, that of the Hopi has not been increased, but actually has been decreased. The Navaho, some of whom were already living within the boundaries of the original "Moqui" Reservation when it was set up in 1882, gradually encircled the Hopi and took over more and more of the range, until by 1910 they were using practically all of the Reservation land except a small area in the vicinity of the Hopi mesas. Unfortunately this movement coincided with the period of erosion, which has progressively reduced the Hopi land base to a fraction of its former value and made imperative the drastic stock reduction program. Moreover, the Hopi considered that the original "Moqui" Reservation was set up for their exclu-

sive use (although actually it was "for the use and occupancy of the Moqui and such other Indians as the Secretary of the Interior may see fit to settle thereon") and that even this arrangement was an outrage to their vast traditional land claims. Consequently disputes arose between the Hopi and the Navaho, which were finally settled legally by the Government's setting up a grazing unit[37] of 624,064 acres of grazing land and 7,130 acres of farm land for the exclusive use of the Hopi (1943). (See pp 18-19). The result has been to confine the Hopi within an area about one-fourth the size of the original Reservation, a circumstance which, added to past events, has increased the sense of grievance which many Hopi feel toward both the Navaho tribe and the Government.

This is augmented by the fact that although the Hopi were theoretically granted United States citizenship under the treaty of Guadalupe Hidalgo (1848) and were made full citizens by Congressional Act in 1924, the State of Arizona has refused all reservation Indians including the Hopi the right of franchise. In this connection it is interesting to note that the Hopi pay federal income tax, state sales tax, automobile tax, and are subject to selective service. They do not pay taxes on their tribal land or improvements.

Looking at the Hopi today, we realize that a good many changes have taken place on the Reservation in the last 50 years. The material culture has been altered with the introduction of new traits such as improved farm implements, household utensils, machine-made cloth and commercial foods, and the number of traders has increased to 16.[38] Roads have been built, water resources improved, the number of domestic animals and wagons increased and a few automobiles introduced. With the improvement of schools the knowledge of English has become widespread and the number of wage workers has grown. Moreover, a few Hopi[39]

Man weaving a vegetable dye rug in his home

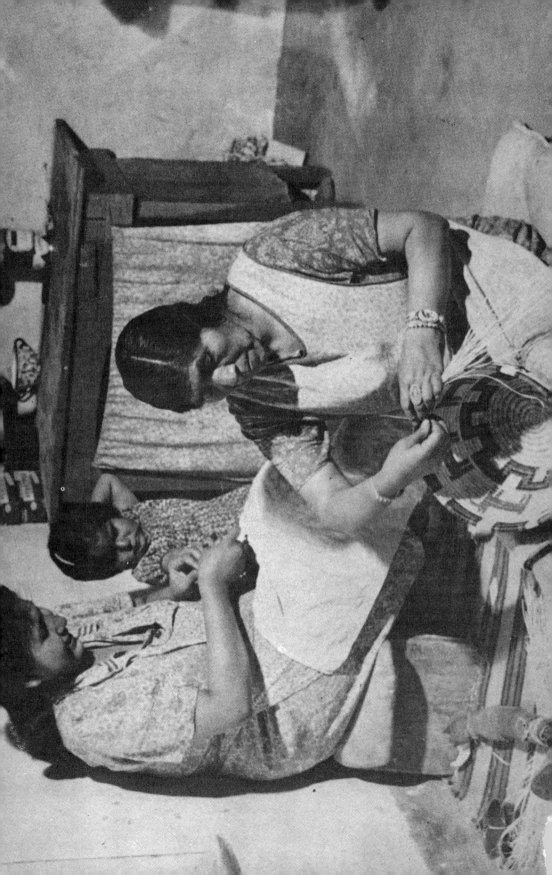

have been converted to Christianity. These changes are most noticeable in the villages below the mesas (Polacca and New Oraibi)[40] where live the most acculturated Hopi—the converts, the cattle owners and the wage workers— as well as the White population composed of Indian Service personnel, Protestant missionaries and traders. Yet in spite of these changes, the Hopi today stand out among the 360,000 Indians of the United States proper[41] as the tribe which probably has been least affected in its basic culture by modern civilization.   This point will become clearer as the study progresses.

In this brief glimpse of the history of Hopiland and its people—covering a span of over a millennium—we have attempted to select and highlight processes and events which we believe may contribute to our understanding of the modern Hopi and their culture. We have seen that out of a nucleus of Pueblo peoples who settled in the vicinity of the Hopi mesas, the Hopi tribe grew and was augmented by accretions from many sources. These apparently sedentary people living in apparently closely knit local groups, when viewed through the perspective of centuries, turn out, on account of the interrelationship between factors of the e x t e r n a l environment (especially drought, disease and out-group aggression) and factors of internal organization, to have long manifested not only

a certain physical mobility but also an absence of rigid internal cohesion, expressed in occasional town segmentation and in lack of tribal unity.

We have also seen that the problem of survival in the desert environment, which faces the tribe today, is an age old problem slightly disguised; and that early in Hopi history a solution to it was worked out by the ancestors of the tribe and a general pattern of culture established, the main features of which have come down to the present, not only on account of their survival value in a particular environment, but also and mainly on account of the complex interplay of that environment with historical factors which delayed contact with the outside world (i. e., the defeat and rebuff of the Spaniards, the success of the Navaho raiders, and the subsequent peaceful encirclement of the Hopi by the Navaho). As the study progresses we shall see that other factors, namely, the internal organization of the group and its interrelationship with Hopi personality played an important part in this complex process.

Having looked at the Hopi from the outside as it were—that is, at their interrelationships with the external environment at long range—we shall now turn inward and study briefly their social structure and ceremonial life in relationship to their exceedingly interesting and original outlook on the world.

3.   THE CLAN MOTHER AND HER BROTHER

So far we have discussed only aspects of the Hopi culture and its setting which, even when presented in a brief and summary form, are easy to grasp because they tie in with our own experience. In the next three chapters we shall explore that part of Hopi collective life which, for the reason that

its basic configuration developed quite independently of our own, is somewhat strange to all of us who have been conditioned by modern western civilization. To stand aside from one's own culture and view another with perspective and with empathy[2] is about the most difficult intellectual

Mother and daughter
making coiled baskets

and emotional task that faces modern man, but this is what we must try to do if we are to make progress toward scientific social planning for world peace.

Whereas often in modern industrial civilization, life appears to be segmented into diverse parts which may be worked into a meaningful whole only through individual effort, life to the Hopi is a single unit, the various aspects of which are obviously interrelated. The familiar categories of the economic, the social and the religious for him do not exist. Sacred and secular are one, for his universe, although complex in detail, is a unified system, all aspects of which are interrelated under a single set of rules.

The formal relationships in this universe are patterned mainly in accordance with the Hopi kinship system, which differs markedly from our own in that it is based on the principle of unilateral descent through the female line, rather than on that of bilateral descent through both parents with emphasis on the male line. Whereas, under our system, kin through both blood and marriage are grouped by families, the individual acknowledging close connection with immediate relatives in the ascending and descending generations on both the father's and the mother's sides, under the Hopi system the emphasis is on kin related by blood through the mother's line only and grouped by clans.

A Hopi clan consists of one or more matrilineal lineages which descend theoretically at least, from a common ancestress.[3] The living core of the lineage is a closely knit group of females, consisting of a senior member, usually the oldest woman (who is its female or "real" head) and her sisters, together with all their female descendants. The brothers of the "real" head (one of whom is its male or "ceremonial" head) and all the male descendants of the females in the lineage are also members of the lineage. It should be noted that relatives of the above mentioned individuals by marriage do not belong to the lineage.

The females of the lineage, together with their husbands and their unmarried male descendants, occupy one or more households[4] which are frequently adjacent to one another especially in the older Hopi villages. And the married men of the lineage, although living in the households of their wives, look upon the households of their mothers or sisters as their real homes, to which they return frequently to participate in the ceremonial life of their clans and secret societies. Moreover, they go back there to live in case they lose their wives through death or divorce.

Each household is practically an independent economic unit, the members of which work together for the welfare of all. The women and girls of the group cooperate in caring for the children and the house; storing, preparing and cooking the food for the group; hauling water from the spring; cultivating the vegetable gardens, and making pottery or baskets. On the other hand the men of the household, with the help of their sons, do all the farming, herding, hunting, collecting of fuel and timber for the group. Many of them also spin, weave and work with leather. Also, they frequently contribute materially to their mothers' or sisters' households. Moreover, as we shall presently see, much of their time and energy is spent in ceremonial activities connected with the clans and ceremonial associations to which they belong.

Since in Hopi theory, ownership is usually correlated with use, the house and its appurtenances, the food stored in it, its seeds,[5] its springs and its gardens[6] are considered to belong collectively to the women who live in it, in charge of the female head. Also the children are thought of as belonging to this group.[7] The men, on the other hand, own individually most of the livestock and the fruit trees, besides their personal effects, tools and ceremonial regalia.[8]

One household in each clan is regarded as its traditional "ancestral house," and the two heads of this household are the leaders of the clan, the woman being the Clan Mother or "real" clan head and her brother being the "ceremonial" clan head. Here the interest of the clan members is focused. Clan meetings and certain clan ceremonies are held in this household and here are kept its fetishes and other sacred paraphernalia, looked after and "fed"[9] by the Clan Mother.

Each clan feels itself very closely related to a non-human partner, called wuya, consisting of a species of animal or plant (for example, Bear or Reed), or a class of natural or supernatural phenomena (Bow, Cloud, or Sun's Forehead), which gives the clan its name, its quality or "medicine," and its protection in return for certain correlative services. The members of the clan refer to their non-human partners by a kinship term such as father, mother, or mother's brother. The fetish, also called wuya, representing this primary partner, is kept in the clan ancestral house. The clan feels related to a number of other non-human partners, which may be thought of as its secondary partners, each of these belonging primarily, however, to another clan. A group of clans which share the same wuya, either through primary or secondary ownership, are considered to be related and members are not allowed to intermarry. They share not only one another's wuya but also their clan names, and take a continued interest and responsibility in one another's ceremonies. Such groups of related clans form exogamous units, called phratries,[10] which function chiefly to regu-

late marriage. These phratries are the largest groups in Hopi society based directly on kinship.

Having outlined the organization and functions of the household and its relationship to the lineage, clan and phratry, we are better able to understand why the Hopi classifies his relatives and patterns his behavior toward them according to a system which differs considerably from our own (also incidentally why it is difficult for him to translate his kinship terms accurately into English or our terms into Hopi). The Hopi, for example, calls not only his own mother but all her sisters and their female cousins related through his maternal grandmother—in fact, any elderly woman of his own clan—by the term ngu'u[11] (mother). His mother's brothers, his mother's mother's brothers and any elderly clansman of his mother's generation, he calls ta'ha (mother's brother). He classes his sisters and female parallel-cousins[12] together as "sisters," and his brothers with his male parallel-cousins as "brothers," but distinguishes in these categories between those who are older and those who are younger than himself. All these relatives are in the same clan as himself.

His father, who belongs to a different clan, on the other hand, he classes not only with his father's brothers but also with his own male cross-cousins and, in fact, with his father's clansmen generally—all under the blanket term naa (father). And his father's sisters he groups with all the women of his father's clan, except his paternal grandmother and her sisters, under the term kyaa (father's sister). The paternal grandmother is classed with her sisters, her mother and mother's sisters (and also with the maternal grandmother, her sisters, her mother and mother's sisters) under the term soo (grandmother). A similar grouping of both paternal and maternal grandfathers is called kwa'a (grandfather).

It is not necessary for our purposes to burden the reader with a complete description of the kinship system.[13] This brief treatment will suffice to show the central position of the women in the Hopi household in contrast to the peripheral position of the men, and to clarify especially the close basic relationship between mother and daughter, which is the cornerstone of Hopi society. Since every kinship term implies a set of obligations and privileges, expressed in prescribed attitudes and behavior, it will illuminate the patterns of reciprocal interaction between relatives.

The kinship system is important because it is applied to (and regulates Hopi attitudes and correlative behavior toward) not only all Hopi related by blood or marriage, but also (through a series of extension mechanisms such as ceremonial adoption and initiation) to practically all interpersonal relations in the tribe, and many relationships with neighboring tribes, such as the Navaho and Zuni. Hence, an individual is related, either through actual kinship or through an extension of it, to practically everyone else in the pueblo and also in other Hopi pueblos, and his behavior in practically all face-to-face relationships with other individuals with whom he comes in contact, except Whites of course, is prescribed and regulated accordingly. Frequently a person is related in several ways to another and in this case he usually acknowledges and acts upon the closest or clan bond. Moreover certain natural and supernatural phenomena are addressed in kinship terms. For instance, the sun is called father; the earth, mother; the spider, grandmother; and clan partners are called father, mother or mother's brother. Thus the kinship system also affects the patterning of Hopi relationships toward the non-human world and functions as one of the most important integrating mechanisms in Hopi life.

As we have noted, the Hopi household, lineage, clan and phratry center in the women of the tribe, and it is the significance given by the Hopi to the function of women in kinship groups attached to specific houses, the most important of which are repositories for clan and secret society fetishes, that gives the clue to their relatively high position in Hopi society.[14] This mother-house-fetish complex also provides the connecting link between the kinship and the ceremonial systems. For, as has been noted, the brother of the Clan Mother is the ceremonial head of the clan and as such he controls the ceremonies (if any) which are attached to the clan, as well as their associated fetishes. This relationship will become clearer as we study the ceremonial and political organization of the village. (See Chapter 5). In order to understand the pueblo theocracy, however, we shall first consider some aspects of the Hopi world view and ritual.

4. A STONE AGE THEORY OF THE UNIVERSE[1]

Implicit in the Hopi configuration of culture is an original and basically integrated theory of the universe by which the Hopi attempt to organize their world in order to cope with their life problems and obtain some degree of security in a highly hazardous environment. They conceive of the world —including man, the animals, the plants, the land base and the supernatural—as an absolute, ordered system functioning under a definite set of rules, which are known to them (and to them alone). In accordance with these rules they believe they can, through regulating their behavior, emotions and thoughts in a prescribed manner, exercise a measure of control over their environment.

Theoretically all phenomena, natural and supernatural, living and dead —including man, animals, plants, the earth, sun, moon and clouds, the ancestors and the spirits—are interrelated and mutually dependent through the underlying dynamic principle of the universe—which we shall call the law of universal reciprocity. This law implies the concept of immanent or cosmic justice. The emphasis is not, however, on the idea of rewards and punishments or on punishments alone (retribution), but on the mutual exchange of essentially equivalent but not identical values according to fixed traditional patterns, in the interests of the common weal. Man, the elements, animals, plants and the supernatural cooperate in an orderly fashion, by means of a complex set of correlative interrelationships, for the good of all.

This concept of the universe is not "mechanistic" in the usual sense of the term, on account of the special role played by man in the scheme of things. Whereas, according to Hopi theory, the non-human universe is controlled *automatically* by the reciprocity principle, man is an active agent who may or may not acquiesce in it. While the world of nature is *compelled* to respond in certain prescribed ways to certain stimuli, man not only responds but also *elicits* response. Hence, man, in the measure that he obeys the rules, may exercise a certain limited control over the universe.

Hopi philosophy, therefore, ascribes to man an element of choice—which, it seems, is dependent on his *will*.[2] And this element of choice, this concept of a free-will-within-the-law, we may ex-

pect to be reflected in Hopi social sanctions and in Hopi personality. In fact it is crucial to an understanding of the dynamics of Hopi society.

To show how the law of universal reciprocity operates, we shall first touch on another basic tenet of Hopi thought. All phenomena, living and dead, which are important, either positively or negatively, to the Hopi in their struggle for existence, are grouped into mutually interrelated orders or classes and these orders are combined into overall, interdependent categories. This web of categorized orders of phenomena gives basic form to the cosmos.

We have already seen that human beings are grouped into orders—namely clans—through the kinship system, and these clans or human orders are linked with orders of non-human phenomena through an extension of the kinship system to include their non-human partners, forming a category of human, natural and supernatural phenomena. This process illustrates the Hopi tendency to classify in order to control, a tendency similar to that operating in other societies which attempt to understand and control their environments. It may be compared specifically to the tendency in our own society to classify and control through the methods of science. Hopi categories, however, are so different from those with which we are familiar that they baffle investigators and remain as yet but little understood. It is only by laboriously piecing together bits of internal evidence until they crystallize into a pattern and then checking the results with other aspects of the culture and the language that we are able to gain some insight into their nature and meaning. Our main clues are found in the grouping of clans with non-human partners mentioned above, in the extremely complex, highly organized ceremonial, and in the symbol system.[3]

Examining the clan *wuya* groupings,[4] we note that some apparently represent significant activities in Hopi life, as for instance, the Waterhouse-Rain-Corn-Frog, etc. unit associated with the growth cycle of corn; some are evidently linked with one of the world's six[5] cardinal points, as the Sun-Moon-Stars-Eagle-Hawk-Turkey is with the Zenith or "Above" direction, and some, like t h e Bear-Spider-Bluebird-Carrying-Strap,[6] are associated by an explanatory myth.

To illustrate, the Hopi say that on leaving the Underworld a part of the tribe went ahead of the rest and finally came to the Little Colorado. Here they looked at a dead bear and from then on were called the Bear clan. A party traveling with them made carrying straps out of the bear's hide and were called the Carrying Strap or Bearhide clan. Shortly thereafter another party found bluebirds eating the bear's cadaver and they became the Bluebird clan. Still another came and found the remains of the cadaver full of spider web, so that part was called the Spider clan. The Bears, after many halts and wanderings, finally settled at Shungopovi, the first Hopi to arrive and hence the leading clan.

An analysis of the phratry groupings in relation to the Hopi traditional symbol system as revealed in ceremonial and myth, shows that they tend to follow an ideal pattern in which each unit, composed of a group of related clans, may also include as non-human partners one or more species of animals and of plants, one or more orders of physical objects, one or more natural elements and one or more deities or parts of anthropomorphic deities. Moreover, ideally each unit appears also to be associated with certain character traits of their non-human partners; with one of the six world directions and its color (each direction has a color as well as other symbolic associations[7]); with a season of the year; with an important activity (economic or ceremonial); with one or both sexes; and with some aspect of the reproduction and growth cycle. This concept of the phratry, as

representing a category of orders interrelated according to an ideal pattern, explains why the Hopi include extinct as well as living groups when asked to name the clans in a phratry and why the Hopi are more accurate in keeping phratry than clan lines distinct. Probably the symbolism expressed in these categories may be interpreted at various levels—from the concrete to the abstract and from the natural to the supernatural—interrelationship b e - tween the symbolic elements being expressed through rituals associated with the clans.[8]

Such basic categories and their subdivisions form the framework within which the law of universal, reciprocity operates. For it is between orders and categories of phenomena rather than between individuals that correlative exchange takes place. Individuals usually interact reciprocally not on their own, but in behalf of a group. For instance, a man functions in a reciprocal exchange of goods or services not as an individual but as a representative of his household, clan or secret society. In similar fashion, the leader of a ceremony theoretically correlates with orders of natural and supernatural phenomena in behalf of his clan, secret society and village, and also, in major ceremonials at least, for the good of the whole tribe and all mankind.

In attempting to understand the Hopi world view, we should bear in mind that some orders of phenomena, e. g., those composed of human beings, animals, plants, spirits or gods, are considered to be living, while others, e. g., those composed of physical objects, are dead. Of the living orders, most animals and some plants, such as the evergreen spruce (which is associated with the kachinas or ancestors)[9], are thought of as being human beings in disguise with "other homes"[10] where they live in human form, and their own afterworld to which their spirits return when they are killed.

This brings us to two important aspects of the Hopi world view, namely the Hopi sense of space and time, a grasp of which will illuminate our whole study. Spatially, the Hopi universe is three dimensional, with six sides, corresponding to the six cardinal directions. It is divided horizontally into two parts: the upper world of the living, and the Underworld, from which mankind emerged originally through the Sipapu (Place of Emergence) to which the individual returns after death. The passage of the individual through the life cycle and the migration of the tribe to its present site are expressed symbolically in the ceremonies by means of a line (usually traced with corn meal) beginning in an aperture, called the sipapu, in the floor of the kiva.[11]

During the hazardous passage from birth to death, the individual is sheltered by means of a house, which has become a symbol of security.[12] At life crises, when the feeling of insecurity is intensified, the individual is provided with a symbolic house; as, for instance, when at the birth of a child the father's mother marks four parallel lines of corn meal on each wall of the house. The clan, in its continuous life through the generations, has, as has been noted, its ancestral house. And all creatures, natural and supernatural, in the universe are thought of also as having "houses."[13] For example, the Sun has a "house" at each of the solstice points; the Hard Substance Women, two female deities who created the earth, have "houses," one in the east and the other in the west;[14] and the clan non-human partners also have "houses." Moreover, as part of the pattern of reciprocity for mutual security, man builds symbolic houses or shrines for his non-human partners and his gods. This house concept expresses the Hopi's need for definite, three-dimensional boundaries, of closed spaces, of fixed points, in his vast and timeless world.

For to the Hopi time as a *dimension* (in the sense that the concept is used

in modern physics) does not exist.[15] The Hopi verb has three tenses but their function is not, like our tenses, to distinguish between the present, past and future of an event but to distinguish between the *factual* (which may represent action in either the present or the past), the *future*, and the *generalized*. Thus verbs in the Hopi language always indicate what type of validity the speaker intends a statement to have: whether it be the report of an event, the expectation of an event, or a generalization or law about an event, and they also indicate exactly the actual sequence of reported events.

Moreover, the Hopi distinguish with much greater precision than we do between the nature of momentary, continued and repeated occurrences. For example, their language is unusually rich in terms for vibratory phenomena and for the punctual events to which they are related. That is, verbs which have a punctual aspect may be given a repetitive or durative or vibratory quality by the use of reduplication and a suffix (i. e., ho'chi— " it forms a sharp acute angle," becomes hochi'chita— "it is zigzag"; wa'la—"it makes one wave" becomes wala'lata—"it is tossing waves;" wuu'ku—"he takes a step without moving from place" becomes wuku'kuta—"he is dancing in one place"). Thus Hopi verb forms establish a general contrast between two types of experience, namely the "particle" and the "field of vibrations" and practically compel observation and classification of such phenomena.

"This contrast," as Whorf[16] has noted, "corresponds to a contrast that, as our science has discovered, is all pervading and fundamental in nature. According to the conceptions of modern physics, the contrast of particle and field of vibrations is more fundamental in the world of nature than such contrasts as space and time, or past, present and future, which are the sort of contrasts that our own language imposes upon us." And the Hopi actually have a language and consequently a world view better equipped to deal with it than our latest scientific terminology. For as we know, the language of a group, in its capacity as a classifying and arranging instrument, actively conditions its world view.

Turning to the concept of plurality and numeration, we find another significant difference between the language and world view of the Hopi and our own, in regard to the concept of time. The Hopi use plurals and cardinals only for entities that actually form an objective group and can be counted. That is, the Hopi would use the expression "ten men," but not "ten days." Whereas with us a "length of time," such as a day, is thought of as a row of similar units, like a row of bottles (in other words, it is objectified and counted quantitatively), with the Hopi our "length of time" is not thought of as a *length* at all, but as a *relation* between two events in lateness. "They stayed ten days" becomes in Hopi "they stayed until the tenth day." Thus "instead of our linguistically promoted objectification of that datum of consciousness we call 'time', the Hopi language has not laid down a pattern that would cloak the subjective 'becoming later' that is the essence of time."

In like manner all phase terms like "summer, morning," etc. are not objectified as nouns but are used as a kind of adverb meaning "while the summer phase is occurring" or "when it is morning." Hopi do not say "this summer," but "summer now" or "summer recently." There is nothing suggested except a phase in a cycle similar to earlier phases in an "ever-later-becoming duration."

Hopi time, in fact, may be thought of as a *duration*, a "becoming later and later," in which existing orders of phenomena develop or change from one phase to another, each according to its own mode or law. Some develop "by growing, like plants, some by diffusing

and vanishing, some by a procession of metamorphoses, some by enduring in one shape till affected by violent forces."[18] The Hopi believe that in the nature of each order "is the power of its own mode of duration: its growth, decline, stability, cyclicity, or creativeness. Everything is thus already 'prepared' for the way it now manifests by earlier phases; and what it will be later, partly has been, and partly is in the act of being so 'prepared.'"[19]

This association of time, in the sense of duration, with development or fulfillment, according to the innate nature of each order of phenomena, and this emphasis on preparation, throws light on much that we have noted in our study of the Hopi so far, and will explain a good deal that might otherwise seem obscure in the ceremonial system, and other aspects of Hopi life and personality to be noted.

Having described briefly some aspects of the Hopi theory of the universe, we shall now turn to its expressions in their code of behavior for the individual. In the Hopi system of mutual dependency, which gives basic form to the universe, each individual, human or non-human, has its proper place in relation to all other phenomena, with a definite role in the cosmic scheme. But, whereas the non-human orders fulfill their obligations more or less automatically under the law, man has definite responsibilities which have to be learned and carried out according to a fixed set of rules. These rules form an ethical code known as the Hopi Way. As we shall see presently, a large part of the training of the child is devoted to learning this code.

The Hopi Way expresses, at the emotional and behavioral level, the Hopi world view. It is an integrated code containing rules for acting, feeling and thinking in every role which a human being, male or female, is required to assume in his life cycle from birth to death. The individual's success in life and also the welfare of the tribe depend on whole-heartedly, and with an effort of the will, cultivating the Hopi Way. Responsibilities increase with age and reach their peak in ceremonial participation, especially in the role of chief priests. And the heaviest responsibility is carried by the ranking priest in his role of Village Chief, as noted in the next chapter.

The rules for ceremonial observance have two aspects, the physical and the psychical. If either aspect is neglected or any regulation broken, failure will result. That is, to carry out a rite successfully, the participants must not only follow the prescribed ritual behavior, perform all the proper acts and observe the tabus, but they must also exercise control over their emotions and thoughts. They must keep a "good heart." A "good heart" means that one must not feel fear, anger, sadness or worry. In other words, one must be inwardly tranquil and of good will.

It is interesting to note in this connection that the Hopi use the same word (na'wakna) for "to will" and "to pray."[20] Praying is willing. The Hopi believe not only that man can control nature to a limited extent by observing these rules, but that if he does not do so, the universe may cease to function. That is, the movements of the sun, the coming of rain, the growth of crops, the reproduction of animals and human beings depend (to a certain extent at least) on man's correct, complete and active carrying out of the rules.

This limited but all important control of nature is possible through definite mechanisms, mainly of a magical nature,[21] which are integrated into a unified ceremonial system. If these mechanisms fail, if rain does not come, if the crops fail to yield a rich harvest, then the Hopi believe that one or more individuals have failed to follow the Hopi Way—and since their failure brings misfortune on the whole community, gossip pins the blame on specific individuals and severely censors them.

When failure assumes the proportions of a crisis, such as drought, pestilence, disease or death, however, then the Hopi believe that one or more individuals have not only failed to work for the common good but that they have worked actively against it. Such individuals are considered to be witches who possess specific death-dealing powers through association with a species of animal partners, such as little black ants, coyotes, owls, crows, bull snakes, cats, or dogs.[22] Witches are "two-hearted," having both an animal and a human heart. They are thought to be organized into a secret society which obtains membership not only by voluntary recruits, but also by the initiation of little children secretly while their parents sleep. The major activity of witches is supposed to be that of causing illness and death among their relatives. Hence they are greatly feared, and fear of witchcraft is a strong sanction in Hopi society.

The constriction experienced by the individual in the rather rigid Hopi social system is expressed not only in the above-mentioned scapegoat-witchcraft motif, but also in the concept of the Spider Woman, a major deity, who may be thought of at the center of the cosmic web. The Spider Woman, who is called grandmother, is considered to be responsible on the one hand for giving the Hopi their major properties and skills, and on the other, for the origin of witchcraft and death. (In fact, according to some accounts, she herself is a witch, from whom all witches have descended).[23] In other words, she not only gives out that which sustains life but also, like the spider, draws in and destroys life. This concept reveals in a rather dramatic way the basic ambivalence of the individual toward the whole matrilineal system, especially the Clan Mother. A similar ambivalence, but in this case with emphasis on the male sex, is shown in the concept of Masau'u, a male deity, the god of the Underworld, fire, war and death (who is thought of as appearing in the guise of a handsome man and also as a skeleton). Masau'u not only represents death, but also fire, a symbol of the creative male principle. (Note the role of Masau'u in the Wuwuchim ceremony, page 43.)

The Hopi Way is expressed formally at high intensity in the Hopi ceremonial cycle. Examining this ceremonial, we find that though highly organized and exceedingly complex in detail, it follows a basic pattern that is quite simple. Each ceremony "belongs to" a secret society, the members of which (under the leadership of the chief priest of the society, who must belong to the proprietary clan) carry out the rites. For example, the Winter Solstice ceremony, held in December, is conducted by the Soyal Society under the leadership of a Patki clan priest at Walpi-Sichomovi and of the Bear clan chief at Oraibi. The organization of these secret societies, which forms a pueblo theocracy, will be discussed in the next chapter.

The major forms of the main ceremonies are performed annually,[24] according to a traditional calendar,[25] the dates of which are determined chiefly by the position of the sun and moon. According to this calendar, the year is divided into two parts by the solstices, the period between the winter and summer solstices (when farm work is relatively light) being devoted to the main ceremonies. During this period the ancestors or kachinas,[26] in the form of masked impersonators, are believed to return from their home in the San Francisco Mountains to visit the Hopi. The kachinas are believed to intercede for the Hopi with the major deities and to bring rain. In fact, they also appear in the form of rain-bearing clouds. In the second half of the year (when the men are busy with the crops and the harvest) the less important and less time-consuming rites are performed.

As has been noted, the Hopi believe that there is a close reciprocal relationship between the living and the dead and this is expressed in their ceremonial. For instance, the bisection of the ritual year is duplicated in the Underworld, only there the order is reversed, the main ceremonies being performed in the second half of the year, and the lesser in the first, the Underworld rites reciprocating those of the Upperworld throughout the annual cycle.[27]

Main ceremonies last either nine or seventeen days,[28] part of the rites taking place in the kiva or subterranean ceremonial chamber[29] to which the ceremony is traditionally attached. During the rites a hole in the floor of the kiva, representing the Place of Emergence of the Hopi tribe, is opened to provide a means of communication with the Underworld.

Moreover, each main ceremony,[30] although emphasizing a certain phase in the annual agricultural cycle coincident with the seasonal calendar, deals with the whole of life as the Hopi see it and may be interpreted at various levels. The sequence starts in December with the pivotal Winter Solstice ceremony which, while emphasizing the annual cycle of the Sun, a major deity, and its crucial significance in the cosmic system, also expresses symbolically the whole Hopi world view with its emphasis on interdependence and reciprocity, the history or the migration of the tribe from the Emergence, fertility and long life. As part of this complex, rites are performed to turn the Sun back northward, and prayer sticks are made for nearly every order in the universe: human beings (living and dead), clan partners, animals of the chase, useful plants, houses, fields, crops, livestock, and the places where clan ancestors stopped enroute to Hopiland. In February comes the Powamu ceremony or "Bean Dance" (conducted by the Powamu Society), which stresses preparatory cleansing, germination and the early stages of growth of the crops, also the purification and early development of children——the first initiation of boys and girls occurring during the performance of this ceremony at four year intervals——and the reciprocal relation of the living to the ancestors (kachinas). This rite complex involves the forced growth of beans and corn in the kivas, and the arrival of large numbers of kachinas, and it opens the racing season designed to bring rain and speed growth. The Niman ceremony or "Home Dance" (conducted by the Kachina Society) in July marks the return of the kachinas to the San Francisco Mountains and emphasizes the maturation or ripening process. At parting the kachinas give the children gifts, including sweet corn from the first planting, which symbolizes and anticipates the main harvest in September. The Snake-Antelope or the Flute ceremonies in August continue the process of rain bringing and crop ripening and are emphasized by the running of races. And finally, the cycle is brought to a close in November through a complicated series of rites called the Wuwuchim (Grown Man) ceremony. At this time, after all trails to the pueblo have been closed, all fires extinguished, and the women and children hidden in the houses, the chief priest impersonating Masau'u kindles a "New Fire," which is distributed later to all the kivas and households. This ceremony, which includes periodically the initiation of the young men to full adult status, emphasizes spectacularly the Hopi concept of the active function of the male principle in the creation of life, the Hopi concept of death and rebirth of the individual in the Underworld where he continues to live in a manner similar to that in the Upperworld, and the Emergence of the tribe. The Wuwuchim is complemented by ceremonies[31] conducted by the women's societies in the fall of the year, which stress thanksgiving for the harvest, the central role of women in the clan and household, and the Hopi concept of the function of the female principle in the life process.

Furthermore, each main ceremony involves a complicated series of rites (many of which are of a preparatory nature), including the formal announcement by the Crier Chief; acts of purification (as head washing with yucca root, smoking, fasting and continence); the gathering of materials for those parts of the paraphernalia which must be renewed each year (prayer feathers and sticks, sand paintings, costume details, etc.); preparing and setting up the sacred objects in the kiva (such as the altars, sand paintings and "medicine water," masks and properties to be used in the ceremony); the practice of dances and songs; and finally the performance of secret rites in the kivà, as well as public dances on the plaza, and frequently also races and games. Most ceremonies are accompanied by reciprocal exchanges of food prepared by the women, between the various social groups.

For every kachina dance about a dozen new songs are composed and all the masks used are repainted, except those representing the highest deities. Occasionally new dances are introduced, as well as new kachinas. Moreover, although participation is most intense among the actual celebrants or dancers who carry the responsibility for the success of the rites, all the villagers and visitors from other pueblos as well, who turn out to watch the public performances at the climax of the ceremony, are supposed to participate passively in the ritual by keeping a "good heart."

Comic relief during these performances is afforded by the clowns, who burlesque slight deviations from the conventional Hopi Way by such pranks as satirizing the ceremonial, caricaturing individuals including White visitors, drenching spectators with urine, and feigning copulation with women. The clowns provoke an immediate response and their antics are greeted with shrieks of laughter.

Although the major ceremonies follow a fixed annual cycle and are performed regularly by individuals in prescribed roles, a certain elasticity is given to the year's program by the fact that any individual may suggest performing certain activities of a minor ritualistic nature, such as a dance of the Butterfly or Buffalo type, a hunt or a working party (usually on behalf of the Town Chief).[32] Under these circumstances the initiator takes the responsibility of leadership in the activity and in certain cases even relieves the Town Chief of his duties for the duration of the rites.[33]

The Hopi ceremonial cycle provides an annual series of elaborate and colorful mystery plays which combine rhythmic movement, singing, impersonation, painting and other creative media in a typically Hopi way, and regularly express and reaffirm the Hopi world view in a symbolic, variegated and highly spectacular manner. It thereby provides a means of expression and release to the whole community, spectators as well as dancers, and intensely recreating interludes in the daily routine. As such it is one of the most important integrating forces in Hopi life and acts as a strong and deeply entrenched bulwark against the encroachment of White civilization, which offers the Hopi no adequate substitute. The breakdown of the ceremonial system in Oraibi and New Oraibi is bound to have a disintegrating effect on the native culture.

This glimpse of some aspects of the Hopi world view and its expression in prescribed patterns of behavior including the ceremonial, the full comprehension of which requires study and multidimensional thinking on our part, reveals that the Hopi way of looking at the universe is quite different from our own and accounts for much in Hopi culture and personality which may seem strange to us. It shows that the conception of change in linear, cause-and-effect terms, common among us, is absent in the thinking of these people, who see life in terms of interrelated, multi-manifested wholes in the process of metamorphosis, each according to its own mode, rhythm and tempo. Moreover, the Hopi concept of the balanced, correlative interdependence of the manifold aspects of reality excludes an arbitrary over-all dual division, such as that which structures our own thinking and forms the basis for our traditional ethical concept of the competing forces of good and evil. Duality in the Hopi world view exists only insofar as it represents two correlates in a reciprocally balanced universal scheme, and each correlate is conceived as an indispensable part of the whole, neither one being essentially subordinate to the other.

5.   THE THEOCRATIC PUEBLO STATE

Having considered some aspects of the Hopi world view and its expression in the Hopi Way and the Hopi ceremonial, we now have a background for understanding the pueblo organization.

Traditional Hopi pueblo organization is based on and grows out of the ceremonial organization mentioned in the last chapter. As has been noted, each major ceremony in the annual calendar is conducted by a secret society under the leadership of a chief priest (or priestess), who belongs traditionally to a certain clan and is usually the male (or female) head of the clan. As a symbol of office, the chief is given the society fetish which consists of an ear of corn, feathers and other wrappings, and is called the "mother" or "heart" of the ceremony. The fetish is kept in the clan ancestral house of the chief priest, in the custody of the Clan Mother.[1]

There are about a dozen of these secret societies functioning in Hopiland today, but not all of them are found in every village. We know of several instances of a society's ceasing to function in a pueblo and its ceremonies lapsing, due to the conversion of its chief priest (or priestess) to Christianity.[2] The status of each society depends on the importance of the ceremony or ceremonies it conducts in the annual cycle, and hence on the degree of responsibility for tribal welfare with which it is charged—the Soyal Society, which conducts the Winter Solstice ceremony, and especially its chief priest, having the greatest responsibility in each pueblo where the Winter Solstice rites are performed. Regarding the concept of status in Hopiland, it is important to realize that the emphasis is always on responsibility for tribal welfare attached to a role, rather than on the prestige or power of the individual who assumes it.

Of these societies about nine, including all those controlling major ceremonies, are open to men and youths only, while three societies conducting minor ceremonies are open to women and girls.[3] Moreover, whereas the ceremonies belonging to the men's societies are carried out entirely by men and youths except for a few minor roles performed by women, those belonging to the women's societies are conducted by women, assisted by men in several major roles. Thus the major responsibility for the pueblo ceremonial falls on the men.

A secret society draws its membership, with the exception of its chief priest, from the whole pueblo and frequently also from other pueblos, irrespective of clan affiliations. Initiation into any one of the societies is open to any individual who fulfills the society's requirements regarding sex and age, and membership is voluntary in all except the tribe-wide Kachina group (open to both boys and girls) and the Wuwuchim (open to men only). A boy, however, usually joins the societies to which his godfather belongs and a girl those of her ceremonial aunt. This pair of ceremonial sponsors is acquired when the child is launched on his ceremonial career through initiation into the kachina cult, to be discussed presently.

To prepare for and conduct their annual rites, the members of a secret society meet in the particular kiva to which their ceremony is attached, and during the secret observances the kiva is closed to all other persons. At other times, however, the kiva is used as a sort of club and work room by a group of men, consisting mainly of those who live in the neighborhood or who are associated through their clan affiliations, ceremonial fathers or Kachina initiations.[4] Here men (and boys who have gone through the first initiation) meet to smoke, talk and plan foot races, to spin, weave and engage in other craft pursuits, and on occasion also to sleep. A kiva belongs to the particular clan whose members took the initiative in building or repairing it, and is in charge of the clan's head man, who has certain responsibilities and duties regarding it.

The kiva chiefs and the chief priests of the societies, as well as the head men of the clans, choose and train successors from among their sisters' sons to take over their offices when they retire or die. In choosing a successor an attempt is made to select, from among those eligible by birth, the individual best fitted for the office. If a society chief dies or is converted to Christianity without having trained a successor the society's ceremony as well as the society itself is likely to be discontinued.

Almost every secret society is believed to control a particular form of sickness, called its "whip." For example, at Walpi the Wuwuchim controls a kind of paralysis; the Kachina, rheumatism; the Snake, body swellings; and the Lalakon, venereal disease.[5] An extinct group was associated with "witch-sent" disease.[6] The society's "whip" afflicts not only those who trespass on its rites, but also its own members unless they discharm themselves after conducting their ceremony.[7] Moreover, in keeping with the belief that what causes a disease may also cure it, each member of the society, and especially its chief priest, has the potential power of curing the society's disease and hence may function in the role of a specialized medicine man. This concept seems to be more highly developed on First Mesa than at Oraibi.[8]

The ceremonial of each pueblo[9] is reaffirmed by a "Chiefs' Talk" or council[10] composed of the chief priests of the leading pueblo societies, which meets, according to tradition, at the end of the Winter Solstice ceremony Membership and status in the "Chiefs' Talk" is determined by the part each group plays in the Winter Solstice rites, chief priest of the Winter Solstice being the chief of the "Talk," with the title of Village or House Chief.

The Village Chief in all villages except Walpi-Sichomovi, Hotevilla and Bakabi is the head of the Bear clan, which owns traditionally all the pueblo and farm lands. As has been noted, the Bear clan is reputed to have arrived first in Hopiland. The group is supposed to have founded Shungopovi and from there spread to other sites, the mythical chief taking possession of all the land and allotting pieces to the heads of the various clans as they arrived, in exchange for ceremonies. On the basis of these traditional claims, the Village Chief is considered theoretically to own all the pueblo lands, and one of his main functions is the settling of land disputes. As interpreter of tradition and spiritual guide of the village, however, he should be protected from ordinary secular matters and from petty worries in order that he may devote his attention to concentrating and praying for the welfare of his people and to guiding them in the Hopi Way. In return, his people look upon him with reverence as their "Father" and cultivate the land attached to his office for him, by means of voluntary, informal, communal work groups.[11] As insignia of office, the Village Chief keeps in his possession the Village Chief's Stick and has the privilege of wearing the Village Chief's Markings, symbols painted on the face and body on certain ceremonial occasions.[12] Moreover, the Oraibi Chief has in his possession a sacred stone, on which is incised a sort of map apparently representing among other things the Bear clan's migration and traditional land claims.[13] Just as with the ceremonies, it appears that the markings on this stone may be interpreted at various levels from the individual to the cosmic.

Under the leadership of the Village Chief, the "Chiefs' Talk" reaffirms the Hopi Way and traditional land claims, certifies successors to aged members, and makes decisions regarding ceremonial participation and plans for the coming year. As in all pueblo meetings, matters requiring decision are usually discussed until a unanimous opinion is reached, and the concept of majority rule is absent. The "Chiefs' Talk" is not a law-making body Hopi common law being implicit in the mythology and the Hopi Way which, besides being an ethical code for the individual, functions as a sort of unwritten traditional constitution for the group. The "Chiefs' Talk" acts occasionally in a judiciary capacity, however, and enforces the customary procedure when necessary through its members who belong to societies formerly associated with war, especially the War Chief. This dignitary is aided if need be by several *kachina* impersonators of a disciplinary character (such as the Giant Kachina) who function, for example, as supervisors of village work groups and have been known to enforce their role on occasion with whatever weapons they bear.[14] Force is seldom requred in Hopiland, however, for public opinion operates as an effective sanction.

Under this system, a good deal of responsibility is thrown upon the individual, who is expected to conform and cooperate *voluntarily*, that is without the use of *physical coercion*. He is, however, under considerable pressure from the whole group, since any lapse on his part will be detrimental to the general welfare—according to Hopi ideology—and this pressure takes the form of ridicule, gossip, and accusations of witchcraft.

As a result there is a good deal of gossip and petty wrangling in the pueblo—apparently more than in most small communities, according to literature.[15] But these intra-pueblo quarrels almost never break into physical violence, and murders are rare in Hopiland, a situation to which the almost total absence of liquor on the Reservation must also be an important contributing factor. A major crime committed on the Reservation would be handled by the Federal Court, but all civil cases and misdemeanors are taken care of by a Tribal Court, which operates without interference from the Indian Service, unless advice is requested, under a code established by the Secretary of the Interior. The officers of the Tribal Court comprise a Hopi Judge (who usually is an older man belonging to an important clan), a Hopi Associate Judge, and two Hopi Police.

A Hopi quarrel occasionally develops into a feud which involves the entire pueblo, and when this occurs the feud may grow into a split, as has been noted in the history of Oraibi. In such a case the predominantly non-coercive mechanisms which give cohesion to the group may not be strong enough to hold the pueblo together and the factions may separate into two or more' pueblos (even without loss of life, as at Oraibi). It should be noted, however, that after such a split the segments may reconstitute themselves and build up a complete pueblo organization again, including a full ceremonial system as was done at Hotevilla.

A pueblo may segment, however, for reasons other than strife: notably, for economic advancement (witness Moencopi, an offshoot of Oraibi, with a permanent water supply on the Moencopi Wash); for additional living space (as, for example, with the founding of Sichomovi apparently on account of overcrowding at Walpi); and also perhaps for ceremonial survival (e. g., Shipaulovi, according to tradition, was founded by people from Shungopovi to preserve the Shungopovi traditions when the latter village was threatened by Spanish reprisals). But these are not complete splits, for in each instance the daughter pueblo has maintained ceremonial connections with the mother and become a sort of colony.

The habit of pueblo segmenting is old in Hopiland, as evidenced by the archaeology[16] and history, but it is important to realize in this connection that, although complete splits do occasionally occur, they are uncommon, and the pueblo organization is sufficiently cohesive internally to permit under certain circumstances the survival of a single pueblo on the same site for many centuries—apparently over 700 years in the case of Oraibi. As our study progresses we shall see that this predominantly non-coercive internal cohesion has its roots deep in the control system of the individual.

Turning from the relations within a single pueblo to those between the several Hopi pueblos, however, we find a somewhat different picture. The historic cases of Sikyatki (destroyed on account of land and water disputes, according to tradition, by the inhabitants of Walpi) and of Awatobi (annihilated by some of the other Hopi pueblos ostensibly because of its reception of Spanish priests) show that quarrels between the pueblos have not always been settled peacefully in the past, but have on occasion broken into open and devastating warfare.[17]

The traditional pueblo organization, which has been described, is politically autonomous, each unit of mother and daughter groups being independent from the rest. Although meetings of the chiefs from several villages do occasionally take place, especially in times of crisis such as drought[18] and other external dangers which threaten the whole tribe, there is no formal traditional mechanism by which the leaders of one pueblo may confer regularly with those of another, and no traditional precedent for regular inter-pueblo cooperation. The only instance of concerted tribal action recorded in history was the Pueblo Revolt in 1680, when the Hopi towns united with the other pueblos (including those of the Rio Grande) to expel the Spaniards from their land.

As has been noted, Government officials, in accordance with the new Indian Bureau policy, have attempted recently to help the Hopi develop political unity as a tribe through a system of representative government. The new Constitution, framed with the help of Hopi and adopted by the tribe, authorizes the establishment of a Tribal Council, and groups the villages for purposes of council representation into nine political units or voting districts, based as far as possible on the tradi-

tional ceremonial organization.[19] Of these nine divisions, all but two (New Oraibi and Upper Moencopi, both of which have village constitutions) are organized according to the traditional pueblo pattern under the Village Chief, who is looked upon by the inhabitants as the highest pueblo authority.[20]

As might be expected from what has gone before, although the Tribal Council has met sporadically since 1937, it has not established itself as a regular functioning body, representative of the tribe. Moreover when the Council does meet, it rarely takes any positive action. Since there is no formal traditional mechanism for inter-pueblo cooperation, a period of experimentation and education, under expert, patient guidance from the administrative staff, will probably be necessary before a mechanism for political unity and self government, which is truly Hopi in design and leadership and adequate to the present needs of the tribe, may be devised and implemented among the traditionally autonomous and theocratic Hopi pueblos.

Summarizing our study of Hopi pueblo organization, we find that each village is composed of groups of individuals, related through an intricate social structure based mainly on kinship, ceremonial and traditional bonds, sharing a common value-system which demands conformity to a rather rigid, anti-aggressive ethical code requiring a high degree of self-control on the part of the individual (not only at the overt behavioral but also at the covert psychological level)—a code sanctioned by a complex and integrated world view expressed in ritual and myth, enforced to a considerable extent, but *by no means exclusively,* by public opinion, and oriented to the problem of group survival under the particular environmental conditions that have faced the Hopi throughout the centuries.

Moreover, the Hopi tribe is not traditionally a formal political unit. It is

Sheep corralled for culling

rather a group of historically autono-mous pueblo states of common breed, culture and language, united by a net-work of reciprocal kinship, ceremonial and economic ties and by a long mem-ory of common and similar experien-ces through the centuries. In Hopiland apparently many different groups and individuals, each carrying his own cul-ture and physical heritage, have through time and the accidents of his-tory been molded by the multi-fac-toral process of cultural and biological change, interacting with a common and particular external environment, into a basically similar cultural configura-tion and a common physical type.

This pueblo set-up provides the background for an understanding of Hopi personality development, includ-ing the abstention from physical ag-gression for which the Hopi have long been known, and also of the tensions that develop in pueblo interpersonal relations and lead to petty quarrels and witchcraft accusations. It also il-luminates the problem of Hopi inter-pueblo relations and provides the basis for a study of how these villages may be helped to develop political unity for their mutual benefit in meeting the problems which they as a minority group, however small, face in the na-tion and the modern world.

Having discussed Hopi society in re-gard to both its external and its in-ternal interrelationship patterns, viewed historically, we shall turn now to the development of the individual within the society. We shall approach the problem of Hopi personality devel-opment from two points of view. First we shall describe briefly what may be considered the expected course of de-velopment of Hopi male and female in-dividuals through the life cycle, and then we shall describe and analyze the actual behavior of boys and girls at the various age levels, as revealed by tests and interviews on our sample of selected children from two Hopi com-munities.

Trading post
Hopi owner behind counter

II. THE JOURNEY FROM BIRTH TO DEATH

6. CHILDHOOD

As has been noted, the Hopi conceive of the human life cycle as a journey along the road of life from birth to death. The journey involves a gradual growth and development of the individual through four phases: childhood, youth, adulthood and old age. This concept is symbolized graphically in a Powamu ceremony sand painting in which a yellow line (road of life), running southeast from the *kiva si'papu* is marked by four crooks.[1] Each phase of the journey, representing one segment of a gradual maturation process, is thought of as growing out of the previous ones and preparing for the phases that are to come. Passages from one phase to another are marked by ceremonies, which stress their transitory character by symbolizing the idea of birth or rebirth, until finally death marks the rebirth of the individual in the Underworld. And the ideal patterns of behavior[2] of an individual of either sex, as well as the roles he or she is expected to assume in each phase, are prescribed by the Hopi Way,[3] which if followed, will further the common weal and lead to a long and happy life.

The first crisis, birth, is an important event in the kinship group, for it marks the introduction of a new member and the renewal of the group life force. Children are very much desired by the Hopi and, in keeping with their basic philosophy, are considered to be individuals of central importance from the time they are born.[4] The concern of parents for their children is expressed in legends in which children are transformed into witches, snakes, turtles, etc. Although both sexes are prized, girls are considered absolutely essential on account of their role in the perpetuation of the clan.[5] The central position of women in the Hopi kinship system and their well-defined and highly valued function in the household group give Hopi females, in contrast to the males, a more stable position and greater security throughout life. This, as we shall see, is reflected in their behavior patterns and personality structure at every age level studied.

As has been noted, the child belongs to his mother's clan and his closest affiliations from birth to death remain with it. He is, however, considered to be the "child" of his father's clan and this relationship is initiated by a series of rites actuated mainly by his paternal grandmother and ending at dawn on the 20th day after birth, in his being named and officially presented to the Sun, the great father deity of the Hopi. These rites establish a pattern of the ceremonial exchange of gifts and services between the child and his father's clanspeople which continues throughout life. In due course, the child is "adopted" into other clans, including that of his godfather and godfather's sister at his first initiation ceremony, and that of any medicine man who may cure him of a severe illness. It is through these rites and those initiating him into secret societies that he builds up the network of ties and reciprocal obligations which encompasses practically everyone in the village and extends throughout the tribe.

The birth takes place in the maternal household, the woman's husband and also one or more maternal female relatives frequently in attendance. A medicine man may be called in if delivery is delayed, but if the Government nurse or doctor is called in at all it is not until the woman has been in labor several days. Although a few of the most acculturated Hopi women bear their children in the hospital at Keams, most Hopi lack confidence in the hospital and its representatives, particularly since they ignore customs which the Hopi consider of prime importance, such as omitting salt and meat from the new mother's diet and shading her from the sun, according to informants.[6]

The afterbirth, together with the parturient blood, the sand which covered the birth place floor, and some sacred corn meal, are placed in a basket and thrown from the mesa into a special crevice, as are also a stillbirth and the body of a child who dies before the first initiation.[7] The cord, however, is usually tied to a stirring stick, if that of a girl, or to a bow, if that of a boy, and hung to the rafters of the house, for the navel has special significance as the locus of the spirit of life.[8] This ancient rite, which symbolizes the adult roles of the two sexes, illustrates the Hopi tendency to foreshadow, prepare for, and attempt to control the future by the use of magic.

During the first 24 hours the newborn infant is bound in supine position to a cradle,[9] usually consisting of a flat board with an arched wicker guard at one extremity to protect the baby's head.[10] Except when he is being bathed, the infant spends practically all his time, for the first three months of life, bound to the cradle. And he is never hung up or placed vertically in it, as among the Navaho[11] for instance, nor is he often taken out of doors. Thereafter the use of the cradle gradually becomes restricted to periods when the infant is actually sleeping,

both during the day and at night, and according to the desires of the child, it is usually discarded entirely between the ages of six months and one year. Although this restriction of the mobility of the growing organism apparently does not affect appreciably the development of motor control,[12] it probably contributes to the infant's feeling of security and also conditions him to the expectation of restrictions, which though not recognized at first as socially imposed, gradually as the child grows older become a part of the great social web which, while holding him fast within its reciprocal system, gives him a sense of security and wellbeing in an exceedingly precarious environment.

During the first year of life, the baby remains particularly close to his mother and other female relatives of the household. He is never left alone lest harm befall him through evil spirits,[13] he sleeps at night next to his mother, and he is nursed and soothed whenever he cries or shows other signs of desiring food or comfort. He is allowed to suck until satisfied and is never tickled or tossed up in the air,[14] but is petted and protected from disturbances which might interfere with his wellbeing and contentment. Observers agree that Hopi babies are usually happy, smile frequently and seldom cry.

At the age of about three or four months the baby is taken out of the house occasionally, slung in a shawl on the back of his mother or a female relative. If the mother already has other children and her family duties are absorbing, the day time care of the child may pass into the hands of an older sister, or even of an older brother though this occurs only when no female is available. His child nurse, who is usually between the ages of five and twelve years,[15] takes him wherever she goes as she participates in the activities of her play group and does her work as usual.

The child begins at this time to eat his first solid food, and since he is given practically anything he desires, gradually becomes acquainted with the whole range of Hopi diet from tortillas soaked in coffee to peaches and other fruit. Weaning is accomplished gradually and with little difficulty as a rule. It is usually completed before the child is two years old, although some children continue to nurse until the age of four or older. In difficult cases, chili or a worm is put on the breast to burn or frighten the child. An older child who persists in nursing is teased out of the habit by his playmates.

With the onset of walking and talking, expected at about the age of 15 months, cleanliness training begins. This also proceeds gradually and with the minimum of shock. When the child shows signs of discomfort he is taken outside the door, and he is told to go outside when he needs to defecate or urinate. If he does not do so, he is told again, and if he still disobeys, he is scolded or spanked. Later he is expected to perform these functions outside of the village. Most parents say their children have no trouble in learning toilet habits, and it is interesting to note that constipation is rare among Hopi, especially Hopi children.[16]

Control of elimination at night is not expected until the second year. However, occasionally enuresis persists until the age of six or seven years. In such a case, a girl is merely made to wash her bedclothes, while a boy is carried on the back of his mother's brother, with other boys, at daybreak to a Water Clan house where he is sung over solemnly and doused with cold water, along with the other boys. This institutionalization of the enuresis treatment for males only, indicates that the habit is more prevalent in boys than in girls, an inference that fits in with the observed facts concerning other maladjustment problems in Hopi children, such as thumb sucking, temper tantrums, fighting and stealing, which, as we shall see, although uncommon in either sex, are more frequent and persistent among young males than females.[17]

Training in the basic disciplines and other types of self control demanded by the Hopi Way, as well as initiation into the intricacies of the kinship system with its complex reciprocity patterns, is the responsibility of the household group, which continues to exercise a certain restraining influence on the individual throughout life. During childhood and youth for girls, and up to about the sixth year for boys, the learning process is chiefly in the hands of the mother and other females of the household, aided by the mother's brother when stricter discipline is needed, and also by the father and the maternal grandfather. All these relatives may scold the child on occasion or ridicule him for wrongdoing, the mother and the mother's brother spanking him if necessary. They are also aided by the gift-giving kachinas, who by rewarding children for good behavior, serve as important behavior motivators, and on rare occasions, by the cannibal kachinas, who appear at their door and threaten to eat or carry away bad little children.[18]

The Hopi pattern of discipline, however, is in general an absorptive and permissive one, the child learning largely by imitating and experimenting and being treated as an important member of the group with individual rights and privileges as well as incipient duties and responsibilities. On the one hand he is given considerable freedom of mobility to explore his environment; on the other he is gently but firmly held within the limitations of physical safety and protected from supernatural dangers.

Some of these dangers, such as those connected with witches, evil spirits, drought, sickness and death, are very real from the Hopi point of view, but others, such as those connected with the kachinas, are feigned and dramatized realistically by the adults to reward or frighten the child into obedience without arousing his hostility toward themselves. These shocks have a particular aspect as they are not given from individual to individual, but from the external environment, natural or supernatural, to all children, so that the quality of the shock lacks the feeling of personal persecution and hostility against individuals. Such fear-provoking experiences, whether due to real or imaginary dangers, apparently condition the child at a very early age to the hazardous nature of the Hopi environment.

In this connection it is important to realize, however, that in the face of these threats to his existence, the child is never allowed to feel isolated or abandoned but always has whole groups of relatives to whom he may turn for comfort and reassurance.[19] Outstanding among these, besides his father, are his father's clansfolk, especially his paternal aunts in whose households he is at all times welcome. The relationship between the paternal aunt and her nephew is particularly warm and may serve somewhat to counterbalance the exceedingly close bond between the females of the maternal household, especially mother and daughter.

Although most Hopi children learn the basic disciplines with little difficulty, thumb sucking, temper tantrums and even stealing begin to be manifest in a few individual boys in the third year, whereas no "behavior problems" have been reported for girls until the fifth year.[20] These early signs of adjustment difficulties among the boys coincide with weaning and cleanliness training for both sexes, and also, in some cases, with the arrival of another sibling in the family and the removal of the child from his mother's bed to that of a female relative or his grandfather. Their early appearance among males only, is understandable, however, when we consider the differences between the position of the female and the male child in the household and the expectancies in regard to each sex.

As has been noted, the little girl is born into a household group in which she is expected to grow up, marry, and even in many cases to continue to live until she dies as a member of a closely knit and powerful group of females. On the other hand, the little boy is expected to break away from the group into which he has been born, beginning at the age of four or five years, for the less stable and more hazardous world of *kiva*, field and range, and to remain throughout life in a marginal position in regard to the household.

While the roles of both sexes require endurance, industry and patience, that of the Hopi male, in contrast to the female, requires constant vigilance and a high degree of adaptability in order to cope with the natural, supernatural and social forces of the less restricted and less secure masculine world. Hopi character delineations were built up in the past when a man had to be not only an expert dry farmer, rain maker and stone age hunter, but also a warrior in the struggle for survival. But they still persist and are functional today, for as we have seen, in spite of the cessation of defensive warfare, the reduction of game and the increase in herding, the essential Hopi life problems have not changed intrinsically in modern times.

Apparently almost from birth the child begins to be aware of these sex-differentiated expectancies, which are constantly impressed on him in his interpersonal relations. The efforts of the little girl are encouraged by telling her that she will grow up to be a good cook[21] and those of the boy that he will be a swift runner. Even the gift giving kachinas aid in defining the sex roles by presenting the girls with kachina images which are fertility symbols designed primarily to be hung up in the house and not to be used as dolls, and the boys with arrows which, although used in play, are important symbolically and are highly valued. In fact, the whole training process is oriented toward these ends.

In view of these facts it is not surprising that the business of growing up presents more problems to the boy than to the girl, and that cases of men who assume the dress and perform the role of women occur among the Hopi, though rarely, whereas instances of women rejecting their role for that of the opposite sex are unknown.[22]

Of course the girls also have adjustment difficulties, for the female role, aside from its procreative function (which is particularly hazardous in Hopiland, to judge from maternal mortality estimates and population statistics), offers less mobility and stimulation and fewer actively creative outlets than that of the male, which allows abundant, though stylized, self expression in ceremonial art and craft work, as well as the intense excitement of the hunt and formerly of war.[23]

The little Hopi girl apparently begins to feel the restrictions of the female role in the fifth year, at the age when her male agemate begins to break away from the women's household group, while she must remain at home, helping her mother with the household tasks or caring for the younger children. Now cases of maladjusted behavior such as temper tantrums, stealing, thumb sucking, and fighting—though less prevalent than among the boys— first appear among the girls.

That the adjustment problems of the little boy also increase in the fifth year is shown by the rise in behavior problems at this age, which include fighting as well as all those manifested earlier. His difficulties in escaping from the female-dominated household are illustrated symbolically in the following incident from the autobiography of a Hopi.[24]

Don, aged four or five years, begged to go with his father to the fields and, when his father refused to take him, followed him along the path down the mesa. At the sacred shrine of the Spider Woman[25] he saw "the old woman herself," sitting beside a square hole in the ground. She called to him to come into her house. "You have been walking on my trail," she said, "and now I have a right to you as my grandson." Just as Don was being drawn into the hole, he was rescued by a passerby. Don felt sick and finally was taken to a medicine man who said the boy had been caught in the Spider Woman's web and she held him tightly. (In another version of the story, the medicine man said the boy's body was wrapped in a fine spider web which was choking him to death).[26] He rubbed the boy's legs and belly and advised his father to make a prayer feather for the Spider Woman. This was done and the boy recovered.

In spite of their early responsibilities, however, Hopi children have a great deal of time for fun and play. Duties come first and when they are finished, children are free to wander about the village and amuse themselves as they wish, so long as they do not interfere with the activities of the adults.[27] At this age little boys and girls play freely together. They usually form two types of play groups, however, one comprising the older girls with their small charges and the other, uninitiated boys of four years or older. The little girls build houses with wet mud. They use sticks or bones as dolls to represent the individuals in the household. They also play at grinding and pottery making. The little boys play at farming and herding and practice shooting with bows and arrows. They also run races and play at horseback riding. Although most Hopi children have no toys except those which they receive from the *kachinas* or make themselves, they often keep small animals such as birds, rabbits and prairie dogs as pets and these they handle so roughly that the creatures frequently are mauled to death. A certain cruelty to animals is also noticeable in the behavior of adults.

Children begin at a very early age—when they can barely walk and talk—to practice dance steps, singing and drumming. And as young as four years they may begin to participate in certain ceremonials such as the Snake and Buffalo dances.[28] Moreover, as part of some festivities, special children's events are planned such as the children's race day which may initiate a kickball contest.

But there is no well defined boundary in the learning process between work, play and ceremonial, the child spending his time in one or another of these activities, which to him are events in the "ever-becoming-later" duration which is Hopi childhood. And when this first phase of life ends with the kachina initiation between the ages of six and ten years,[29] the child is expected to have mastered not only the basic disciplines, the fundamentals of the kinship system and the main tenets of the Hopi Way, but also to have become a useful member of society with social and economic duties, responsibilities and privileges, in accordance with his sex and age.

7. YOUTH

The ceremonial initiation of the child into the kachina cult marks the second great crisis in his life cycle, the transition from Childhood to Youth. This first initiation, as has been noted, takes place every four years in February as a part of the Powamu or "Bean Dance," which is designed especially to speed the early stages of development and is marked by the forced growth of beans and corn in the kivas and their distribution to the young children by masked kachinas. As the birth rites introduced the child to his father, the Sun, and inaugurated a series of life-long, mutual obligations and privileges between himself and his father's clanspeople, so the kachina initiation introduces him to his ancestors, the kachinas, and sets up a pattern of regular, correlative obligations by which the kachinas give rain and thus food and other essentials to human welfare in exchange for prescribed ritual behavior. It also marks his adoption into another clan, namely that of the man and his sister who become his godfather and godfather's sister and sponsor him in his ceremonial career. Henceforth the child is considered to be related to these ceremonial kin and their clansmen and phratry members, as he is related to his father's clan, and with similar reciprocal obligations and privileges.

The child's godfather and aunt are chosen by the child's parents with regard to their ritual affiliations,[1] for a boy is expected in due course to join the secret societies to which his godfather belongs[2] and a girl those of her ceremonial aunt. Moreover, on Third Mesa the affiliation of the godfather in the kachina cult—whether with the Kachina Society in which the novices are whipped, or with the Powamu Society in which they are not—determines whether or not the child must go through the whipping ordeal.

Informants say that a "bad" boy is usually given a Kachina Society godfather and hence the initiation serves as a sanction for behavior in the case of the boys at least. It may be less potent in the case of the girls since, even if whipped, they are allowed to remain clothed and are dealt with much less severely than the boys.

The whipping rite,[3] illustrated on page 65, symbolizes the Hopi child training pattern. In it the Mother of the Kachinas, represented by a masked female figure, holds a large supply of yucca switches while the Whipper Kachinas, represented by masked male figures, apply them to the nude boy (or clothed girl) supported and shielded by his godfather and his godfather's sister. Both the boy and his godfather stand on a large sand painting which represents the Kachina Mother and the Whipper Kachinas, while a segmented line drawn from the kiva si'papu southeastward shows the road of life with its four phases. Afterwards the Mother Kachina steps on to the sand painting and is whipped by the Whippers and then the Whippers whip each other.

This ceremony, in which the Mother Kachina may be interpreted from one point of view as symbolizing the mother, the Whipper Kachinas the maternal uncles, the godfather as the father, and the godaunt as the father's sister, illustrates dramatically the complementary functions of the maternal and paternal kin in steering the child along the road of life. It emphasizes especially the role of the Hopi mother as the source of order and control in the child's life, that of her brothers as her active partners in maintaining discipline, and that of the father and his sister as the child's supporters. It also shows the difference between the treatment of boys and girls. And finally, through the discipliners' castigating of one another, it shows that the adult pattern of social control is not one in which one group, namely the adult matrilineal kin, originate action and another group, namely the children, terminate it, but one in which each adult individual is expected to exercise a certain amount of control over the others. From now on the censorship of the group, i. e., public opinion, will gradually replace, to a considerable extent at least, the maternal household group as the principal negative sanction of the child's behavior. On the other hand, the positive role of his paternal

kin in motivating his behavior will remain the same.

During the kachina initiation the child learns that the supernatural beings whom he has known from infancy as bringers of gifts and rain and also as dispensers of punishment, are really only people he knows dressed up to impersonate them, but he also learns of the kachinas' key role in the scheme of things and his own part in the cosmic exchange for the mutual welfare of all. His godfather gives him a new name and from now on he may participate in the kachina rites and gradually assume his share of responsibility for the great annual cycle of ceremonies which gives significance and zest to Hopi life. He has acquired a certain status in the tribe as a whole and may return to the Underworld when he dies.[4]

Some time after his first initiation the boy is expected to join one or more secret societies usually those of his godfather, and the girl is expected to join those of her ceremonial aunt.[5] Each of these has its own secret initiation which represents a variation on the general "rebirth" ceremonial pattern, the neophyte observing part of the ritual as well as certain tabus, having his head washed and receiving a new name.[6] This means a gradual expansion of ties, responsibilities and creative activities especially for the boy since it opens the definitely male world of the kiva to him and a new field of esoteric knowledge. It also gives him a well defined place in the ceremonial organization of the village which tends to compensate for his position in the household group, to build up his self confidence, and to steer him toward the adult male role.

At about the age of eight the boy is expected to kill his first game, usually a rabbit, according to the rules of the chase, and consequently to acquire a "hunt" father and to be formally initiated as a hunter.[7]

With these changes in status, the

boy is expected to increase the observance of certain "strength" building practices which were begun in childhood, including bathing in the spring before dawn, drinking "medicine water,"[8] and long distance running. This Hopi ideal, taught him by his father, his grandfather and the village elders, is no longer practiced quite so rigorously as in the past when the boy was preparing to be a warrior and hunter of big game. It should be remembered that "strength" to the Hopi means strength of mind or will as well as of body,[9] and the boy was and still is expected also to be happy, and to cultivate a "good heart" and the ability to concentrate in behalf of the common weal.[10]

The economic responsibilities of the boy during these years increase gradually. Whereas formerly his chores consisted mainly of helping his female relatives with water and fuel hauling, now he frequently accompanies his male relatives, particularly his father and grandfather, to the fields and sheep camps where his work changes with his growing skill from guarding the orchards and fields to helping with planting, harvesting and herding, and finally, at about the age of 14, to being able to take charge of his own herd (if he has one) and his mother's fields. In the winter months, when farm work is slack and the men gather in the kivas, he also learns the Hopi men's crafts—carding, spinning, and finally weaving, moccasin making and other handwork—to the accompaniment of story and song. The learning of all these skills contributes to his understanding of the Hopi Way, which is systematically taught him in kiva and camp. During long, quiet days and nights away from the distractions of the household, he is expected to master the secrets of his clan and society rituals and to learn the tribal lore.

The initiated boys form their own play groups from which the uninitiated, as well as peers of the opposite sex, are usually excluded. These groups are spontaneous and unrestricted as to clan or other affiliations, as are all Hopi play groups. Most of the youths' play occurs in the late afternoon and evening after the day's work is done.[11] Besides imported games such as basketball, which is very popular, the boys play a number of organized Hopi games, many of which are seasonal and competitive. An analysis of these reveals that rivalry is expressed between teams rather than individuals and in the form of running, throwing, shooting with arrows or darts, and striking or whipping balls or tops—activities which, according to Hopi ideology, have magical efficacy. Moreover, each activity occurs at the season of the year when it is part of the ceremonial pattern used as an aid in the fertilization and growth of crops. For example, the archery game,[12] in which two teams chosen alternately by leaders take turns shooting arrows at a rolling hoop, and which has to be won three times before the final victory is assured, is played only after the Niman ceremony in July, when bows and arrows are given as presents by the kachinas and is associated with the bringing of rain and speeding of maturation. Shinny,[13] in which each team tries to make its own goal by striking a ball with a club, is played only after the Powamu in February when shinny balls and clubs are distributed, and is associated with the whipping or purification rites designed to aid the early stages of growth.

Besides providing a socially approved outlet for aggression, and the display of skill and initiative, the boys' games afford an opportunity for the expression of peer preferences. They also channelize sport into a pattern of give-and-take or reciprocity between two teams, neither of which can expect to win the goal[14] easily even with a high degree of skill and teamwork. Moreover, the interest is centered not so much on winning as on the actual playing of the game for its own sake, and even in the case of imported games such as baseball, there is little or no interest in the score.

Compared with the boys, the girls have few organized games and these are mainly non-seasonal. The girls rarely compete through opposing teams except in races such as the ceremonial Basket Race, but seem rather to follow either the big-girl-little-girl set-up of the girls' play groups or the cooperative pattern of the women's household groups. The former is illustrated by the Pursuit Game[15] and the latter by the Grinding Party.[16] In the Pursuit Game the leader chases the other players along a complicated and twisted path marked in sand from the outside of the play area to the center, while any girl who steps off the path must drop out of the game. Here the guidance role of the mother and the difficult and centripetal life course of the Hopi girl are faithfully portrayed. On the other hand, at the Grinding Party, a group of girls grind together for several days, each girl working each day for a different relative who reciprocates by supplying her with corn. This takes place before the Niman ceremony and serves not only as a social occasion but also as a means of accomplishing necessary work in a pleasant manner.

Through interesting experiments with Hopi girls' play groups made by Dr. Solomon Asch, we learn that these provide an opportunity for the expression of verbal aggression in the form of mutual criticism and through this of the development on the part of the individual of an objective attitude toward her own and others' work, as well as for the expression of a sort of reciprocal praise pattern by which praise of another's efforts or disparagement of one's own calls for a compliment in return.[17]

All these activities and learning processes are quite apart from the school experience which, although usually beginning in the Indian Service Day School at about the age of six and continuing until the age of 12 to 16, occupies only a small percentage of the child's time until, as is frequently the case in the communities studied, he leaves home at the secondary level to go to boarding school, either on or off the Reservation. When a boy is ready for boarding school, at about the age of 14, he is expected to have mastered the main adult male skills, especially farming,[18] as well as part of his share of the ceremonial. The expectancies for a girl of this age will be discussed presently.

Although school attendance is not compulsory, it is urged by many of the village leaders and most Hopi boys and girls go to school for a period of from six to ten years. Regularity of attendance differs among families and villages, children in the more acculturated groups having the highest attendance records. When school interferes too greatly with ceremonial or economic activities, however, the children are likely to drop out for two or three days. To overcome this difficulty, last year the principal of the Polacca Day School persuaded the First Mesa leaders to hold some of their ceremonials on weekends, rather than during the week, and since this time, he reports, regularity of attendance has increased.

In school the children are expected to acquire, first and foremost, a speaking knowledge of the English language and also certain tools of the White culture such as the three R's, together with a knowledge of White ways which will be of use to them in their future life on the Reservation. There is little interest among the parents in many aspects of White culture included in the curriculum, and even some active opposition to such subjects as arts and crafts, which many parents consider to be within the teaching sphere of the clan and ceremonial groups. There is also some objection to the fact that school is coeducational, according to the American pattern.

ing to carry a heavily loaded basket on the journey to the house of the dead.[33]

Thus by the time a young Hopi, whether boy or girl, is 15 or 16, besides having attained physical maturity, he is expected to have mastered the technical skills and to have gained the self control and sophistication in the Hopi Way so that he will have completed the requirements of the Youth phase of life's journey and be prepared to take on the full responsibilities of adulthood.

8.   ADULTHOOD AND OLD AGE

The transition from youth to Adulthood is marked not by a single crisis as is the passage from Childhood to Youth, but by a series of crises involving adolescence and marriage ceremonies for both sexes and also, for the girls, rites which accompany the birth of the first child. The girls' puberty rites, briefly described in the last chapter, take place some time before the corresponding adolescence ceremonies for the boys, which are expected to occur between the age of 15 and 20 years and usually precede marriage.

Practically all Hopi youths go through this second initiation.[1] The ceremony takes the form of an introduction into one of four tribal secret societies (Agave, Horn, Singer or Wuwuchim), conducting the annual Wuwuchim (Grown Man) ceremony, of which it is periodically a part, and it is a prerequisite to membership in the tribewide Soyal Society which controls the supremely important Winter Solstice ceremony. Hence it is frequently referred to as the tribal initiation.[2]

Each of the four societies has a different role in the ceremonial system, the Agave and Horn being closely associated with war, hunting and death, the Singer and Wuwuchim with fertility. Each has its "home" in the Underworld whence its members are believed to repair after this life. A young man is expected to join the society to which his godfather (who sponsors him as he did at the first or kachina initiation) belongs and thus to establish his position in the Underworld.

The boys' adolescent rite is one of the most complicated of all Hopi ceremonies, and no outsider has witnessed its most esoteric parts. In connection with the annual "New Fire" ceremony (described on page 43), it seems to emphasize the death and rebirth motif of Hopi ideology on not only an individual but also a cosmic scale, the youth apparently actually undergoing a realistically dramatized death and introduction to the spirits of the dead. He is then born again,[3] delivered by the Dawn Woman (a major deity), a concept linked with that of Emergence from the Sipapu, and he receives a new name and is aided symbolically by his godfather to grow up to full, vigorous manhood.

With the second initiation the youth is expected suddenly to become a man, with the responsibilities and privileges of manhood, to eschew quarreling and petty fights and to follow assiduously the Hopi Way. (It should be noted that no such injunction is placed on the girl in connection with her adolescent rite). He may now take part in dangerous missions on behalf of the group, such as the salt and trading expeditions which formerly reestablished contact with the Underworld[4] and in the crucial Winter Solstice rites.

In the past his career in defensive warfare began at this time and, with the taking of his first scalp, he underwent another initiation of the "rebirth" type, marking his acquisition of warrior status.[5] It is interesting to note that the "prayer" or "wish" for the warrior neophyte was that he would be rich, "happy with women," successful in war, and free from evil spirits and witchcraft; that he would live a long life; and that there would be rain, fertility and happiness.

By the time a young person of either sex is about 20 years old he is expected to marry, although many young men and also some girls marry at a later age, and a few men do not marry at all. Bachelors (i. e., men who have never been married) over 30 are rare in Hopiland, and spinsters are unknown.[6] In this matrilineal, matrilocal society, where adult males outnumber adult females, it is said that some men cannot get spouses on account of "defective speech or singular appearance."[7]

Although young people are advised by their parents, uncles and clan heads to select mates who are industrious, thrifty, reliable, and even-tempered, and who belong to families of some means and good repute, there is no compulsion regarding the choice. The selection of a spouse, within the limits imposed by the incest tabu and the "basket carrier" tabu (see pp. 61), is left to the individual, each sex being free to accept or reject the advances of the other, and the girl as well as the young man having socially accepted and formalized patterns of behavior by which she may make known her preference[8] or propose marriage.

A Hopi wedding is an important ceremonial, economic and social occasion, lasting several weeks or even months and involving most of the members of the inter-marrying clans, as well as practically all the villagers and usually individuals from other villages. It centers in the correlative exchange of bridal garments, supplied by the groom's relatives and made by the men of the village, for food and plaques supplied by the bride's relatives and prepared to a considerable extent by the bride. As has been noted, the bridal garments and plaques are believed to be necessary to the bride and groom respectively for safe passage to the Underworld, and their significance emphasizes the preparatory nature of the wedding rites in respect to the phases of life cycle that are to come, particularly after death. The magical function especially of the wedding garments renders their acquisition through the prescribed long and arduous rites indispensable to a Hopi woman. And it is mainly for this reason that most Hopi are married for the first time according to the Hopi Way, even though they may also go through a civil ceremony as well.[9] Moreover since only one wedding outfit is needed per person, an individual goes through the Hopi marriage rites only once, regardless of how many times he may wed.

The actual marriage rites are initiated by the bride's four-day grinding ordeal which takes place in the household of the groom's mother. During this time a mock attack is made on the bride and the groom's parents by the groom's paternal aunts who, by means of water-pouring and mud-throwing, formally express their "anger" over the "loss" of their "sweetheart."[10] On the fourth day the heads of the bridal pair are washed in one basin by their mothers, the couple prays to the Sun and henceforth they may sleep together. However, the bride remains in her mother-in-law's house, doing the major part of the cooking, until the long process of spinning, carding and weaving her nuptial costume has been completed and then, clad in her new garments, she returns to her mother's house. A final exchange of food gifts between the intermarrying families concludes the ceremony and the groom, bringing a share of his father's property, including part of his herd if he has one,[11] takes up residence in his mother-in-law's household, and assumes the difficult role of a Hopi son-in-law.

Since he now begins to work the clan lands of his wife and to contribute most if not all the yield to her household rather than that of his mother, the bride's household gains economically by the marriage while the groom's suffers a corresponding loss.[12]

Before or soon after the wedding rites have been completed the bride is expected to become pregnant, although it is not uncommon for a girl to bear a child before marriage. During pregnancy both parents are expected to observe certain tabus, and continence during gestation is apparently the ideal.[13] Although the marriage rites prepare a woman properly for the afterlife and raise her status in the clan and the village, it is with the birth of a child, especially a girl, that she fulfills the aim toward which her whole existence is oriented, namely the perpetuation of life—the life of the clan. As has been noted, children are welcomed into the Hopi household and a family increases a woman's prestige. The central importance among the Hopi of the female function of childbearing and the perpetuation of life is stressed in every phase of the culture.

Although matrilocal residence is still the rule,[14] there is a tendency in Hopiland today for a young man to build his wife a house of her own[15] after the birth of two or three children. But whether or not the couple establish a separate residence, the ties of a daughter with her mother, sisters, and clansmen remain paramount throughout life and those with her husband and his relatives, secondary. If the union endures, however, a man tends to identify himself more and more with his wife's household, fulfilling at the same time his ceremonial and economic responsibilities toward his ancestral household and clan.

Notwithstanding the fact that the wife's position in the home is socially and economically much more stable and emotionally more secure than that of her husband, the relationship between spouses tends to be an equalitarian one, with the emphasis on individual freedom within the limits of the Hopi Way, which is so characteristic of Hopi interpersonal relations. Hopi spouses rarely make decisions for each other and, if marital obligations be fulfilled, each tends to allow the other to follow his inclinations, even in such vital matters as religion. Hence, it sometimes happens that the wife, but not the husband, officially becomes a Christian or (less frequently) vice versa.[16]

Moreover, either spouse is free to terminate the relationship at will, the wife by putting her husband's personal possessions outside the door of her home, the husband by moving to his mother's or sister's house or that of another woman. In spite of the comparative lack of restrictions and social censorship in regard to divorce, it is interesting to note that apparently about two-thirds of the first marriages in Hopiland are stable, the remaining third being characterized by one or more divorces, most frequently occasioned by extra-marital relationships on the part of one or the other partner.[17] Opportunities for such relationships occur especially when a man is away from home at sheep or field camp and when he is sleeping in the *kiva* during his wife's 30 to 40 day confinement or during a ceremony when participants are supposed to observe a period of ritual continence varying in length from 13 to 20 days.[18]

In the case of divorce, each party retains his property, the young children remaining with the mother, and the older ones, although free to follow either parent, usually staying also. Since a woman with her house, clan lands and clan backing is not necessarily dependent on her husband so far as her material welfare is concerned, divorce does not disrupt the household organization.

Divorce is often followed by remarriage but frequent divorce and remarriage on the part of either sex results in a loss of respect in the community, social censorship being somewhat more tolerant in the case of a man than a woman.

In fact, in the journey through Adulthood there are various ways by which the individual may expect to gain or lose prestige. Status in Hopiland, as we have noted, is correlated primarily with social responsibility and participation—within the kinship group in the case of women, and within the ceremonial group in the case of men. Age in itself, or the mere duration of time does not bring position or influence. These come mainly as a function of the complete assumption of role, the whole-hearted, effortful cultivation of the Hopi Way. This does not mean the slavish following of dogma, the rigid conformity to rules, it means the concentration through an effort of will on living the good, the peaceful, the "happy" life, as defined by the Hopi ideal. Successors to head positions in ceremonial and clan are chosen and trained not by seniority but on the basis of character and understanding, and traditional leadership, within the limits of the clan system, is the reward of wisdom and effort on behalf of the common welfare.

Of course, with the increase of White influence in Hopiland new avenues to power are being established such as the acquisition of wealth through herding, running a trading post, or developing a craft commercially, and of influence through a knowledge of White ways and the English language or conversion to Christianity. These are developing new types of leadership on the competitive American pattern, the effects of which are particularly apparent in local politics—but it is significant that, in spite of these new trends, the ultimate authority in all Hopi villages, except two,[19] still lies in the traditional system with the Village Chief and his sister at its core. Thus a Hopi's main channels to power apparently still are in the traditional system: ceremonial chieftainship in clan, society and village for a man; and clan headship and leadership in the women's societies for a woman.

No rite marks the transition from Adulthood to Old Age ("when a man grows small again")[20] but as the individual becomes old and feeble he is expected to pass his responsibilities and duties on to a successor whom he has chosen and trained to assume them. He is still respected and continues to work at whatever tasks he can perform, for there is no old age retirement in Hopiland, but he gradually drops out of the active life of the community. Such a person has fulfilled the Hopi ideal of a long life[21] and his impending death from old age is accepted,[22] for he has completed the journey and arrived at the end of the road. On the other hand, premature death from sickness is considered to be the fault of the individual who is believed to have deviated from the Hopi Way.

Mortuary rites are simple and quickly accomplished, the Hopi showing a marked aversion to anything connected with death. The hair of the deceased is washed by his paternal aunt[23] and the body is wrapped and quickly buried by the oldest son on the day or night of death. It is placed in a flexed position with a "cloud" shroud over the face and a stick is inserted upright in the grave to serve as an exit for the soul, which is believed to stay in the grave for three days and on the fourth to begin its journey to the land of the dead.[24] The spirit of the deceased is propitiated with prayer feathers to forget and not to bother the living and the trail back to the village is ceremonially closed.

Thus with rebirth in the Underworld ends the Hopi journey of life.

Hopi ceremony

III. SOME YOUNG HOPI EN ROUTE

9. SIX PORTRAITS OF HOPI CHILDREN

We have described briefly the environment in which the Hopi live, and the culture which they have developed through centuries. In the preceding section we have noted how Hopi children are brought up, how they are subjected to various forces and constellations within the family and community, and it is assumed that their position and their attitudes are, in a general way, channelized by the same forces. Now, we shall introduce the reader to some of these children, as they may be found on the plaza or in school, today or tomorrow, in our two communities. In doing this we hope not only to give an impression of the actual, living, individual Hopi child, but also to describe the methods which contribute to our study and on which our conclusions are partly based. From seeing how the method works on the individual, the step to the group analysis in the next section will be more natural and more comprehensible.

We know that, just as in sickness the same symptoms may come from entirely different sources, so the attitudes and the behavior of normal individuals may appear alike or similar, while in reality they are based on essentially different personalities and are motivated by different factors. For instance, a child may be ingratiating and solicitous because he or she is warm-hearted and affectionate, or because he is terrorized by the general idea of punishment, or because mischief has already been done and he wants to cover up his guilty con-

science, or because he calculates the prospect of a certain reward, etc.

Understanding t h e personality which determines behavior will have much bearing on the success of education, guidance and social planning. Misunderstanding of it has been at the root of many failures to establish good relations with individuals or groups; e. g., it was one of the many reasons why a disastrous appeasement policy was attempted at Munich. Words are untrustworthy without confirming actions, but the reliability of actions rests mainly upon their motivations.

Aware of this, we were not satisfied in our aim of knowing the Hopi as well as possible, with what they themselves or other people told us about them and what, besides, could be observed in their overt behavior by the occasional onlooker; but we thought it necessary to use a certain number of tests, which would supply us with comparable and less biased results and also make possible or—for the doubtful—probable, an insight into personality and motivation. Explanations of the selection, nature and limits of these tests are found on pages 91 and 92.

In presenting portraits of individual Hopi children, we have contrived to integrate all the data we have—interviews, reports, observations and test results—in order to give a personality picture as coherent as possible. The reader who is expecting amazing and complete findings as they are obtained in psychoanalysis will be dis-

Child being whipped at
Kachina initiation ceremony

appointed. Our means and our time have been limited, and we have had to use methods which might prove to be easy tools to apply in future studies with practical aims. We ask the reader to think of our work as a well meaning attempt for better understanding and better relations. Evidence of our success or failure will come mainly, as in medicine, *ex iuvantibus*, i.e., from the success or failure of practical plans and actions based on our results.

The children whom the reader will meet now are not representative of Hopi society in a quantitative sense. If one child is a prosperous man's son, that does not mean that there is a corresponding percentage of children of prosperous men in the two communities studied. What we are attempting here is to show how the Hopi personality reacts to a certain range of psychological situations. If, e. g., we present two children of widowed mothers, it is to point out two different adjustments made to a situation which is a potential danger to every Hopi child. Similar considerations have determined the other choices. Because of the limitation of space, many psychological situations have been left out. In spite of this, we hope to arouse the reader's curiosity and interest toward a better acquaintance with Hopi children.

As we have already hinted, the problems and the aims which in our minds are connected with the individual personality studies go, however, beyond the sketching of mere portraits which may be introductory to the next section on group analysis. First of all we are convinced that any psychological method which is by nature qualitative requires, if it is to be applied later to quantitative material, a previous testing on individuals where its interpretative validity can more easily be checked. The mere fact that the findings of tests in the single child are accompanied by a life

history, to which these findings can be related and on the background of which their proportional significance can be measured, is here of greatest importance for the evaluation of the method itself. Thus generalizations, and the establishment of an "average type of Hopi child" who is not a mere shadow-like product of figures and percentages, can approach actual conditions of life only if based upon the careful examination of corresponding results found in individuals.

Working with children who belong to a culture different from our own, and operating not with one test but with a whole battery of tests, we had to face two particular problems. Among the manifestations of an alien culture there will always be some which catch the observer's interest and attention because of their exotic quality, while others less colorful or less obvious are relatively neglected. Only the analysis of individuals can show conclusively how far the various manifestations of a culture determine the lives of the people at the time of the study, and how far, for instance, we are dealing with features which have a greater influence in appearance than in fact.

Using several tests, the results of which had to be integrated, we had to establish the degree and the quality of reactions to each of them, their relative reliability, and their range, which again could only be done on individuals. In order to reduce as much as possible the influence of preconceived opinions on the interpreters of tests, the following procedure was adopted.

Blind interpretations were made by different examiners for each test independently. The results were matched separately by every one of them, and then compared and discussed at length in a general meeting. In regard to the reliability of the tests and the psychological ability of the interpreters, we can say that even on the level of blind matching, the various results of this procedure showed a surprisingly high agreement.

Concerning our aims, which in a general way may be expressed as the establishment of better understanding of and better relations with members of a different culture, especially minorities, we know from experience that, while opinions and prejudices of important political and administrative consequence concern whole groups and are usually based upon considerations of the socio-economic roles of groups only, the nature of the direct contacts between individuals who constitute the group, and between these individuals and the out-group factors may have an influence on the time required and the way in which measures on behalf of the group need to be conceived, applied and adopted. As in international affairs where a diplomat's particular ability or, on the other hand, his unfortunate tendency to blunder, will not determine his government's fundamental policy, but may aid in and accelerate, or delay and hinder, its effective application, we have observed again and again that good or bad relationships between single officials and single members of a minority, and in a small minority group such as the Hopi—the good will of one superintendent, one teacher, one physician, the open mind and active loyalty of one Hopi—may have an immediate bearing on the speedy and successful course of general practical procedures.

Our psychological study is concerned with Hopi children with whom in the future we shall have to deal as adult representatives of the Hopi tribe. We are interested in the development, the reactions and attitudes of the well adjusted and maladjusted, the exceptional, the problematic and the normal children, because as they are and as they are trained they will

act, and thus will have their greater or smaller share of influence in the sequence of events within their family, their village, their tribe, state and country.

With regard to our relationship to them, the potential and existing spheres of influence are numerous—partly used, partly neglected—and it is one aim of this study to consider the results of our efforts at influence, and to trace the psychological basis for a future improvement of mutual relations in specific areas of contact. School, for instance, is or can be a powerful instrument for directing the mind and character of a child. Incompetence, malevolence, but also disregard for psychological needs and demands, may turn it into a predominantly negative factor. School brings the Hopi child into early and long lasting contact with representatives of an alien culture, on whom he may more or less model his attitudes toward other representatives of that culture. Understanding of the individual child's needs and character structure on the part of the teacher will not only ease his task of teaching, but also will largely determine the child's adjustment to the requirements of a way of life foreign and often incomprehensible to him.

Similar considerations apply to most modes of contact between White Americans and Hopi, be they institutionalized or casual. In situations which render spontaneous understanding difficult, as is almost the rule where individuals of different cultural backgrounds are brought together, socio-psychological methods may be called upon as an aid in the guidance of individuals and in their education towards good will.

LAWRENCE[1]

Lawrence, 12, his two-years-younger sister, and a baby girl of three, are the only survivors of his parents' nine children. Another boy, eight years old, the father's brother's son, lives with them and is considered and treated as the family's own child. Lawrence belongs to a clan which is one of the most powerful in social prestige and ceremonial significance.

While the family lives on top of the mesa in one of our communities and follows the traditional ways, the father farming and taking care of his herd of sheep, the mother doing the work at home, it seems that they also take advantage of what White material culture offers them as an improvement of their daily comfort. The house is quite spacious, extremely neat and unusually well furnished, and parents and children alike are remarkable in the good quality of their clothes. The economic condition is above average for Hopi in general.

Both parents are handsome, friendly and very dignified in their manners, industrious in their work. The home atmosphere seems happy and harmonious, and it is perhaps significant that no gossip about the family has reached our informants. The children's training, though not unduly strict, is a matter of weight and thoughtful planning, the mother tending more to limit and discipline, while the father, who views education not only as to its advantage for his own family, but also as to its significance for the whole community, directs in a broader sense. As an admired creator of Hopi songs, the father teaches his son about the values of Hopi thoughts and beliefs.

Visitors, even those who frequently go to the house, say that they find Lawrence around very seldom. He loves to herd the sheep and to stay with them on the ranch. The lambs are his favorite playthings. From the one sheep his father gave him some time ago, he has now a small herd of 15 as his own property, and he is proud and embarrassed when he is talked of as having a "lucky hand" because he has not lost any of his animals. When he is not with the sheep in the desert, alone or with his father, he helps in the fields, chops wood for his mother at home, or roams around with the boys of his age, mainly those of the most conservative set. Whenever there is a ceremonial in a *kiva* or on the plaza of one of the neighboring villages, Lawrence is present.

At school he is a rare guest. Often he brings an excuse from his parents that he has had to herd the sheep or to do other work, but sometimes he stays out without any justification. Although the father makes an issue of his son's getting a good school education, there is a definite streak of humor in the way he deals with the school authorities, and we may assume that the pressure he exerts on his son is not too hard. The fact that Lawrence, because of his frequent absences, was put in the second grade together with children two or three years younger, may have increased his dislike of school. Whenever he is there he is rated as doing "good work." His manners are usually shy and embarrassed with Whites, respectful with Indian adults, and lively and natural with his agemates.

Lawrence is a handsome, healthy boy, with a somewhat sleepy or dreaming expression on his face. His I. Q. is 111 (i. e., high average), the projective tests show his intellectual capacities as superior, one of them (Rorschach) as outstanding among the Hopi children, particularly with regard to his high synthesizing, imaginative and creative capabilities. He is observant, logical, critical, and at the same time shows originality and flashes of humor. His mental approach is well balanced and so is his whole personality. He is spontaneous, capable of outgoing happiness and, on the other hand, has a strongly developed inner life, constructive ideas and a tendency towards introspection. All the tests agree on his good social adjustment, which seems to center around life and thoughts of specific Hopi character. There are two points which cause him some difficulties: he seems to resent the too neat regularization of his life by his mother, and he shows a slight sexual anxiety. While he appears much more mature in his interests and ideas than his agemates, he is still immature sexually.

In summary, we are dealing here with a boy remarkable through his high natural gifts and his good adjustment. The few difficulties under which his personality seems to suffer are well comprehensible as symptoms of a transition from the period of prepuberty to that of puberty. Deeply imbued with Hopi values, his strong creative and imaginative trend does not seem to find enough response and satisfaction in lower grade school work. That, in spite of this trend, he is capable of good practical achievement, is shown by his success in building up a herd of his own. The well balanced family life, in which both parents have their share of influence, has probably been a determining factor in the good social adjustment Lawrence has made.

ELLEN

Ellen belongs to a conservative Hopi household which can be called average with respect to its members' general way of life, their economic conditions and their social position in the village. Nine persons are living in the small stone house which contains three rooms: the parents, a married daughter with her husband and a baby girl, 15-year-old Ellen and three younger sons of school age. The father and his sons work the mother's fields and take care of a moderately large herd of sheep, the father's own property, while the two women and Ellen do the housework.

The native ceremonials are attended by all, and, during the winter months, the ancient legends and stories are told by the father or the grandmother. The Hopi language is used almost exclusively, and the facts that the son-in-law has a high school education and makes an additional living as a trader, and that Ellen and her brothers go to a Government Day School, do not seem to have altered the slow and traditional rhythm of life. Those influences which may threaten the stability of the family are of purely personal character.

The father, a strong, handsome, jovial man of 44, is a very good runner, participates in the traditional foot races and is greatly admired by the village boys, who crowd around him whenever they can. At the same time, he is the Don Juan of the community, openly talked about, appraised and criticized as such. His relations with married or widowed women are numerous. At intervals he leaves his family entirely, "marrying" another woman and becoming a member of her household, but always, so far at least, returning to his original family. Even when he lives there, however, he often goes away during the night, and his sons who love him dearly have recently started to trail him, for fear of losing him for good.

The mother, a rather plain woman, does not show her resentment openly, and frequently voices her confidence that her husband will always come back to her. She is, however, very sloppy, and her household is considered the least clean in the village.

While Ellen, within this family situation, is said to get along well with her mother, "as long as she has her own way," her relationship to the father seems to be more intimate. From him she has learned weaving, an unusual privilege for a Hopi daughter, and we hear about the amused glances of mutual understanding passing between her and the father when the older sister states that "Ellen runs the whole house." The brother-in-law accuses her of bossiness which, according to him, has lately caused much strife in the family. While mentioning her strong bond with the father, he does not think that the paternal authority would have much weight in disciplining her, since she seems to realize that her father's own behavior is no shining example.

In school, Ellen uşed to be boisterous and "boy crazy," but she is now quiet, serious, studious and, at the same time, friendly and polite to everybody. Her work seems to vary with the teacher under whom it is done. While it is just satisfactory with one teacher, it is extraordinarily good with another. She participates in all social events and associates mainly with a few girls who are known to have similar trouble with the amorous escapades of their parents.

Ellen is healthy, stockily built, has pleasant but rather coarse features, and looks more like a fully developed woman than an adolescent girl. Almost always she shows a friendly smile. Her movements are slow and heavy but not altogether ungraceful. Her I. Q. being of high average (119), her intelligence is characterized by an almost complete lack of imagination and creativity. Her mental approach is extremely cautious and calculating, showing her great preference for common-sense values, determined less by a desire for conformity than by a tendency toward deliberately playing safe in all situations. Her range of interests is conventional and concerned with matters of daily life within the Hopi traditions. Although a natural extrovert, she transfers her cautious and calculating attitude into the areas of her emotions and interpersonal relations, thus restraining her spontaneity and the immediacy of her reactions. In a counterplay of desire and distrust, the latter has apparently

won out. While her manifest personality appears placid and compliant, there exists underneath a feeling of dissatisfaction with, and even of disaster in, her present situation, a feeling of inability to escape, and of powerless hostility which has to be covered up. Her sexual adjustment seems to be determined by the same factors of desire and cautious, calculating distrust. Her whole personality is limited in scope, partly by her natural earthbound disposition, partly as the result of a superficially inhibitive defense which, though sufficient for quite a clever handling of the various situations and problems of daily life, leaves her in the end dissatisfied.

In summary, Ellen is similar to a person who, desiring to cross a swamp, aware of the dangers, very carefully probes the terrain before each step. In her life in an average conservative Hopi family, regulated by the endless repetition of work and ceremonials, the father has apparently been the one great source of glamour. Pleasure-giving in his intimacy and the distribution of his favors, he is probably at the same time, as the object of hero-worship for his own sons and other boys and as the successful hunter for female companionship outside his family, eternally eluding her efforts toward a stable attachment. While in earlier years this may have caused suffering without depriving his image of splendor, it has, since she has grown up and understands the whole significance of the village gossip, now driven her against her will into her mother's camp. The fact that in his marital life her sister's husband follows her father's example helps to generalize her resentment and distrust. Still secretly admiring the father, she seems to realize that she as a woman would only be a victim of such ways of life, like her mother and her sister. She feels, however, that inhibiting her drives on the surface and very cautiously calculating all her own moves may do the trick, so that she can keep her cake and eat it too. That this is impossible shows up in the underlying dissatisfaction and hostility which she demonstrates in her overt bossiness at home (not in school!). Her recent attempts to give a great deal of attention to her school work point to a desire to find a better solution for her difficulties. Her outer adjustment can still be called good. How far she will be able to find inner happiness, will largely depend upon the experiences with which she will have to cope in the future.

ROGER

Roger is a tall, slender boy of 15, whose handsome and rather delicate features show traces of the eighth of Navaho blood he has. He is undernourished, has a slightly stooped posture, and his facial expression is somewhat sullen. From the tests, after they have been integrated, we conclude that he is a boy who has made an ambivalent and deceptive kind of adjustment. Passive, quiet, conventional on the surface, he is basically not only deeply insecure and depressed, but also quite aggressive. Behind a facade of submission, he is rebelling, reticent and negativistic. Attempts to restrain his natural vitality have led to a conflict within himself. The Thematic Apperception test points to the dominant influence of a neurotic mother, who has made his achievement of independence difficult. His intelligence, though of high average (114), is affected by his conflict, and shows that his efficiency is lowered by evasiveness on one side, and an over-critical attitude on the other.

In his overt behavior Roger appears shiftless and unpredictable. In school, the quality of his work used to be fluctuating. Sometimes excellent, it would suddenly become careless during intermittent periods of indifference and laziness. Friendly and polite in his manners, Roger gave the impression of keeping aloof from too much intimacy.

His teachers said that "it was difficult to crack his shell." He seemed to like social contacts, but changed his friends frequently. He showed much affection for his younger brother and his little nephews.

Last year, his attention and interest were concentrated on one girl, and he showed all the signs of puberty love, such as general lassitude, the drawing of intertwined hearts, the etching of her name and sexual symbols into the stones of the mesa, etc. This year, he preferred the company of boys, mainly of those concerned with Hopi ceremonial life. For a time, this and his own active interest in Hopi ceremonials seemed to stabilize him to some extent, but his mother was greatly worried about his behavior—staying out late at night, associating with "bad" boys and girls, signs of stubborn disobedience—and openly expressed her fear of having lost control over him. A few months ago, after pleading unsuccessfully with both his parents to let him leave home for work, he made a pleasure trip to town with their permission, and there obtained a job secretly at a hotel. He did not send any message to his parents and expressed the wish never to go back home again. Visited a month later by one of our informants, he appeared unhappy and homesick.

Roger is the seventh born of eleven children, nine of whom are surviving. The father being absent from home for weeks and even months on his sheep ranch, and an older brother being away in boarding school, Roger was the only "man" of the household among his mother, two older and three younger sisters, one brother, age nine, and two small nephews. The quite large house, in which the family lives, is remarkable on account of its slanting roof and the furniture, which is very much according to White standards. The house is very neat and apparently kept with great care. The family's economic condition is average, but since the mother has been working for wages for many years, the family is used to having and spending ready cash money. Within this household, in which the female element prevails, the mother is the dominant personality; the main source of gratification and also the main disciplinarian. She had been raised by missionaries, is now one of the most important and most eager members of the mission in her village and is greatly attached to, and concerned with the problems of, her religion. The husband has kept his tribal beliefs, but seems to sympathize with his wife. All her children are Christians, except Roger and his younger brother. Often the mother expresses her deep preoccupation with this point. She feels herself "punished in the sins of her children."

While she herself states that she disciplines her children only by talking to them at length and by exhorting them alone or with the missionary's aid, Roger says that both his parents beat him and his younger brother with whatever they find at hand. The relationship between the parents is seemingly quite good, though there is gossip that the father is staying most of the time on the ranch because of his love for Navaho women. The mother thinks that Roger, in his childhood a lively and very social boy, received less affection and attention than his older brother, because her two older daughters married and left her alone with the whole care of the children. The father talks in a matter-of-fact way about Roger, and apparently prefers his brothers as helpers with the sheep.

Roger's difficulties to adjust seem to rest mainly on the following points: A dominating mother, attempting to make her children well-behaved according to White standards, and at the same time to influence strongly their spiritual life, a woman not overly affectionate and, in her Christianity, different from most of the other mothers in the village; and a father apparently uninterested and absent most of the

time. And equally important and connected with these factors, a family which belongs officially to a small but active minority within a community, the native religious traditions of which are still alive and functioning with strength. In order to render a child content with and willing to accept the difficult role of an outsider, much affection and continuous, understanding support is needed, more than apparently Roger's family has given him. While during his earlier years the directed training he received succeeded in making him submissive and conforming, it did not give him other bases on which to solve the emotional problems of puberty and manhood than the obedient suppression of his natural tendencies. This has apparently caused a deep inner conflict. Not knowing how to solve it, he rebels against Christianity and against his family which he considers the source of his stress. Still, the mother's influence is strong enough to make it a secret rebellion, one which does not boldly face the responsibilities.

We must hope that his first experience of independence—his running away from home; his contacts with White culture; his earning money with his work—may help him to consider his problems in a more objective way, and thus to achieve a solution of his own.

MARJORIE

Marjorie is a 16-year-old girl who lives with her parents and five of her brothers and sisters on the mesa. She is the third of her parents' nine children, only one of whom died in babyhood. The oldest son being married and living off the Reservation, and a sister, six years older than Marjorie, working near Albuquerque, Marjorie has been, at least for the last three or four years, the oldest child of the family. There are two other brothers, 14 and 12 years of age, two little sisters, six and four years old, and a baby girl born only a year ago. The family is considered to be slightly above average in economic status, which in this village means a condition of very labile economic security, to be kept up through constant hard work of all the members. It also means that the parents, though only 45 and 47 years old, look much older than their actual age, and that all members of the family are undernourished. The father, and also the two boys when they are not in school, spend the days away from home on the farm land or the sheep and cattle ranch, while the mother has to take care of the smaller children, the house, the orchard, the storing, drying and grinding of the products of the fields, the cooking and the laundry. In all these duties Marjorie assists her mother and takes her place, whenever the mother is kept from work by pregnancy or sickness.

The family is counted among those conservative ones which follow the tribal religion, participate in all native ceremonies, and teach their children the ancient Hopi crafts and customs. At the same time, there is a trend in the family not only to accept, but to acquire and to utilize those values of White culture which may contribute to their prestige and to an improvement of their economic status. Both parents have been to boarding school and seem to welcome the idea that their children should receive an education according to White standards and also should seek jobs off the Reservation. Their pride in the children's achievement in school is outspoken and not at all usual for a family living in the conservative set-up on the mesa. Their prestige among the neighbors is apparently not disturbed by this fact and they seem to be well respected.

Reared in such an environment and in a rather harmonious family atmosphere where the relationship between the various members seems to have been stabilized early, more through the whole family's concerted effort for security and achievement than through the strict and enforcing discipline from one domineering parent, Marjorie is now a well developed, attractive adolescent girl. During the last years she increasingly has had to take over the hardships and responsibilities of the roles of adult female housekeeper, of mother and disciplinarian to her younger siblings and, at intervals, of a nurse to her own mother, who often suffers from gastro-intestinal disturbances and, on the whole, gives the impression of a person who, worn out by too much work, easily and willingly yields to feelings of exhaustion. At the same time, Marjorie has to do her school work and to keep up in concentration and interest with her schoolmates, many of whom are not burdened to such a degree with responsibilities.

This whole accumulation of tasks she seems to master perfectly. Her father speaks with great pride of her, her mother agrees that she needs her help, her smaller siblings obey her. She is an excellent worker at school, the second best in the eighth grade, an obvious favorite of her teachers and, apparently, popular among her agemates, boys and girls alike. She attends school regularly and also takes books and school work home with her, quite an unusual feature among Hopi children. She even has started to take piano lessons and likes to assume a leading part in all kinds of school performances which require an exhibition of her capabilities in front of a public of Hopi and Whites.

The teachers praise her "ladylike" behavior, her ability to keep the boys at a "proper" distance, and her efforts to teach and to supervise the younger children. A recent incident, in which Marjorie had been told by an intelligent and lively classmate "to go to hell"—and this in answer to a friendly "good morning" from her side—and then by letter had communicated this fact to her teacher in the tone of a deeply offended queen who retires into exile, and another incident, in which she, though not a Christian, had been competing for days with a Christianized Hopi girl in praying aloud and exhibiting pictures of pious content, did not seem to arouse the teachers' suspicion. It was therefore with a great deal of interest that the various examinations and tests were analyzed, because they would give a more complete insight into a personality which seemed to meet with so much approval from all sides.

The medical examination shows that Marjorie is definitely under weight, and has also certain signs of malnutrition, i.e., of vitamin B and C deficiency. Her tonsils are enlarged, and the findings over her lungs point to the possibility of a tuberculous infection. Her vision is somewhat below normal but, while a great number of Hopi children have the same or a worse degree of shortsightedness, she is, in her group of agemates, the only one who wears glasses and who seems to attribute to them not only a value of usefulness, but also a significance of prestige and authority. Among the large number of children, she alone volunteered complaints about her health, telling the physician about occasional attacks of vomiting, for which at the time no physical equivalents were found.

Toward the psychological tests Marjorie showed the attitude of a person who willingly, but unsmilingly, has to perform an important task which is both a duty and a serious occasion for competitive achievement. All the tests agree on her high intellectual level (I.Q. 129), the projective tests specifying her as an excellent observer, a logical, critical and conscientious thinker with a good deal of common sense, but with limited imagination, low creativity and originality, and a preponderant interest in the analytical discernment of details. The most outstanding and determining feature of her personality is a strong compulsive drive for pedantic accuracy and perfection, which deprives the world of its attractions and pleasures for her, unless it be an object for conquest, and which lowers her spontaneity considerably and transforms her genuine emotions and instinctual drives into intellectual aggression. Together with this goes a rejection of her own femininity and of intense and intimate interpersonal relations in general, a strict and unbending tendency for judging right and wrong, and a definite awareness and acceptance of the implications and gradations of authority. She appears deeply egocentric, self righteous and socialized only with a constant eye to her prestige. On the whole her personality is, according to the tests, firmly set, tense and inelastic, with its high potentialities rigidly channelized by her drive for perfection.

Summarizing the test results and the various reports about her and her family, we come to the conclusion that Marjorie is a girl of high gifts and capacities, the development of which has been greatly influenced, directed and limited by the constellation of her specific environment. In a family situation undisturbed by gross discrepancies and conflicts, regulated by the unifying effort toward survival and achievement of all its members, with a father very fond and proud of her, and a sickly and weakened mother relying upon her ready help, Marjorie responds to the great demands on her strength with eagerness. However, the gratification she receives from the father, who is usually absent, does not seem to be sufficient, and the ever present factor of an exhausted and increasingly inefficient mother who is the immediate source of these demands, is apparently too trying to make her efforts genuinely enjoyable. She reacts with a rejection of the feminine role, of which she sees an undesirable example at home, and defends herself, since she cannot and does not want to rebel, with a conversion of her spontaneous emotions and instincts into the one overwhelming drive for perfection and achievement which keeps her still in harmony with the aims of her family, but at the same time shall lead her away from and above it.

So far, she has made an excellent outer adjustment but at the expense of a full and natural development of her inner resources and with a "second hand" satisfaction as compensation. The approval she receives is a well merited reward for her efforts. The uncritical favoritism and the special attention she meets in school is, though understandable, a dangerously enhancing factor in her trend toward the rigid confinement of her personality in one direction. While she should be encouraged in the utilization of her intellectual capacities, this ought to go hand in hand with a careful deepening and broadening of her concepts of values. Otherwise, in the event of shocking situations—particularly if they include personalities superior to her—she may find herself helplessly frustrated and may fall victim to hysterical reactions.

IRENE

Born off the Reservation, Irene, now 14 years old, spent the first 11 years of her life in a small town in northern Arizona, where her father had a good job. The environment in which she grew up is therefore decidedly different from that of the other children studied. Her early training at home, the first impressions she received of the world—streets, stores, traffic—the language she heard around her, her toys and White playmates, the public school, everything was saturated with the elements of modern White culture.

Within the family itself, the father was the one who presided over the household, providing comfort and security and a nice house of their own from the good salary he earned. The mother did no other work than taking care of the house and the children. The ties with Hopi culture were, however, not severed. There were Hopi friends in town, travels to Indian festivals at Flagstaff, and also trips to the Reservation to visit relatives and to attend the ceremonials, where the family made their appearance as interesting and slightly exotic visitors from town.

This state of affairs began to break down quickly when the father developed a heart disease. After about a year of unrest, hope, and worry—filled with a trip to the west coast for cure, a temporary return to work, and again other doctors and hospitals—the father died. Without a penny, the widow returned to the Reservation, together with Irene, one older and two younger sons.

From then on, the family's way of life changed completely. The mother's social position, after being for years mainly that of her husband's wife, became that of a representative of one of the most powerful Hopi clans. It had also become, however, that of a widow without married children and without property, that of a receiver of her brother's support, begrudged by his wife, and of Government relief. There was no field, no herd of cattle or sheep which slowly and organically would have drawn the family into the ordinary cycle of Hopi life. It was not even easy to find a place to live.

After two apparently unsatisfactory years in the house of the father's brother, the family moved into the mother's native village, where her own brother was a high official. Here, the mother started a relationship with a man much younger than she, from whom she had a son and, recently, a daughter. During her first pregnancy, her lover hurriedly married a village girl, but continued his former relations. The mother, in order to better satisfy the needs of her large family, has taken over a small job for Whites, doing quite reliable and good work. Occasionally, the oldest son earns some money through odd jobs. The whole family inhabits a very small house, living, cooking and sleeping in one room, which shows traces of an effort to recall the time of well being in town. Within the village, the family associates almost exclusively with their closest relatives. While there are no open sanctions against them, there seems to be a good deal of gossip, criticism and hostility.

In this situation Irene moves, quiet, serious, poised, helping her mother with the housework, being herself a second mother to her younger brothers and the baby, not only in efficient care and in her attempts at disciplining them, but also in her affection for and obvious attachment to them. The children, in turn, seem to respond with equal affection. In contrast to Irene, they are a vivacious group and get into fights among themselves and with the village boys, so that the mother, who does not seem to have sufficient hold over them, sometimes has to give them a whipping. It is, however, characteristic that all the children, including Irene, form at once a close and loyal unit of defense, whenever they are attacked from the outside.

Not only the mother is a target of gossip. The boys are said to be stealing, a misdemeanor which they have supposedly learned in town, and Irene herself is said to give her favors to the men and boys of the village. In school, she is very cooperative and does excellent work. There too, her manners are quiet and modest and, unlike her behavior at home, where she appears more determined, very shy. Usually she is alone, and if, sometimes, she is seen with a group of girls around school, there are no indications of close ties of friendship.

Irene is a slim, delicately built adolescent girl with a sweet face and serious expression. She is much under weight and shows signs of vitamin B deficiency. The findings over her lungs point to the possibility of tuberculosis, significant in that her mother has suffered the same disease, and that her oldest brother is suspected of having it too.

All the tests characterize Irene as passive, shy, full of fear and of a desire to escape. The projective tests reveal a warm-hearted, kind, very sensitive personality, deeply disturbed by an overwhelming fear of the world which she tries in vain to overcome by withdrawing into herself and into the refuge of her imaginings. Basically vital, passionate and trusting, she has kept her spontaneity. Her originally active drives have, however, assumed a decidedly yielding character. Satisfaction is sought for in "service" to others and in the retreat into an unreal fantasy world of her own. Though this kind of a defense protects and even overemphasizes her inner development, on the other hand it leaves her fully exposed to attacks from the outside. It is interesting that the Thematic Apperception test specifically points out her "need of the helpful yet authoritative affection of an older man." Irene's intellectual capacities seem to be of superior quality. Her efficiency (I.Q. 121) appears somewhat affected in times of emotional stress by the escapist function of her thinking.

Irene's case is almost self-explanatory. It seems to be significant that the first ten years of her life were apparently happy, harmonious and secure, and thus a good foundation for a rich development of her personality without need for building up a specific defense. The change to a life of insecurity came suddenly, shock-like, and as an unavoidable blow from the outside. The impact of changes was great and almost completely of a negative, depriving character. Responsibilities increased in disproportionate degree. All this happened during the period of prepuberty where we also normally find a strong tendency toward withdrawal into the inner world of the imagination. In Irene, it accentuated this tendency. On the other hand, the sudden increase of demands on her own self, deeply affectionate, but unprepared for and inexperienced in resistance, made her defense largely a yielding and passive one. It is in this light and in that of her need to find a substitute for her father, that her sexual relations to men (if they are true) have to be viewed. Regularization and clearing of the environment i n which she lives, would not only help her greatly in her own development, but also make her a social being of high value.

BERNARD

Bernard is a 14-year-old Hopi boy, whose family is distinguished in its clan membership and prominent through its relative prosperity. Hopi beliefs and ceremonies with the whole elaborated system of worship, tabus and initiations, are followed and cultivated with intensity by the entire family. At the same time, the father has been working for over 20 years at a trading post, which has meant not only a regular and secure income of cash and a savings account of several hundred dollars, but also continuous contact with Whites and particularly with Navaho, who frequent the trading post a good deal and are a rich source of news, tales and the broadening exchange of opinions.

In this family, which lives in one of the largest and most comfortable houses below the mesa, Bernard is the last born of five children. While his mother was pregnant with him, the youngest daughter, a girl of six and everybody's favorite, died by accident and left the family in such dejection that the mother wished the child she was carrying to be born dead. It was not until about six months after his birth that first the father and then his mother could accept him with affection, but from that time on, as if to compensate him for their early neglect, the whole family has made him an object of special care, attention and love.

He was nursed by his mother until he was three years old and finally quit of his own accord in response to the teasing of older children. In his early childhood he played mostly with the "less rough" girls, thus staying more than other little Hopi boys under the watchful protection of his adult female relatives. His two brothers, nine and 12 years older, and his only sister, 14 years older than he, were rather so many more caretakers of his than playmates or objects for competition. Now that the sister and one brother are married and the other brother is in the Army, Bernard has become the only grown-up son of the immediate household who, besides smaller duties at home, has taken over the responsibility for his grandfather's and brother's large herd of sheep, and on the other hand, sees at least part of his mother's attention held by a number of small grandchildren.

In his overt behavior Bernard is described as a very bright boy, who is respectful toward his parents and all older people, and courteous and refined in his manners. While he qualifies as quite a good worker in school, there is not much said about industriousness or conscientious striving— he seems even to loathe arithmetic— but great emphasis is given to his pleasant personality and to his artistic interest and achievement. Reading and writing he learned first from naming the pictures he drew. Throughout the years he has excelled among the other children in the quality of his paintings and at the same time has shown so much delight and interest in music that he is now the best guitar player in the community and the leader of the harmonica band at school.

From early youth he has participated in the native ceremonials which culminate in an intricate and highly rhythmic play of dancing and singing. Last year, probably in connection with his second initiation, his attention and his time was greatly caught by them, at the expense of his attendance and work in school. Bernard is very popular and gets along with everybody but, while the girls seem to feel attracted toward him, he prefers at present to confine himself to a gang of three or four boys, his agemates, who have the same interest in music and whose unquestioned but also unobtrusive leader he seems to be.

Bernard is a healthy, slender boy with strikingly handsome, delicate features and a happy, frequently smiling, expression. His I.Q. is 142. In the projective tests he is characterized by the outspoken dexterity with which in all situations he chooses the easiest and most comfortable way, in order to avoid harm and to obtain the moderately pleasant. He is sensuous and sensitive, a social being by nature but, since he evades penetration in his thinking and in his emotional ties, not socialized in an ethical sense. His creativity appears quite superficial, in so far as it does not seem to influence his basic personality structure other than by being one of his many natural outlets and means of expression; a matter of easy defense, still conventional and not an imperious and determining force of original concept formations.

Emotionally he is unaggressive, highly receptive, though not impulsively yielding to stimulation, but again instinctively selecting the safe and evading possible impacts. Still greatly attached to his mother, he is insecure and slightly depressed by the problems of puberty, and this seems to have given his spontaneous reactions a certain restraint and to have developed, within the last months, a trend toward withdrawal into himself. The equilibrium of his personality is genuinely excellent, but, in its reliance on a defense of evasion and conformity, light and precarious.

In an attempt at summary and explanation, we see Bernard as a boy unusually favored and conditioned by his superior intelligence, his various talents, and the particular family in which he grew up. For him, economic security and family prestige are realities, unquestioned and established. But there is more than that. The family situation is not the traditional one among the Hopi. While the mother is still dominating in the house and in her role within the clan, the father is not only a laborer in his wife's fields, but also an independent worker who provides his family with a steady income and special comfort and besides, in Navaho fashion, has a very large herd of sheep, which facts establish his sons quite probably as future heirs. The balance between the spheres and the strength of influence deriving from both parents is thus exceptionally well kept and also extends into areas of spiritual significance, where we find a very active observance of ancient Hopi beliefs, together with a clever and well founded utilization of the advantages of White culture.

In such a family Bernard has, until lately, been the constant receiver of protection and attention, and it is at this point that we discover the one essential weakness in the direction of his development. In a household where the perpetuation of the clan rested on one daughter only, the whole impact of resentments and emotions caused by the second daughter's loss was thrust upon him; at first, for a short time, complete rejection, and then overprotection and overaffection which, at least in the mother's efforts to keep him under her watchful eye and in the companionship of girls, seems to have been stained by guilt feelings and by the half conscious idea that this boy had to take the daughter's place. It is fortunate, and probably due to the sufficiently strong male influence in the family and to the boy's own constitutional superiority, that he has been handicapped only slightly by this attitude. As it is, he not only rests in the security offered him, but has become dependent upon it, happy to please, willingly conforming and anxiously avoiding any possible disturbance of a situation so pleasant to himself. He is psychologically an epicurean among the Hopi, with all the implications of artistic refinement, receptivity, and slightly melancholic tinge inherent in the epicurean idea. The latest development within his family—his taking over new responsibilities typical for males, and the balancing factor of the grandchildren in his mother's affection—may help him to solve the too strong maternal ties. How far it may influence his range of depth, which has most been affected by his attempts to avoid harm, remains to be seen.

10. FIVE MORE PORTRAITS

LENA AND LARRY

Lena, 12, and Larry, nine years old, are members of a large family which, while living below the mesa and having contacts with White people, consciously and deliberately keep to the Hopi pattern of life. The father, who seems to be quite a dominant personality, is a very good stone mason and carpenter. Though for a time he was working off the Reservation and even got a raise in salary for his good work he used to express openly his dislike of leaving the Reservation and his family, and he gave up the job at once when he heard that Lena was sick. Sending all his children to school, he sets the Reservation High School as a limit for their education, determined to make them "stay Hopi."

The mother, unobtrusive and not outspoken like the father, presides over the household and is an excellent pottery maker. While not hostile to White contacts, she shows the same trend towards conservatism in her quiet reserve and her preference for the medicine man rather than White methods concerning health. The native ceremonies are faithfully attended, and all the children are initiated into the *kachina* cult. Within the community, the whole family is very popular and respected.

There are eight children. The oldest daughter, whose husband is in the Army, lives with her baby in a little stone house which her father has built very close to the nice, neat family home. Lena is now the oldest unmarried daughter. Except for a little girl of four, all the other children are boys, ranging from 16 to one year of age, with Larry exactly in the middle. The tie between all the members of the family and their cooperation seems to be very strong. Everybody has his share of work; the parents' affection appears equally distributed among all the children, and discipline is kept up with persuasion and scolding, coming from the parents, the oldest daughter, and now also from Lena.

In this family Lena and Larry have been brought up according to the average child training pattern of the traditional Hopi: tied to the cradle-board for most of the first year of their lives and nursed by the mother for about one year, later playing around the house with dolls and wagons, and early starting to work—Lena in the house, learning how to cook, to wash and to make pottery, Larry helping the grandfather and the father on the fields or with the sheep.

Apparently they have not been away from the Reservation, except for the one time when Lena had a check-up for tuberculosis (with negative result) at a sanitarium in a railroad town and Larry had a fractured arm set in a hospital, after first being treated by a Hopi bone doctor. When the mother visited her husband for several weeks off the Reservation, she took with her only the small children, and left the older ones in the grandfather's house on top of the mesa. During that time Lena and Larry often got "into mischief" in school and had to be punished. Usually they are well behaved and always active and busy.

Their work at school is outstanding, Lena particularly excelling in arithmetic, Larry being very good in all school situations which require abstract thinking. Both children got a double promotion last year, and it was a surprise to the teachers to find out that Larry, contrary to the impression he had given, had actually missed a good part of the work. Because of their constant activity both children are considered by their teachers as extroverts.

Larry plays with boys and girls alike, seems to be a leader in his class, and loves to perform before an audience. He even took the part of Santa Claus at Christmas. He enjoys playing with construction blocks and gives all his attention and effort to copying the design of the patterns in minute detail.

Lena too seems popular, but she does not like to get in the limelight or to take solo parts. She has a close friendship with a cousin, a girl of her age. They walk together arm in arm, hug each other, and even hold hands comfortingly, when one has to perform at the blackboard in class. The cousin's home is that of a well-to-do, progressive family which lives very much according to White standards. Lena seems to play less with the boys than the other children, and while her cousin had a boy friend last year, she thought herself too busy for such things. After school she never stays with the other children on the playground, but hurries right home. In her relationship to the teachers she appears indifferent, and her cooperation depends on the mood she is in. Sometimes she shows a streak of stubbornness and does not like to be bothered with anything. She can be very talkative and chatters endlessly with her

girl friend in Hopi, not giving much heed to the teachers' admonition to speak English.

Lena is a very attractive adolescent girl, healthy and well developed. Larry is short, stocky and so well nourished that he is almost obese. His tonsils are enlarged and his eyesight is poor. A fracture of his right arm has not affected its strength and mobility.

The tests reveal certain similarities of more general character and, on the other hand, differences in the degree and mode of development between the personalities of the two children. They are of high, Lena even of superior intelligence, Larry's I.Q. being 117, Lena's 130. Their intellectual capacities are characterized by a good ability for abstract thinking, by creativity, originality and rich, but overemphasized, imagination. In their mental approach both give most of their attention to subtleties, and are apt to lose themselves in matters of small detail. At the same time, they have sufficient common sense, and also their fantasy is concerned with themselves and the events of daily life, and not with motifs of fairy-tale unreality. Both are pronounced introverts, i. e., more deeply occupied with their own inner life than being outgoing and truly interested in outside contacts. Both show signs of anxiety and insecurity, and it is the nature of this anxiety and the kind of defense they have adopted which mainly distinguish their personalities from each other.

Larry's insecurity has made him quite obsessed with concern about himself, his health, his position and his achievement. His imagination is centered mostly in these things, and he wants to be a hero, admired by everybody, particularly by his family. In so far as he considers his environment mainly as a background for his fears and a stage for the display of his abilities, his interpersonal relations are rather superficial. Emotionally he

Hopi infant on cradle board

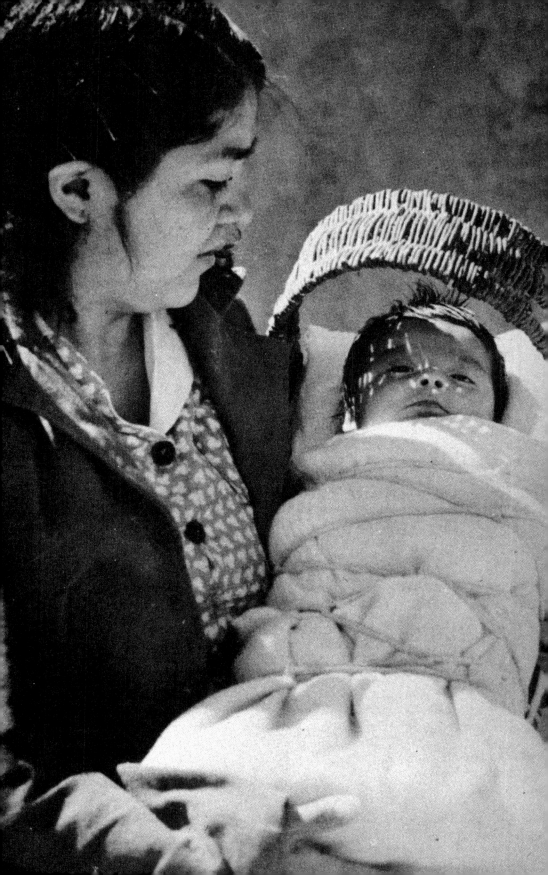

is quite passive and slightly restrained. He defends himself by exhibiting his abilities as much as he can.

Lena has feelings of inadequacy and fights them with a compulsive drive for perfectionism and accuracy. This lowers the freedom and the spontaneity in her behavior and restrains her impulses. She builds a wall around herself, behind which she retires and behind which her inner life functions with great strength. Part of her anxiety and her withdrawal into herself is probably due to the problems of puberty with which she has to cope; but, according to the Thematic Apperception test, a great part seems also to depend upon the specific family situation, particularly upon a hard-bargaining, demanding father. She seems to feel that she must continually demonstrate her efficiency in order to gain the family's affection.

In spite of great conformity to the Hopi pattern, both children show a good adjustment to White contacts. In Lena it seems to be even better than her adjustment to the Hopi.

Summarizing our knowledge about Lena and Larry, we can say that both of them are highly gifted children, whose personalities show the effects of anxiety. What in their behavior appears "extroversion," i.e., their constant activity, their being always busy, does not seem to stem altogether from a spontaneous and happy enjoyment of life, but seems to be mainly a means of proving to themselves and to others their own efficiency. They are both children who utilize their capacities and their strength to the limit, without daring to keep back a reserve for their own, self-desired satisfaction. Larry, still naive, trusting, and not consciously aware of his limitations, thinks that a good show of his abilities and even "going only through the motions" will avail, but already he is insecure and too preoccupied with himself; starting to imagine what he cannot be. Lena, three years older, hides her much

Hopi grandmother and grandson

stronger withdrawal into a rich imaginative life behind the surface of eager activity. It seems possible that the demands coming to both from a family in which the parents, but particularly the father, are extremely efficient, have been too great and have required too much responsibility from them too early. Since not only their anxiety, but also their security in affection and support comes from the same source, namely the family, they have accepted what is demanded from them. So far, they have both made an excellent outer adjustment, but the development of their personalities has been neither balanced nor free of suppression. Already Lena, in her stubbornness and her moods, seems to show signs of rebellion.

HELEN

Helen's father died of tuberculosis when she was seven. He had the reputation of being "very loose in his ways." The mother and her children, Helen, two older boys, a younger son and a little girl, born one month after the father's death, stayed on in their home which they shared with other maternal relatives. With the sons and their grandfather taking care of the fields and the small livestock, they continued to fit into the everyday life of the community as they had before, though their economic situation might have been somewhat reduced. No jobs with White people were taken on. The mother, while fairly active and interested in community affairs, and also a pottery maker, kept to her work at home and in the orchard. The ceremonies were attended too, and the children took part in the dances.

The fact that, after the husband's death, the mother had had three other children, two by a young man who has since married a girl of the village, and one by another man divorced from his wife, did not seem to arouse much objection or resentment in the community. Two of the children died shortly after birth; a little girl, now two years old, survived. Some advantage to the family's prestige seems to derive from the brother-in-law who belongs to a powerful clan, and is also a man of some means. He and his wife live in the same house and have adopted Helen's seven year old sister. The White employees consider the whole family as "not too bright," but agree that they are good workers and easy to get along with. The two older sons, one of whom is married, are now in the Army.

As the oldest daughter, Helen, now 14, helps her mother and takes care of the younger children. She has learned how to make pottery and has participated in the Buffalo and Butterfly dances. Like her mother, she is quiet and unobtrusive but, if rumor be right, can also be quite determined and aware of her position as oldest daughter. Gossip has it that when the man who is the father of her mother's last baby came to stay with them in their home, she objected and the man left. The teachers find her phlegmatic, plodding, not giving any cause for difficulties, but "hard to make a dent in." Her school work is fair; she does what she is told to, without showing any initiative. With the other children she gets along well.

Helen is quite a nice looking young girl usually with a serious expression on her face. She is short and underweight, looks younger than 14, and is physically less developed. She also shows symptoms of vitamin B and C deficiency. Her eyes are inflamed and she wears glasses to correct her moderate myopia. The results of the tests given to her are very interesting. Her I. Q. (80) obtained from the Grace Arthur tests puts her intelligence on a level of low average. Both projective tests (Thematic Apperception and Rorschach) independently judge her intellectual capacities as superior or of high average, emphasizing her good imagination, creativity and originality. At the same time, the Rorschach reveals an overcautious attitude in her ap-

proach to new situations and an almost total lack of a drive for achievement, which are both based on the anxious overadjustment the girl has made to the world and its demands. Her intellectual energies are introverted, and what she lacks in overt spontaneity is more than compensated by the great spontaneity and vivaciousness of her inner life, into which she seems to withdraw. In spite of this, she does not lose herself in fantasies, but takes up the struggle with a frightening outer world and tries to appease it. Sensitive and introspective, she chooses the way of "being a very good girl" as the most secure to save her inner freedom. In her sexual adjustment she shows a conscious fear of aggression, which is frequently found in puberty.

While some of Helen's withdrawal into herself goes with the usual picture of a personality during puberty, her anxious desire for appeasement does not. We cannot be sure about the causes which have led up to it. It may be that after the father's death the family situation was more insecure than is apparent. If nothing else, it is known that widows and their children are favorite targets for jokes made by the Hopi clowns, and in one of the tests (Emotional Response) Helen herself says that she is sad and ashamed when people say mean things to her or laugh at her during the dances. To a Hopi who follows without rebellion the Hopi traditions that everything has its right place and that sickness and death have a meaningful and fateful interpretation, even a slight deviation in the intracommunal position would call for compensation. On the other hand, as the oldest daughter, Helen has always had a good deal of responsibility, and with her mother's frequent pregnancies and small children in the household, appeasement was probably for her a daily exercise. However it be, her method of adjustment is such that, depriving her of satisfaction based on outer success, it reduces possible friction to a minimum and, at the same time, does not affect the free development of her inner life.

As to Helen's intelligence, the White employees' opinion and the performance test tell us that she is "just dumb." Referring to the projective tests and following the rule that a test may show lower but never better results than the subject's capacities, we strongly doubt this conclusion.

RUSSELL

Russell's family is very much like the average Hopi family, following the old traditions without being prominent in their ceremonial expression, leading a daily life of hard work and relative scarcity, and, at the same time, using here and there a few devices of White culture which may increase their well-being or their prestige, but which do not seem to affect deeply their way of life and thinking.

Here it is the father who apparently worked for the Government in the past, and who now receives a disability pension of $45.00 a month because of his "bad eyes." He uses it mostly for the upkeep of his truck, with which he hauls his food, wood and water. He farms and has a few sheep. Both he and his wife have been married before, and have lost their first spouses through death. The wife has one son by her first husband, and two by her second: namely Russell, age 11, and an older son of 20 who is now with the armed forces. Several other children she bore in between the 20-year-old son and Russell died. The lack of a daughter as a perpetuator of the clan has apparently been much felt, for about eight years ago the family adopted a little girl, the daughter of the mother's son by her first marriage, and thus her own grandchild.

The father is an industrious, friendly man, at ease in contact with other people. His wife is a very good housekeeper who keeps her home very clean and dresses her children well, giving perhaps more attention to the adopted daughter who has the nicest clothes of any school girl. The mother appears quite withdrawn, seldom speaks up in conversations and does not take part in any of the community activities which attract the other women to the school house. She usually keeps to her home below the mesa, leaving it only to go to her husband's ranch and to the ceremonies on top of the mesa. Russell's older brother has always been a very active and exceptionally bright boy in school, and parents and teachers alike compare his brilliant qualities with Russell's shortcomings.

Russell himself was initiated into the *kachina* cult three years ago and sometimes dances in the ceremonies. During planting and harvesting time he helps his father in the fields. He seems to make good at home. The worries he causes his parents apparently concern only his school performance, in which his older brother so greatly excelled. Until recently he overslept in the mornings, often claimed that he felt sick and too weak to go to school, and tried with all kinds of tricks, like tales about abuses suffered from the teachers, to cut down his attendance, which has therefore been very spotty. In class he was so unresponsive that, for quite a long time, the teachers thought him deaf; now their verdict tends more to extreme inattention. Due to his poor performance he was kept in the lower grades together with the smaller children, and was there a target of much teasing which he seemed to resent deeply. In vain his parents scolded and sometimes spanked him, and taught him in the evenings words in English which he might use in school. Last year as a final resort he was moved into a higher grade with children of his size. From then on he has not missed a day of school even when he really has had minor ailments like sores on his foot or his face, and he has since done much better work. He is very good in arts and crafts.   In his behavior out of class he seems to be a "real boy." Not quarrelsome nor timid, he gets along well with his agemates. He does not talk very much and appears very conscious of the way people feel about him.   He plays a good deal with his adopted sister who, in contrast to him, is a very talkative and vivacious girl.   He refers often to his older brother whom he apparently likes very much.

Russell is a lanky, awkward boy whose facial features are definitely not handsome.   He is well nourished and healthy.   Eyesight and hearing are normal.   The results of his tests were quite a surprise to his teachers.   His I.Q. of 123 puts his intelligence on a level of high average.   His thinking seems to be very solid and is characterized by highly developed common sense and a definite preference in interest for the obvious realities of daily life.

Though not particularly vital but showing an emotional life of normal strength, he knows how to keep his spontaneity under a layer of superficial restraint with which he consciously covers his real emotions and drives. Not aggressive and tending to withdraw into himself, he may sometimes startle his environment with actions which, by contrast to his usual behavior, appear impulsive and seem to constitute pent-up emotions breaking through his self-imposed defensive restraint. He apparently sometimes tries to swallow more than he can stand.   He is sensitive and there are signs that he feels uncertain of his own worth.   He seems to be greatly dependent on and clinging to his mother, but hostile towards the father.

Russell is a boy who shows in his overt behavior a definite, one-sided maladjustment in his attitude toward school.   At home he seems to get along quite well.   However, according to his personality picture in the tests which reveals that he is very much on the defensive, there is apparently more

behind this than a simple boyish dislike of being tied .up in school.   To keep the appearance of a deafmute for hours daily and for years in sequence, while one's intelligence is higher than that of most of the other happily successful children, is quite a show of determined resistance, of self-torture and of emotional mastery. The nature of Russell's feelings toward his parents, as they appear in the tests, seems to give us a hint for the solution of this problem.

The first surviving child after ten years, he has probably been quite babied by a mother who in her type and constitution shows traits similar to his, reserve and silent withdrawal; while the father in his easy, outgoing ways seems to have found a more congenial replica in his oldest son.   This son has apparently been held up to Russell as the one desirable and brilliant model for his own development with an over-playing of his excellent achievement in school.   Thus quite a good foundation for resistance was laid. Aggravating factors were Russell's own temperament which made successful competition with his sparkling brother probably hopeless from the beginning, and the fact that his mother, if not in her words, then in the way of her life exemplified his own attitude toward school.   It should be added that it was the father who made a constant issue of his school performance, talking to him, teaching him in the evenings, and discussing again and again his problems with the teachers.   This would of course create feelings of unworthiness in Russell, and also hostile resentment which, similar to the way of his mother, he expressed in mute resistance, and only in the one area which appeared most precious to his father.   That he was kept in the lower grades was probably fuel to his father's scorn and to Russell's own feeling of abasement.   The presence of the adopted daughter, who has apparently attracted much of his mother's attention and affection, has perhaps made his situation still more difficult. It is quite possible that through his promotion into a higher grade and through further encouragement and training of Russell's specific talents in school, without dwelling on his brother's different abilities, his difficulties may be overcome through a more organic adjustment.

EVE

Eve, eight years old, is living with her mother and her two-years-older brother in the house of her maternal grandparents. She was born and spent the first five years of her life at the Reservation Agency, where her father, a full blood Navaho, has a good job. There she became used to contacts with Whites. The first language she spoke was English and she learned Hopi only when, three years ago, her parents got a divorce, and mother and children moved from their small, confined household into the larger one in the mother's native village.

As cause for the divorce the mother mentions her ill health and acute sickness after childbirth during the year previous to the separation. The child, a boy, died at the age of four months, and the mother spent quite a long time at a hospital, several miles away from home. On the other hand, her former husband has the reputation of being "fond of women." He married a Navaho girl immediately after the divorce and has had three children by her.

The household, in which Eve is now staying, comprises besides her mother and her brother, the grandparents, a great grandfather, two maternal aunts (one divorced and the other married to a soldier), and a crippled uncle. There are no other children. The whole family, except the two old men, are Christians and affiliated with the mission of the village. The tribal ceremonies are not attended. The family's economic conditions are average, part of the support being provided by the aunts who frequently work as housekeepers in town. Eve's mother receives a good alimony from her husband, and also works, as much as her ill health permits, either for the teachers in the village or for White people off the Reservation, leaving the children with her parents. The family appears to be fairly respected in the community, but they are called ka'hopi (i. e., not Hopi) because of their Christianity and their approaches to White culture.

While the grandmother still lives much according to the traditional style, making and selling Hopi pottery, the mother seems to value possessions like a .radio, a sewing machine, an alarmclock, etc. quite highly, emphasizes her children's cleanliness and tries to dress and groom them and herself after town-fashion. Her moral reputation is good. She is an outgoing, talkative, rather gossipy woman who does not appear overly strict with her children, though quite concerned with their looks and behavior. She states that in matters of discipline the father used to take the children's part and to be quite indulgent.

Though at first afraid to go to school, Eve is now a star pupil. While there are other children in class who do better work, she receives more credit "because she knows how to get along with White People." Lively, frank, and quite a chatterbox, she is said to have a sweet disposition. Her playmates are her brother and the children of her neighborhood. During the last year there have been occasional fights between brother and sister, in which the brother seems to have been the aggressor. We do not hear anything about other children attacking her, but we do know that her brother is occasionally teased on account of his being half Navaho.

Eve is a very pretty, healthy little girl, with sparkling eyes and a ready smile. Very much at ease, she approached the tests eagerly and asked questions and made remarks about them. Her I.Q. is 116, and one of the projective tests (Rorschach) shows her quick and alert comprehension, her excellent sense of observation and her good creative potentialities. All the tests characterize her as naive, spontaneous, rather outgoing, and at the same time, imaginative. Her adjustment is excellent, still strongly determined by her tie to the mother and by her own efforts to please. Ambitious and self assertive, she shows slight traces of anxiety over the adequacy of her performance.

Eve's personality shows a natural and balanced development and does not seem to have suffered from the early change of her environment and the separation from the father. In her grandmother's house she has found a number of adult relatives ready to give her affection and care. No new responsibilities for her were involved. There has been no crude deprivation and she has remained essentially trusting. As a little girl in a prevalently female household, her natural inclinations are more encouraged than limited. The fact that, as a half Navaho and a Christian, she is to a certain extent an outsider will probably not affect her deeply at her age, and may be outweighed by the approval which she generally enjoyed in her earliest environment and which she still receives from her family and the teachers.

A few words at the end of this section, without coming to conclusions which will be drawn later. Among the reader's reactions may have been one of surprise that the personalities of the Hopi are so similar to those of White children. Part of this impression will be due to the language and the analyst, a language of our own culture and a White analyst. Besides, though, and mainly, the similarity is a fact. Security and insecurity; acceptance or rejection by a loved person; strict, inhibiting training or no training

at all, will evoke reactions of like or dislike, of defense or yielding in every personality in every culture. To us it does not seem a coincidence that in many cases where, by means of the tests, we found an irregularity of the personality according to our standards, we also found irregularities in the child's environment from the Hopi point of view. Where the irregularities were of a more subtle nature and e.g., were only implied in the parents' behavior, we may have been wrong in our emphasis and, on the other hand, may have missed hidden factors. With regard to this we can only say that we thought it better to use our knowledge as we have it at present than not to use it at all. Opposition to our findings will be more productive than inertia.

As to the "Hopiness" of these personalities, we want to point out now that the adjustment which the Hopi children seem to be able to achieve in trying situations is remarkable in resourcefulness, strength and even sophistication, and shows in its variations certain trends which distinguish them from children of other tribes which we have studied with the same methods. In the following chapter we shall deal with all these qualities in detail.

With regard to the question of a better understanding of individuals and its desirability for the sake of better adjustment, we hope that our personality sketches, though they are presented in very short form, condensed from the abundance of our original material, may give at least an inkling of the help which a child's educator may derive from the use of standardized psychological methods, correlated with a knowledge of the child's home environment and life history.

No individual enters the world with a ready-made personality. Constantly his natural qualities are worked upon by his surroundings and those other individuals with whom he comes in contact. The behavior and the reactions which he shows in one situation are intimately connected with his various experiences and the influences exerted upon him in another. A child does not leave the security or insecurity, the joy or sadness of his home-life outside the door which leads into school, and he does not leave his pleasant or unpleasant experiences with teachers and schoolmates along with his books in the classroom. Knowledge of the *various* forces of influence to which a child is exposed and of his reactions to them is therefore apt to explain attitudes which otherwise, considered as direct functions of cause and effect, appear inexplicable, and should provide a more successful basis for educational modes of action. For the acquisition of such knowledge, sociopsychological methods have, as we have mentioned and as we have tried to demonstrate, the advantages of saving time and of supplying a more objective means of evaluation and comparison.

Take for instance the striking case of Russell. Here six years of observation and the coincidental advent of a teacher with greater abilities and wider interest in his pupils, were required to destroy the myth first of deafness, then of mental deficiency. A medical examination, an intelligence test taken five or six years ago would have settled the question of his deafness and his mental capacities, and correlation of such findings with his home life would have modified the attitudes assumed toward him in school, probably with better educational results.

And this is not a very exceptional case of misunderstanding and consequential failure in educational influence. Symptoms of the same kind we find in the history of Lawrence, with the difference that there the harmful effects of misinterpreted behavior and intellectual achievement at school on a personality of outstanding qualities and gifts are more than neutralized by a happy home situation.

These are examples of a compara-

tively simple and obvious nature. The more complex the situation the more frequently we may find reactions which, just because of their complexity, are less obviously definable and less open to mere observation. Think of Marjorie. She is a girl who loves to study, who is ambitious—why should she not be favored by her teachers and set up as a model for other children? The tests show us, as otherwise only intimate personal friendship could reveal, the narrowness of her pursuit and her interests, the danger of a development into cold righteousness. In connection with them, small observed incidents apt to be looked upon as "cute" or "funny" take on quite another significance and, remembering that competitive ambition is severely condemned and leads not rarely to accusations of witchcraft in Hopi society where this girl has to live, we come to the conclusion that a guidance different from and much subtler than the encouragement of her ambitions will be necessary to prevent serious maladjustment.

Think of Irene. A good, quiet, submissive pupil at school, a good worker —and talked about as prostituting herself at home. Interviews reveal her extremely difficult life situation within Hopi society. Should she be encouraged to leave the Reservation and to get a job in town? The tests show a high imaginative intelligence, a considerate, kind character, and, the deep threatening influence of her experiences on her personality. Remaining off the Reservation without guidance would possibly make her a victim of her own submissiveness. In terms of Irene we are interested in developing and using the high qualities of an individual for the benefit of the society. With the absence of behavioral problems in school, only the tests and their correlation with the life history in Irene's case show us the necessity and the value of very careful guidance.

Thus in each child we may, to a

greater or smaller degree, detect the usefulness of socio-psychological methods for a more complete understanding of overt behavior, and for such modes of relationship with the individual as do not inhibit but may further his adjustment to the conditions of his life. The range of effective guidance and its acceptance by the individuals themselves are naturally limited, the more so as coordination and cooperation of all agents of influence in a plan of guidance usually cannot be achieved.

But the amount of indifference and misunderstanding, on the other hand, are unnecessarily great in all areas of human contact, and their reduction by whatever means are at our disposal is urgently desirable. There is certainly no danger that an increase in interest, attention and active good will in human relations will suddenly reduce the sum of human suffering so much as to result into "softening, debilitating life conditions," as is not uncommonly argued. If resistance provokes growth of strength, too much resistance is destructive to effort and life itself. Helpful understanding at the right time may channelize an individual's, and particularly a child's, energies into greater strength and more productive development than his own "hit and miss" trials of action do.

In this regard we shall point out as a last example from our study that all reports and all casual observation which we obtained about Roger did not contain one hint of the possibility of deeper-lying conflicts in his personality. The tests—every one of them—revealed with great clarity his conflicts, his sufferings under the home-situation and his inability to cope with them. Their verdict was *subsequently* proved against the indifferent tenor of observations and reports by Roger's own actions—his escape from home and his breaking off relations with his family. Better knowledge, not only of his personality but of his whole family situation, might have modified his maladjustment and shown him the direction toward a happier solution of his problems.

IV. GROWING UP TO BE A HOPI

11. THE USE OF TESTS AS TOOLS

After attempting to sketch the personalities of a few Hopi children in the last section we found that they impressed us as being surprisingly similar to those of White boys and girls. This is also an experience which many a person has who approaches single individuals of a group or culture other than his own, with a certain degree of interest.

"Why, this woman is as decent as Cousin Bertha, and that one is as mean as Aunt May," he says, "even though Bertha would not be afraid of witches, and May would never eat lamb stew with her fingers." In short, he considers and treats some of these strange and different people just as human beings of the kind or similar to the kind he has known all along.

So far, he may see his impression well confirmed. The friend whom he finds in an alien group may visit him as the friends did at home; he may do small favors for him and be helpful when help is needed. With advancing intimacy both may agree in common reactions and emotions. They may be smilingly happy when they mention the affection or appreciation which they receive from other persons, and be sad about the death or sickness of dear relatives. They may relish together the hatred of a common enemy. The stress of want and poverty, or satisfaction at the improvement of economic conditions may still be common ground for their mutual understanding. In such a relationship, differences of beliefs or habits are likely to be overlooked or tolerated or may even act as curious and interesting attractions. Everything is functioning well as long as the ordinary course of events goes on without gross interruption.

But what will happen when a crisis arises which concerns both friends? Let us assume that the White American who has a Hopi friend learns that, through circumstances which have a specific meaning within Hopi culture but are without importance in his own, his friend finds himself in a situation in which the whole village seems to have turned against him. The Hopi feels like an outcast. He complains. The White man does for him exactly what he would do for his brother. He obtains a job for him in town, recommends him warmly to the boss, installs him in the house of other friends of his. Soon he hears that the Hopi is doing excellent and reliable work and that he will get a promotion in due time. The White man is delighted. He imagines for his friend a bright future, and himself as its founder.

Suddenly he receives the news that the Hopi has left the job without apparent reason and has returned to his village, where he is still treated as an outcast. At this point, despite all possible explanations, the White man sees his feelings of friendship dangerously threatened. Until then he had considered the Hopi as "just a human being as we all are." Now this opinion may turn into "Well, he is just a Hopi, mean and ungrateful as all Hopi are."

Both opinions stated as they are here—and they are very common indeed and widely spread—are essentially faulty. Both can and do, however, pass as true and may apparently be confirmed by facts, for the following reasons. For the more generous-minded persons, who have a brotherly feeling for all human beings, the crisis in which the existing cultural difference becomes a personally felt proof may never occur. On the other hand, many people with an over-developed sense for details and an unquestioning conviction of their own cultural superiority experience even small differences of habits, like eating stew with the fingers, as *moral* shock and crisis, and therefore have difficulty in conceiving the idea of similarities.

In our example, both the White American and the Hopi were equal in feelings and reactions common to all human beings. The asking for and the giving of sympathy, the desire to escape from an unpleasant situation, and the kind urge to help belonged in this unifying area. But some of the ensuing actions—procuring the job and leaving it—derived from divergent, culturally determined factors. Beyond a certain point both men were not only human beings, but a White American human being and a Hopi human being. This did not change their basic personalities. They were still essentially what they had been before—kind or unkind, outgoing or withdrawn, sensitive or callous, etc. But to each other they now *appeared* changed and appeared so only because a factor, which had always been functioning within their personalities but had been overlooked as negligible, suddenly obscured the familiar picture.

Everybody has emotions, opinions, concepts or values which are directly or indirectly influenced by the group in which he lives. They are responsible for those qualities which distinguish the rural inhabitant from the city dweller, the nomad from the settler, the Hopi from the Navaho, the Hopi and the Navaho from the White American. As a group reaches sufficient consoli-

dation to acquire and require a certain molding influence on its members' way of life, these members will respond more or less with the development of personality characteristics specific for the group. This applies to professional, political, economic, and religious groups, to groups living under different forms of government, to national groups, etc. Their influence on the personality varies considerably according to the strength and organization of the group itself and according to the responsiveness of the individual, which in turn varies with his age and other contributing circumstances. Of these, a personal crisis is one of the most important.

While under special conditions, as for instance in times of collective stress or enthusiasm, the group influence may even produce in the individual temporary or permanent personality traits like a sense of self sacrifice, it usually affects not the amount and efficiency of his mental capacities but the areas of his interest and attention, not so much the depth and quality of his emotions as their range and direction, not his basic temperament but the freedom or limitation of its expression. To a certain degree—by no means entirely—the group also channelizes the individual's attitudes toward persons inside and outside of its realm, gives him a feeling of security, and provides him with a specific set of values which may assume the more or less imperative character of moral standards. Thus, even though the influence of the group may not reach the whole personality, it is at times dominant, and usually far-reaching enough to give its imprint to behavior and actions. It is, therefore, understandable that in periods of the formation of new groups and their influence, and during the breaking down of existing ones, as happens, for instance, in the so-called processes of acculturation, the personality may be more or less deeply disturbed in its balance and also disturbing in its outward effect.

If we believe that good will between groups and peaceful relations may be achieved essentially through the relative freedom of development of everybody within the limits of group living and not through a continuous state of aggression and defense, daily warfare and mutual extermination, or the establishment of a well-organized but deadly sterile relationship of masters and slaves then, approaching alien groups, we shall have to take into consideration the function and psychological significance which the group has for its members, and the degree and quality of its influence on them. Otherwise, we shall not only be unable to build up lasting good personal relationships, but also shall act against our own interests, wasting time, money and energies in futile efforts at good will or in the rigid enforcement of our own principles, which procedure from the beginning carries the germ of failure because the resistance created will require a further continuous supply of energy, money and time for their enforcement.

In order to avoid misunderstandings: those missionaries, administrators, traders, workers and visitors who have been successful in alien groups, have been people who have known that much more important than giving orders is asking, listening, thinking about the matters heard and seen, and waiting with conclusions and generalizations. On the other hand, they have not been sentimentalists who have given up the essential values of their own culture. They have known their limitations and the great potentialities of successful planning and acting which lie in knowing them. They have had respect for themselves and other people, genuine interest in, and patiently and often painfully acquired knowledge about, these others.

In our study of Indian children we contrived to get this knowledge and to convey it to those who want or need it, not through long years of personal experience, but through experiments with tests.

Of the 190 selected Hopi school children, aged 6 to 18 years, 109 from Oraibi and 81 from First Mesa, a number (varying according to the children's availability) received the following tests:[1]

1. The *Grace Arthur Point Performance Scale (short form)*[2] was given to 92 children from Oraibi and 54 children from First Mesa. The test does not necessarily require the use of language (this is its greatest advantage) and consists of six separate test parts of the puzzle, maze and block-design type. In our final scoring one of these parts was omitted, since it appeared charged with elements of White culture, incomprehensible and often confusing to Indian children. The Grace Arthur Test is an intelligence test designed for children through the age of 15 years, and its score is given as an Intelligence Quotient (I. Q.).

II. The *Goodenough Draw-a-Man Test*,[3] another intelligence test, used by us on children through the age of 11, was given to 46 Oraibi children and 32 children from First Mesa. The child is asked to draw a man to the best of his capabilities, and certain items in the picture thus obtained are scored and evaluated as an I. Q.

III. *Stewart's Emotional Response Test*.[4] Here the child is asked, "Have you ever been happy?" and if the answer is affirmative, "Tell me about it." The question is repeated three times and is followed by similar ones about sadness, fear and shame, and the best and worst thing that could happen to the child. This test works psychologically by provoking selective associations which are more or less limited by the child's actual experiences. It throws light not only upon the range and points of emphasis of these experiences, but also upon the child's overtly admitted emotional attitudes toward various situations, persons, and objects, and the importance and kind of the role which these situations, persons and objects admittedly occupy in the child's mind. This test was given to 101 children from Oraibi and 73 children from First Mesa.

IV. *Bavelas' Test of Moral Ideology.*[5] The children are asked: "What is a good thing to do for a boy (or a girl) of your age?" and "Who would praise you?" and "What is a bad thing, etc." and "Who would blame you?" The questions are repeated three or more times. The answers give valuable information about the most common official moral standards of a group and, to some extent, about the range of their variations. Besides, the test deals again with the children's attitudes toward persons of their environment, but, in distinction from the Emotional Response, only in view of their role as disciplinarians, i. e., as rewarding or punishing agents. Ninety-four children from Oraibi and 67 from First Mesa were thus tested.

V. *The Story of the Stolen Melon and the Axe.*[6] A story is told in which two boys steal a melon. While one of them is punished on the spot, the other gets away, but chopping wood a short time afterwards, he cuts his foot with the axe. Three questions are asked:

1. "Why do you think Paul's foot was cut?"

2. "If Paul did not steal the melon, would he cut his foot?"

3. "Did the axe know that he stole the melon?"

Of a series of similar stories or questions which were given to the children of our study, only this one has been analyzed so far. It was devised after the model of stories used by Piaget and others in order to reveal:

1. If a person's moral concepts contain a belief in "immanent justice," i.e., if he thinks that misdeeds are inexorably followed by punishment through a justice other than that instituted by man; and

2. If an object, like, e. g., the axe, is believed to be animated and capable

of thinking, feeling and acting.

It has been found that very young children of White culture have both beliefs to a high degree and show a gradual decrease with advancing age. Thus the test gives information about a specific aspect of the personality, prevalently interesting to us because of its cultural implications. The story was told to 98 children from Oraibi and 71 from First Mesa.

VI. *Free Drawings.*[7] A set of eight watercolor or crayon drawings was obtained from the child who had free choice with regard to subject, color and size of the paper. This test has been analyzed in respect to the content of the pictures which throws light on the degree to which Hopi children have been influenced by modern Western material culture. Eighty-three children from Oraibi supplied 644 drawings and 58 children from First Mesa supplied 451.

VII. *Murray's Thematic Apperception Test (revised).*[8] The child is shown a series of pictures, the content of which allows a practically infinite range of possible interpretations, and is asked to tell a story about each picture. It is assumed that the child projects more or less of his conscious and subconscious emotions, attitudes and experiences into his stories. The test was given to 65 children from Oraibi and 40 from First Mesa.

VIII. *Rorschach's Psychodiagnostic (Inkblot) Test.*[9] A sequence of standardized inkblot cards are shown to the child who is free to give as many interpretations of them or of parts of them as he wants to. The test gives a complex picture of the basic personality, and includes information about mental capacities and efficiency, emotional attitudes and drives, the balance of the personality and the defense mechanism adopted against outside pressure or inner conflicts. It was given to 105 children from Oraibi and 80 from First Mesa.

We thought it necessary to give this

rather perfunctory account of the tests in order to convey to the reader at least an impression of the kind of work and methods on which our results and interpretations are based. Psychology is still, sometimes, met with diffidence, like a vague and disquieting game of guesswork, and we naturally do not wish to further such an opinion by omitting to mention our tools of research and to define the ground on which we stand, as well as our limitations. Those who are interested in greater details about the methods and aims of the various tests, will find the references for these in the footnotes. (See Appendix).

Which traits of personality—as far as they can be established from our tests—distinguish the Hopi children from other groups like, e. g., the Navaho or the White Americans? By checking and rechecking, combining and comparing the results of our analysis on one hand, and by comparing and integrating them with reports from other branches of this research, we may be able to reach certain conclusions. However, before we discuss personality in its strictly psychological sense, we shall give some attention to the physical conditions, i. e., the health of these same Hopi children.

12. HEALTH, FOOD AND SICKNESS

Health and personality influence each other in varying degrees in different individuals, and in varying degrees, in one and the same individual during different periods of his life. Sad and shocking experiences may temporarily disturb the physical condition of a person, and these in turn may change his outlook on life and his behavior. The reactions of a group too may show the influence of its general state of health. It will, for instance, be remembered that undernourishment in large parts of the population was an important contributing factor in the German revolution of 1918. Epidemics, as sources of widespread panic and its resulting attitudes, also have some significance in this regard.

However, the average general conditions of health, particularly the state of nutrition and its long-lasting physiological effects, appear of greater importance. How far-reaching the influence of a certain diet may be on the strictly physiological conditions of a whole group, may be illustrated by the following example. "The Masai and the Akikuyu, two African tribes living side by side, subsist on quite different diets. The diet of the Masai has a high protein content; it consists largely of meat, milk and blood. The Akikuyu live on a vegetarian diet composed of cereals (chiefly maize), legumes, plantains, sweet potatoes and other tubers, and green leaves. The members of the meat-eating tribe are some five inches taller and 50 pounds heavier than the vegetarians, and their muscular power is about 50 per cent greater. The Masai are comparatively free from disease, whereas bone deformities, dental caries, anemia, pulmonary diseases; and tropical ulcer are prevalent among the Akikuyu. Arthritis, however, was found to be much more common among the Masai. Though these tribes come from different original stocks, there is a considerable amount of intermarriage and the differences in physique and health between them appear to have a dietary rather than a racial basis."[1]

Thanks to a study of the Hopi food habits done in the spring of 1942 by James Watson and Michel Pijoan, M. D., in the villages of Old and New Oraibi, we have the following information about Hopi diet.[2]

There is a certain monotony in the average diet, tending to be less extreme in more prosperous households. The basic foods are corn, white flour, beans, potatoes, oats (to some extent), sugar and coffee. Meat is eaten very rarely. The amount of fresh vegetables and fruits consumed does not seem to be truly abundant at any time of the year. Within the stated diet the seasonal variation in the available foods is quite high, winter and spring being the seasons of greatest scarcity.

A quantitative analysis of the winter and spring diet in a number of Hopi households indicates "that the Hopi diet is notably deficient in protein, somewhat less deficient in fats, and perhaps in certain cases or at certain times of the year slightly deficient in carbohydrates." It also seems that the amount of caloric intake is "just adequate and no more" in adults, less than normal in children. With regard to the average vitamin consumption it was found that the dietary intake of vitamins A, B, and C was about two-thirds, one-half, and one-third of the requirements established by the United States Department of Agriculture.

We may probably assume with safety that during the other seasons (summer and fall) the supply of carbohydrates and vitamins is approximately adequate. This, however, still leaves a rather long annual period of lowered resistance, and exactly during seasons when climatic influences favor the development of respiratory diseases.

The diet of adults and children is practically the same from the time that the child is able to chew solid foodstuffs. It should be added that, except for ceremonial purposes, children are apparently not urged to eat a certain amount and a certain kind of food. In this regard their choice is free and determined by actual hunger, the likes and dislikes of taste, and the degree of their preoccupation with other things. Food education consists mainly in the emphasis given to the sacred, life-giving value of food in general and of certain ceremonial foods in particular, as well as in the serious, early and daily admonitions against any waste.

It has been pointed out that babies are usually breast-fed for a varying length of time—from one year to two or more—and are nursed whenever they cry. From a very early date they receive, as more or less frequent additions, corn mash and soups or juices from various Hopi dishes, and whatever else their fancy happens to desire. It is for instance no exception to see a baby, 8 to 14 months of age, sucking and licking the not very clean rind of a melon or the peel of an unripe apple. While no statistics are available, there is the impression that the incidence of, and the mortality from, intestinal disturbances in infants are extremely high in the summer months. Another factor important for the health of a breast-fed baby is the quality of the mother's milk, and considering the deficiency in the intake of fats and vitamins of adults, we may find again that the nutritional source is not quite adequate.

How far are these dietary observations (which we should remember concern only two Hopi villages and, in their quantitative analysis, only a limited number of households) borne out by the actual conditions of health?

In 1942, clinical examinations of 56 pupils of Oraibi Day School made by Dr. Michel Pijoan gave the following results:[3]

Vitamin A Deficiency . . . . . . none apparent
Vitamin B Deficiencies (B complex) 43%
Vitamin C Deficiency (probably). 4%
Vitamin D Deficiency (all stages). 31%

The evidences for vitamin D deficiency, which causes rickets, were mostly obtained from bone changes observed in x-rays. Dental caries was found in 61%, primary inactive tuberculosis of the lungs (x-ray) in 31% of the examined children.

In 1942-43, as part of the Indian Education Research field program, the writer of this chapter (A. J.) examined medically 153 Hopi school children, from 6 to 18 years of age; 91 from Oraibi and 62 from First Mesa. The examinations were similar to the usual routine health surveys, i. e., their findings did not include any obtained through biochemical methods or x-ray.

Weight and height were established for all children, with very few exceptions. The general condition and possible deformities were determined; eyes, ears, mouth, throat and skin were inspected; lungs, heart, abdomen and reflexes examined. Pulse and blood-pressure were taken, vision and hearing tested. Special attention was given to possible manifestations of nutritional deficiencies. Considering the children's modesty and reluctance to strip entirely, and considering the fact that "White medicine" is still in a stage of persuasion and propaganda among the Hopi, and that the enforcement of its principles would only cause prolonged absence from school, no data concerning the genital organs and hernia were obtained.

The results of this kind of examination are the following. Looking for children in good health according to medical standards, we find an extremely low percentage even if we include those who show a few decayed teeth or very slight shortsightedness: 18.7% in Oraibi and 14.5% in First Mesa. The picture looks somewhat brighter, though not at all encouraging, if we concentrate our attention on good nutrition or underweight alone: 48.4% of Oraibi children and exactly the same percentage of those from First Mesa are undernourished, 51.6% being well-fed. The only difference in this regard between the two groups lies in the proportion of children with fair or poor nutrition; the number of almost emaciated children is somewhat higher at Oraibi than at First Mesa.

What is usually called malnutrition, combining under this term all symptoms of specific nutritional deficiencies such as rickets, scurvy, etc., is present in 41.8% of the Oraibi children and in 32.9% of those from First Mesa. In these figures the evidences of disturbances in the formation and structure of the teeth are not included. We find at Oraibi irregular teeth in 40.7%, decayed teeth in 32.9%; at First Mesa, in 32.2% and 33.9% respectively.

Comparing these figures with those obtained by Dr. Pijoan and realizing their difference, we anticipate pointing out that the percentages concerning malnutrition and teeth vary strikingly according to age. We have no data concerning the age distribution of the children examined by Dr. Pijoan, but it is probable that this would account for most of the discrepancies.

For a clearer view of the health conditions of our Hopi children and for better comparison, Table I presents the most important findings for Oraibi and First Mesa separately. (See page 96)

The organs most affected by disease seem to be eyes, teeth, lips and gums, tonsils, lymph glands of the neck, and lungs. Organic heart disease was found in only two cases, chronic abdominal disturbances in none, bone deformities only as far as a few cases of old fractures were concerned and the low percentages of those children who, in consequence of rickets, showed slight deformities of their ribs or of the shape of the head. The occurrence of skin diseases, like impetigo, acne, etc., was negligible.

Often examinations of children at school do not give an entirely reliable picture of the conditions of health because those who are seriously sick or incapacitated are not included in the survey. In our case the reports of the school authorities at the time did not suggest absences from school because of sickness, except for one little boy in Oraibi who, after a fracture of his leg, had developed osteomyelitis. As far as we know, absences were at that time caused by the preparation for and the attendance at ceremonials. Children with obvious mental disturbances were not included in our study from the very beginning. One case of the kind is known to the writer at Oraibi, none at First Mesa. There may be some who are kept at home and have thus escaped observation.

Among the examined children, one girl from First Mesa showed actual symptoms of an organic disease of the nervous system. Two girls from Oraibi offered in their history signs of nervous disorder which could not be ascertained during examination: one was reported to have attacks of epileptic character, the other complained about neuralgia.

Regarding our results, the small number of children in perfect or almost perfect health and the kinds of disorders which we find prevalent in the others seem to us quite significant and may in fact very well point to a dietary influence on the actual physiological conditions. Apart from real undernourishment, many of the children show one or the other sign of a vitamin deficiency, as cracked lips, inflamed tongue, bleeding gums, etc., which even if their weight is adequate, indicates malnutrition. And assuming that part of the relatively high percentage of decayed teeth is due to poor care, we have to consider at least the possibility that a lack of vitamin D may be a contributing factor, and certainly more than that if we take into account the high incidence of irregularity in the arrangement of the teeth. The great number of children who have either enlarged or removed tonsils (and in Hopiland only clearly diseased tonsils are removed) may show the disturbing influence of climatic conditions—dust in summer, snow and humidity in winter—and the inadequate protection from them. But it also should remind us that general undernourishment increases the susceptibility to infections;

TABLE I[4]

CONDITION	ORAIBI	PER CENT GIRLS	TOTAL	FIRST MESA	PER CENT GIRLS	TOTAL
	BOYS			BOYS		
Good Health	11.6	25.0	18.7	10.0	16.7	14.5
Good Nutrition	32.6	68.7	51.6	25.0	64.3	51.6
Fair Nutrition	27.9	14.6	20.9	55.0	14.3	27.5
Poor Nutrition	39.5	16.7	27.5	20.0	21.4	20.9
Malnutrition	44.2	39.6	41.8	25.0	38.1	33.9
Vitamin B Deficiency	30.2	18.7	24.2	15.0	16.7	16.1
Vitamin C Deficiency	16.3	20.8	18.7	10.0	21.4	17.7
Vitamin D Deficiency	4.7	6.3	5.5		7.1	4.8
Impaired Vision	18.6	58.3	39.6	45.0	66.6	53.2
Conjunctivitis	9.3	10.4	9.9	10.0	9.5	9.7
Trachoma	4.7	2.1	3.3	5.0	11.9	9.7
Irregular Teeth	41.8	39.6	40.7	40.0	28.6	32.2
Decayed Teeth	30.2	35.4	32.9	35.0	33.3	33.9
Swollen Gums	27.9	12.5	19.8	10.0	9.5	9.7
Bleeding Gums	16.3	22.9	19.8	10.0	21.4	17.7
Enlarged Tonsils	41.8	27.1	34.0	15.0	16.7	16.1
Removed Tonsils	16.3	39.6	28.6	55.0	35.7	41.9
Swollen Lymph Glands	23.3	20.8	21.9	30.0	11.9	17.7
Suspicious Tuberculosis of Lungs	16.3	10.4	13.2	20.0	19.0	19.3
Colds	9.3	12.5	11.0	20.0	7.1	11.3

Hopi child nurse with her little brother

that in the light of modern physiology lowered resistance to disease seems to be connected with a low protein intake; and that also lack of vitamin A, through its influence on the mucous membranes, may apparently facilitate the development of infections. In tuberculosis, for which we found a relatively high percentage of suspicious cases (suspicious because they were not checked by x-ray or laboratory examinations) and for which Dr. Pijoan found about twice as much evidence from x-rays, it is generally known that good and balanced feeding is one of the most important means of effecting cure. Important for its incidence and spreading among the Hopi are probably the living and sleeping of many persons in one room and the relative scarcity and preciousness of water, which is not always at hand for cleaning purposes.

A very encouraging side of the picture of health conditions of Hopi children, which may indicate a way for future measures to be taken for the elimination of other disorders, is the very low incidence of trachoma and skin diseases. Only five years ago trachoma was an extremely widespread evil among our Indian population. It is an infectious and highly contagious disease of the conjunctiva and also other parts of the eye, which frequently leads to impairment of the eyesight and sometimes to blindness. Thanks to the ingenuity of Fred Loe, M. D., of the United States Indian Service, who first conceived the idea of using sulfanilamide in the fight against trachoma, and thanks to the continuous efforts of the Divisions of Health and Education of the Indian Bureau, this disease has been greatly reduced among almost all Indian tribes in the United States and has practically disappeared among Hopi children.

For this achievement, health education and treatment at the schools were and still are of great importance, and the same is true concerning the elimination among Hopi children of impeti-

go, a relatively harmless, but extensive, long lasting or often recurring, and quite debilitating infection of the skin, which still occurs rather frequently in other Indian tribes.

Concerning the occurrence of contagious childhood diseases our data are scanty. When asked about previous illnesses, some children denied ever having been sick, which may or may not be true, while many of them remembered having had measles, mumps, whooping cough and chicken pox, without, however, appearing very reliable in their answers.

With regard to the health conditions found in boys and girls and in the various age groups, we observed a few striking differences which are worth mentioning here. Always, but particularly from eight years on and increasing with age, the percentage of girls who are well nourished exceeds that of the boys and shows at the age of 14 and older the great difference of 80% and 30.8% respectively. At the same age level there are only 4% girls and still 23.1% boys among those whose state of nutrition is extremely poor. (See Table II, page 145).

Differences in way of life of the sexes, e. g. the greater amount of physical exercise taken by the boys, and perhaps also the aesthetic concepts of the Hopi, according to which well-rounded female forms are preferred, may be at the root of such findings. But it would also be interesting to know whether the girls consume more food than the boys since, usually being around the house and assisting in the preparation of the meals, they have more opportunities to do so, or whether perhaps they are somewhat favored in this regard by their mothers. As yet no clear observations have been reported concerning these possibilities.

Another important finding is that the various symptoms of poor nourishment and of malnutrition are in boys and girls most numerous and most pronounced at the ages of six and seven

*Little Hopi girl
in school at Keams Canyon*

years. While we cannot be entirely sure about the underlying reasons, it may very well be that we are dealing here with the effects of a faulty diet during infancy. The high percentages of irregular teeth, for instance, may point to a vitamin D deficiency which is probably not great enough to produce other gross manifest signs of rickets, but sufficient to interfere with dentition, to influence the general state of health and to show up in x-rays as disturbances of bone formation, which Dr. Pijoan observed in such a comparatively high percentage of the children whom he examined.

In review it is necessary to point out that, with the exception of tuberculosis, the disorders that have been found are mainly of a kind and degree which do not constitute any direct danger to the lives and probably not even to the immediate working capacities of those afflicted with them. To this extent we can say that Hopi children are healthy, as they will in fact appear to the casual observer. But we have also the definite impression that a large number of Hopi children do not have the reserves of fundamentally good health which are the greatest help in overcoming acute attacks of serious illnesses. Their state of health appears labile and exposed, particularly to infections. We must, however, remember that this is an examination of school children. In order to get a clear picture of the degree of damage and its persistence, we need not only a survey of the health conditions in adults, but also complete figures about birth, mortality and the incidence of illness. During the last decades the Hopi have been increasing in number rapidly. This in itself is an encouraging fact.

Our communities of Oraibi and First Mesa do not present striking differences in their health conditions, except for eyesight which seems worse in First Mesa. In both communities eyesight is worse in girls than in boys. Further examinations will be necessary in order to explain this finding.

Venturing beyond the actual health conditions, it would be indeed interesting to know if and to what extent sickness and death have their influences upon the emotions and concepts of Hopi children. Do they realize the dangers to which they are exposed in the kind of life they lead, are they preoccupied with them to a degree that makes them overcautious and inordinately afraid of sickness?

We think that while the answer to the first question must be affirmative, Hopi children certainly do not appear to be neurotic hypochondriacs, who fear sickness and death more than the reality of their experiences justifies. Masau'u, deity of death—wild, destructive, inapprehensible and elusive as fire, flickering up now here, now there around the edges of the mesa—is a perfect symbol for the realization of the often unpredictable, countless blows from drought, famine and epidemics which have hit the Hopi through centuries. Institutionalized rationalizations of the same order are the numerous tabus against sickness-conveying animals and objects and, partly, the fear of witches. Hopi children, the majority of whom participate in the ceremonial life, will also participate in these concepts. But we must keep in mind that side by side with the unpredictable, dangerous Masau'u has been conceived the abundant number of equally important life- and prosperity-conveying deities who hold the balance.

One of our tests (Emotional Response) gives us some direct information regarding concern about death and sickness. From its results we learn that Hopi children, when asked to tell about occasions when they have been sad, name in fact occurrences of death and sickness more than anything else. In this regard children from Oraibi appear somewhat more concerned than those from First Mesa, and children in both communities living on top of the mesas more than those living below. Possibly the somewhat better living conditions of the First Mesa group and the ready help which the school children receive for their small ailments from the field nurse show their influence. On the other hand, difficulties and dangers of life are definitely greater in the villages situated on top of the mesas, where the water supply alone is an ever present problem which has its effect on the actual health conditions. It is interesting that about half of the mentioned responses are accompanied by the naming of family members who have died or have been sick in the children's experiences. Considering the fact that in almost every household group we studied, one or more members, particularly babies, are noted as deceased, the degree of preoccupation with death or sickness found does not seem to be abnormal. A suppression of these experiences would indeed have been more so than their mentioning. White children from a Midwestern industrial town, to whom the same test has been administered, give for death and sickness together a not much smaller percentage of sadness responses.

When it comes to the question about the worst thing that could possibly happen, sickness rather than death ranks for the Hopi children as the very worst. Although sickness also ranks quite high among Midwestern boys, these know many other things which are much worse. To be actually sick in Hopiland has nothing of the comfort, the constant care given by the family and the painsoothing effect of our medicaments, which may render the experience of a sick White child less frightening. There, sickness not only implies the whole impact of pain, but also the felt disruption of the minutely organized household group, in which everybody constantly has to do his own share of work in order to keep it functioning. This alone would justify the Hopi opinion that sickness indeed is the worst of all "bad" things.

But apparently it does not entirely account for the fact that sickness inspires such a dread in Hopi children. Dr. Fred Eggan[4] reports that to become sick is usually considered among the Hopi to be the result of unlawful behavior, bad thoughts and bad actions, in short of what might correspond to the idea of "sin" among us. Here *guilt* for the first time in this part of our study, we come upon concepts which are different from those considered typical of modern Western civilization, although similar ideas may not at all infrequently be found. In the following chapters we shall meet thoughts and attitudes of similar nature when dealing with fear and the concept of "immanent justice." Their importance becomes evident if we remember that the institutions of Hopi medicine—the medicine man and his methods of curing, his esteem and his actual psychological power—as well as the Hopi attitude against "White medicine," hospitals, etc. are intimately connected with this ideology.

On the other hand, the mystic or magic side of concern about sickness does not seem to occupy an exceptional position in the mind of the Hopi, i. e., to be of hypochondriac nature. It belongs to and apparently does not dominate the wide circle of Hopi concern about all kinds of danger—enemies, bad crops, starvation and accidents—which all may occur as a result of infraction of the Hopi Way.

In conclusion we may say that the existing conditions of health have in fact an influence on Hopi personalities in so far as they make them alert to the realization of those dangers which threaten them most frequently. These dangers do not, however, seem to hold their attention in an exaggerated and unbalancing degree. Actual facts and concern obviously correspond quite well.

13. THE HIGH HOPI I. Q.

In establishing well functioning relationships with an alien group, knowledge about the degree and nature of its members' intelligence is quite important. Of course we do not think seriously that intelligence is group-owned anywhere in the world. When we speak here of intelligence, we are thinking about the particular kind which runs along lines similar to our own, which makes us good or bad pupils in the kind of schools we have, allows us to get along more or less successfully in our world of machines, and might let us starve if we were to be stranded in a jungle where unclad natives find a plentiful living. It is ours and we survive on it quite well. But in dealing with people whose thinking is conditioned differently and who have a different mental approach, we may fail miserably if we either overestimate or underestimate their capacity to follow the ways of our own thinking.

In order to measure intelligence and to achieve a comparison between individuals which is more objective and not dependent on judgments influenced by personal likes and dislikes, numerous intelligence tests have been devised and used during the last decades. There are those which require the use of language and others which measure intelligence by the ability to perform certain manual tasks, the more or less faultless achievement of which may reflect the comprehension, organizing capacity, etc., of the mind, as well as the efficiency and speed of its coordination with the hands. In our selection of two intelligence tests we were guided by the desire to compare Indian and White children without the one-sided handicap of testing the Indians in a foreign language. We therefore chose two non-verbal tests (the Grace Arthur Point Performance Scale and the Goodenough Draw-a-Man test).[1]

Indian children of other tribes have been given intelligence tests before. Often this has been done without much discrimination regarding the selection of tests, and consequently most of the results have shown their intelligence as inferior to that of White children. Variations were not only attributed to different amounts of schooling and varying adaptation to Western civilization, but also sometimes to the degree of White blood.

We found that on the Grace Arthur Point Performance Scale Hopi children made very high scores, which were in fact by far the highest among all those of the Indian tribes studied, and also remarkably higher than those of the White school children on whom the test was standardized.[2] (See Table III). Considering the nature of the Arthur test we may indeed say that Hopi children seem to be extraordinarily puzzle- and maze-minded, and this appears to us quite in agreement with the intricate, elaborate system of social organization, symbols and deities which we have found in their culture. Excellent memory, observation of details and their quick correlation, are probably required to a high degree from the child who early and persistently is trained in the comprehension and practical application of Hopi concepts and values.

In the Draw-a-Man test all the Indian tribes studied rank more or less higher than White school children from an industrial Midwestern town who have taken the same test. (See Table III). Though the Hopi are still among the highest, the difference between them and children from other tribes is relatively small, and Sioux and Zuni children score even slightly higher than Hopi do. This test, devised for children to the age of 11 years, is almost entirely based on the capacity for detailed observation, without involving more complex categories of thinking, and here we find expressed in the high scores those same qualities which gave to the Indians and with them to the Hopi the ancient fame of being superior scouts, i. e., superior observers of minute and subtle, significant details. This trait is strikingly manifest in the records of American Indians in World Wars I and II.

Table III presents the mean I. Q. as found in both tests for Hopi and White children.

TABLE III

	Mean I. Q. Grace Arthur	Mean I. Q. Draw-a-Man
Hopi Children		
Oraibi	115.0	110.5
First Mesa	110.7	117.1
White Children	100.0	101.2

Information about the manner by which individuals approach a problem can be obtained from the Rorschach Inkblot test. It tells us whether a person gives most of his attention to obvious details, or to those which are unusual and even far-fetched, or whether he considers the problem as a simplified or a complex whole. Here we find that Hopi children from both communities show, at the early age of six and seven years and throughout their further development, an average mental approach which differs from that of White children, and those of the other Indian tribes given this test, in that it corresponds closely to the approach used by White adults. Everything gets its appropriate share;

the whole problem is viewed more or less in its complexity, the most obvious is taken into account, and subtleties are observed to quite a high degree. This astonishing result becomes understandable too if we think of the complex and balanced order which seems to be the core of the Hopi concept of the world, and is also expressed in their doctrine of desirable social conduct. Everything in its proper place and at the proper time; each one, from an early age, not only an individual with his personal aims and desires, but also a fully conscious part of a family working group, of a clan, of secret society and *kiva*, the other members of which require his constant attention.

From our tests we have the impression that Hopi children on the average are very intelligent, highly observant, show a remarkably balanced mental approach and are apparently very capable of complex and abstract thinking. Mental activity appears even overemphasized to a certain extent, and we shall see later its influence on the balance of the whole personality. We have also the impression that these qualities are closely connected with Hopi culture and the training which the children receive at home and through the community. In dealing with the Hopi it would indeed be a grave mistake to adopt the baby-talk and the oversimplified methods which are often used toward half-witted persons and those who go under the collective name of "natives."

14. SOME EMOTIONS AND ATTITUDES

The range of the most common and openly remembered experiences of a group, how they stand out as pleasant, unpleasant, frightening or embarrassing, and the generally accepted and officially stated views on what is good and what bad conduct, these are the

factors which appear to have the greatest visible influence on the behavior and attitudes of a group, and usually determine its characteristics in the eyes of the outsider and make the group appear to him as "typical Hopi," "typical Navaho" or "typical American." Convinced that very often limitation to these openly voiced views on emotions and morals has led to generalized misstatements about a group, and convinced that, for the sake of fair judgment, what is being kept back and not stated is just as important or even more so, we still think that these views are significant and have to be taken into consideration. We may assume that, on the average and if not under undue pressure, people mean what they say and, although usually omitting the sacred and intimate, are consciously aware of about as much as they say, and that this will have a bearing on their actual behavior.

What we know about Hopi children in this regard has been obtained through the Emotional Response and Moral Ideology tests.[1] There we find that within the range of those experiences which are connected with pleasant and happy feelings, Hopi children remember and name openly, more than anything else, occasions at which they received gifts either from a member of the family or from the *kachinas*, the supernatural beings who during certain ceremonies give their own images carved as dolls to the girls, bows and arrows to the boys, and food to both. Delight in the affection and attention which go with the gift, or pride in being rewarded as a good child by the deities, and at the same time joy in the property itself are at the roots of this kind of happiness. When we remember, however, that among the Hopi giving and receiving are regulated by reciprocity and that even the *kachinas* give to those who have given to them, namely good thoughts and lawful behavior, then the emphasis on happiness in the mere fact of property-owning is probably not very great. In fact, the number of children who delight in receiving money or in *possessing* property is very low.

Second in importance as pleasure-giving experiences are all kinds of festive occasions—of a Hopi character,

like ceremonies or dances, but also the celebration of the Fourth of July, birthdays, etc., the latter occasions being much more often mentioned at First Mesa (which, it will be remembered, is quite near to the Government Agency in Keams). The native ceremonies hold for the Hopi child's mind and imagination experiences of the miraculous and divine, stimulation and also *amusement* which the White child finds in church, theater, concerts and movies. While the range of pleasant experiences as recalled in the test seems to be only slightly more limited than that of White children,[2] there are certain things which rank high in the minds of Midwestern boys and girls but receive scant attention from the Hopi, and vice versa. (See Tables IV and V, page 145.) In this regard happiness deriving from one's personal achievement is one of the most significant differences. While an appreciable number of White children seem happy about being outstanding, we know that the Hopi child is taught to avoid any demonstration of this kind as much as possible, but to praise the achievements of others and to belittle his own.[3] Accordingly, self-achievement is mentioned rarely. On the other hand, twice as many Hopi as White children see happiness in work, which means chiefly work for the household group and not work for pay.

It is interesting that if the test allows greater opportunity to express desire, as in the question about the best thing that could possibly happen, a much greater percentage of Hopi children dare to voice the satisfaction which lies in possible personal achievement than they do when asked about their actual experiences. It seems that while they follow the rules by belittling their own efforts and keeping in the background, they are consciously proud of being praised and respected by others for their accomplishments. When for instance a child longs to be a teacher, we find here also to a certain extent the influence of our school system which, even in its progressive forms, implies more or less competition. On the other hand and besides the high number of children for whom (as also for most White boys and girls) play and pleasure are the very best things, the strong group-directed factor is still evident in this area of admitted desires. To be a worker for the household, to help the mother, to raise the crops, and to do whatever else concerns social activities without stressing the personal outstanding achievement, is much more often a motivating desire for the Hopi children than it is for White children.

We have discussed how strongly death and illness occupy the Hopi children's minds when they are asked about sad experiences and the worst thing that can happen to them (pages 98-99). Before we go more into the series of negative experiences, let us digress with the tale of an incident which happened at First Mesa recently and which illustrates better than anything else a characteristic Hopi attitude towards the negative aspects of life. One day when school was just over, four children—brothers and sisters, 5 to 13 years old—approached their teacher and asked for permission to stay in the school house until evening. These children usually did not linger around school but hurried home as quickly as possible. What was the matter?

"Oh," said the oldest girl, "it is because our grandmother is dying, and we do not want to become sad."

These children had not been sent from home in order to keep from them a new shock, something unknown and vaguely frightening, as we send young children away to spare their feelings. Hopi children cannot help knowing death from family experiences, tales and observations in the neighborhood. But they avoid as much as possible and are taught to avoid what they already know is sad or frightening or bad. (See Table VI and VII, page 145.)

This attitude is consistent with what we have learned about the Hopi Way and the Hopi belief in the efficacy of keeping a "good heart." What is evil, dead or sick causes worry or sadness and thus endangers the individual and the whole community. Sorrow is not something which must be faced or which may have a constructive effect. It is destructive, and thus is to be avoided.

This is the attitude of a people who have been continuously in a state of defense against enemies, famine and epidemics, and the attitude of children who from an early age are kept aware of these dangers by what they are told and what they have seen. It is therefore not surprising to find that the number of answers given to questions about sad events drops steeply to about half of the number of responses concerning happiness, and that this is the case only on First Mesa where practically the whole system of traditional ceremonies and child-training practices is still intact and functioning. However, we retain our impression (stated on page 98) that, while avoidance of harm is operating and influential in Hopi children, it does not show the degree or quality found in neurotically terrorized persons or groups.

There are two situations which in their negative importance seem to stand out in the mind of the Hopi, while White children pay comparatively little attention to them. Being disciplined by others and being attacked with "bad" words and jokes causes them much sadness, anger and shame. (See Tables VI, VII, VIII, IX, pp. 145-146). In White society disciplining and punishing a child is, except at school, usually a private matter between person and person within the family. The child knows that punishing is done and has to be done everywhere, that if he is punished he probably has been bad, but that practically nobody outside the family is permitted to interfere or to have his say about it. Therefore it is not discipline itself which is resented by the White child so much as the restraint of personal desires and the loss of pleasure and amusements which are connected with discipline.

Among the Hopi discipline and its methods are not private issues. The favorite methods, even if accompanied by slaps or whippings, are "The neighbors will talk about you, you will disgrace the whole family and even the clan," or "that is ka'hopi" (not Hopi, or bad). The facts are that the neighbors will indeed talk about any digression from the Hopi Way, give advice and interfere constantly, and for the bad child there will be the final consequence of all this talk as a prospect or a memory——the official whipping by the *kachinas*. Thus Hopi discipline is exerted to a considerable extent by the group and lies in the imprint of "good" or "bad" which the child obtains in the eyes of the whole community. In comparison to this, the loss of amusements or the pain from the whip are indeed of secondary importance.

The same considerations apply to concern about aggression by others. It is relatively high because there is practically no defense possible against it. To fight openly is almost a crime, "ganging up" is not observed very often. The group judges, advises, teases the individual who has transgressed the common rules or has aroused displeasure. And on the other hand, judging and teasing are encouraged, if not directly, then indirectly through the practices of the adults and the clowns' festivals.

Consistent with these open, group-influenced and group-directed attitudes of the Hopi, seems to be also their ready embarrassment in front of others, which causes shame about as frequently as actual bad behavior does. That this embarrassment runs parallel with and apparently does not exclude the realization of "good" and "bad" is revealed by the fact that quite a high percentage of Hopi, though only about half as high as that of White children, name personal bad behavior as a source of shame, and that they consider it much more often even than White children as "the worst thing." How far the realization of "good" and "bad" coincides here with the observation or transgression of group laws, and how often it may be connected with the particular personal conscience, which seems to play an important role for White children, we cannot determine from this test. Personal failure and inadequacy as such seem to be of as little significance as outstanding personal achievement, while to White children these issues appear highly important. We shall deal with the problem of the development of conscience in the next chapter.

It is in the area of fear and of frightful experiences that we discover the most striking differences between Hopi and White children. (See Table X, page 146.) Fear reflects not only actual dangers, but also the methods which underlie the child's education, the indirect teachings to which he is submitted and the atmosphere which surrounds him. Here we find that, as far as fear is admitted, White children are afraid predominantly of actual dangers, as of the elements, of cars, accidents, injuries, animals, etc. In the Hopi, much more than by anything else, fear is caused by the powers of the supernatural and by the anxiety which arises without apparent reason in the stillness or darkness of the night when the child feels lonely or when he hears mysterious noises which he cannot and will not explain.

Of the other tribes tested, only the Navaho show clearly a similar pattern. The Hopi children's openly expressed fear seems indeed to prove how much alive Hopi religious concepts are in their minds, and how great the influence still is which derives from the frightening shocks received in early childhood and later through the punishing deities and through the tales about witches and the animals of death and evil.[4] But it also seems to indicate something else. Although there are in the child's mind plenty of reasons why his own group should cause sadness, anger and shame, at the same time fear—the deepest sensation of displeasure—is mainly projected into the supernatural, which to him is not of imaginative nature, vaguely to be ashamed of, but of closest reality. Fear is the only area where concern about aggression by other people is less than that shown by White children. Thus, if Hopi beliefs and training methods have succeeded in imbuing the children with great fear, they have apparently also succeeded in concentrating and directing this fear into the supernatural sphere, a fact which implicitly will accentuate (on the other side) the security represented by the mother's lap, the familiar house, the laws and rules, and finally the group itself.

15. CONSCIENCE AND THE OFFICIAL CODE

Keeping within the realm of the security derived from laws and rules, we are interested in the following problem: Which of these sanctions, as far as moral behavior is concerned, are so common, so much in daily use and generally acknowledged that they come up as answers to the simple question, "What is a good (or a bad) thing to do?"[1] Which kinds of behavior give to Hopi children on the average the assured feeling that at least in their open actions they are doing right, or the pang of conscience that they are doing something wrong?

The first striking fact which we find in this regard is that the differences between the Indian tribes which we have studied seem to be much less pronounced than the difference between all of them on the one hand, and White children on the other. For the Indians, for instance, work seems to have the value of demonstrating good or bad behavior in the most unchallenged way. Work or good and ready work, bad work or laziness, are named about twice as often by them as by White children. (See Table XI, page 146.)

We know that, in order to survive, the Hopi have to work hard and constantly. Almost all ceremonies, which to the outsider seem to interrupt quite frequently the sequence of work days, are in fact not *aimed* toward relaxation or amusement but are also intimately connected with work, in which they are designed to elicit the cooperation of the supernatural forces. They themselves constitute hard exertion not only for the men who have to fast, to rehearse, to dance in eternal repetition in the *kiva* or on the plaza under the burning sun, but also for the women who have to prepare the abundance of ceremonial food.

When the Hopi children speak of "work" in our test they mean, particularly and most often, work which is done for the household group—herding sheep, helping the father in the fields, the mother at home, hauling water, chopping wood, etc. Here again the Hopi trend reveals itself. What is done for itself or oneself is not given the uppermost attention—that must belong to the group. Together with it goes a relatively high accent on thoughtfulness and kindness toward other people (which is more outspoken in the Hopi than in the other Indian children) and a practically complete disregard of personal pleasure and amusement, which seem to have acquired moral value in a number of White children's minds.

It is also not surprising to find that acts of aggression—i. e., fighting, quarreling, hitting or killing someone —are considered "bad" by about twice as many Hopi as White children. Everyone who goes to their pueblos may hear the Hopi, the "Peaceful People," condemn such traits in their teachings and conversations. Stealing is looked upon by many children as bad, and since the Hopi do not have the reputation for this trait, we may see herein expressed the care of hard-up people for the fruit of their work, the concern of the town dweller, who is exposed to theft, about his property, and perhaps also a hint of the Hopi's tribal pride and prejudice when he states, "The Navaho steal."

"Bad" language, smoking, drinking, and sexual behavior, which play a role in White children's moral concepts, receive from the Hopi practically no attention as to being either "good" or "bad." Drunkenness does not exist as an actual problem in Hopiland; smoking, being a ritual necessity, is not a moral issue (except to the few Christianized Hopi), nor apparently is sexual behavior, if understood as premarital or extramarital relations.

Discussing moral concepts, we are interested in knowing how far actual behavior may be influenced not only by the conscious awareness of "good" or "bad," by reasoning insight into the preferability of "good" or by the fear of punishment through various human authorities, but also by the belief that a "bad" deed is bound to be followed by punishment, even if this be implemented by non-human agents. The range and degree of this belief are wide and vary in different cultures. In our society (partly influenced by specific interpretations of the Christian religion) we find this belief in adults expressed, e. g., in the conviction that misfortunes, though separated by time and space from former misdeeds, are the latter's just and direct punishment. But usually only young children, as a part of the deeply felt and overpowering importance of their own selves, see this kind of punishment operating in the smallest incidents of daily life and apparently connect it with the belief that everything around them, e. g., the doll, the table, the tree, the sun, is alive and may directly respond to their behavior. In such form the belief in unavoidable punishment has been called "immanent justice," and the belief in the aliveness of all things "animism."[2] In the child these beliefs are considered to reflect egocentricity and perhaps also insecurity from the impact of the yet unknown and incomprehensible, which leads to the attempt to classify according to one's own image what cannot yet be classified from experience. Augmented by actual punishment, the reason for which is often but vaguely understood, these beliefs work psychologically like a diffuse and bewildering conscience, uncrystallized toward definite aspects of "good" or "bad."

If young Hopi children show, as they do, this belief in immanent justice and animism about as often as do White children (Table XII, page 146), it may be that in both groups similar psychological forces are at the base of this attitude. In the average young Hopi child these egocentric beliefs will probably, as far as their moral implications are concerned, be augmented by his belief in the many rewarding and punishing deities, as in the White child they are enhanced through the ever-present, all-seeing Creator. If, however, in contrast to White children, who with advancing age show a great decrease in both beliefs, we find the belief in immanent justice among older Hopi children as high as before, or even higher as is the case at First Mesa, we may assume that here we are probably dealing not with the simple egocentric conscience of early childhood, but with more complex, culturally influenced factors. And in Hopi culture, as has been noted, we find the conviction that not only "bad" actions, but also "bad" thoughts may fatally harm the individual's life and alter the course of the whole universe. Moreover, hard work alone may be futile; only if it is accompanied by "good" thoughts and lawful behavior will the crops grow abundantly. Thus the individual's thoughts may have a certain bearing on the prosperity or misfortune of the whole community. Within this context the concept of immanent justice would lose its infantile egocentric qualities and would express in older Hopi children a conscience of group-bound responsibility on the religious level, which in turn would be related to the insecurity of the actual group situation.

While the belief in immanent justice increases with age, the belief in animism among Hopi children, as measured by our test, decreases, though more slowly than among White children.[3] (See Table XII, page 146.) The belief in immanent justice on the religious level, as a magic or mystic dependency of the world's course on human thought and action—sociocentric but not childishly egocentric—leads in its mature form towards an increasing concentration on the image of man and his spiritual power, on his overall interdependence with nature, and may be closely interrelated with a gradual refinement of animistic beliefs. Thus a decrease of positive answers to a question which implies a more crude

belief in the animism of dead things (in our test, an axe) would be understandable. On such a basis we may conclude from the high percentage of Hopi children who reveal a belief in immanent justice that their actual good behavior will probably be influenced and enforced by a conscience based on their particular religious concepts, which will presumably also pervade and partly determine the nature and range of their doctrines of common decency.

From our tests emerges the "typical" Hopi child as he openly shows himself, and as indeed he is usually referred to by the outsider: Highly intelligent in a balanced, unchildish way; hard-working and industrious; thrifty and careful of his property, but not excessively concerned about it; sober; reticent concerning matters of personal intimacy. Family- and group-bound in his moral standards, particularly with regard to the thoughtful and kind consideration of others, and in most of his openly admitted emotions. Happy about gifts and the tribal ceremonies. Experienced in and concerned about aspects of death and sickness, and at the same time avoiding sorrow in its greatest and unmanageable impact. Sad and angered by aggression from other members of the group and by discipline with its far-reaching consequences. Strictly condemning all individual efforts to rise above the group through fighting or bullying; aware of his own abilities but not admitting and not openly desiring outstanding personal achievement which would separate him from his group. Deeply afraid of the supernatural which also seems to have a strong, even a determining influence on his moral conscience and to be a fundamental incentive for good behavior.

16. WHAT LIES BELOW THE SURFACE?

What lies below the surface of the "typical" Hopi? What kind of personality are we apt to find at the base of his overt behavior? How far have its qualities been influenced by the direct and indirect sanctions of his culture and what are his innermost reactions to them?

It may happen that the overt behavior of an individual appears like a cover over an entirely different being, whose real desires and emotions break through the surface only occasionally to the amazement of his fellow men. In a group it is not probable that such strong, deceiving discrepancies exist. The average overt behavior of a group is intimately connected with its culture, which in turn reflects the personalities of its group members. In reflecting them, however, it not only reflects the present actual personalities, but also their potential and idealized qualities, and, in the rules and laws which are still followed, the true and idealized qualities of their forefathers through generations. Therefore, although the overt expressions of a group and its institutions are never a mask superimposed on different features, these overt expressions and institutions convey more and less than the actual personalities of the present generation with whom we have to deal in daily life, and show us certain points in relief, while others are left in the shadow.

Two of our tests (Thematic Apperception and Rorschach's Inkblots) were devised to give information about the personality structure underlying the overt behavior of individuals. From a quantitative and also partly qualitative analysis of their results, obtained from our sample of Hopi school children, we shall attempt to picture the average personality characteristics which underlie the overt behavior of the group. There are many areas in the basic personality structure of an individual which predominantly represent his own unique experiences and his specific reactions. On them are based those qualities which distinguish each individual from any other existing in the world. But there are some areas which, to a certain extent, represent the fields of reaction to common experiences and influences, and it is with these that we shall deal.

We are fully aware of the difficulties and dangers of generalizations based on this method, but we also think that, until special tests for group characteristics are devised, it may give us some useful data at least, which otherwise we cannot obtain.

This is not the place to go into the theories of depth psychology. We may note, however, that in both of these tests the individual is assumed, without being aware of it, to "project" his emotions, desires, etc., into his interpretations of the test material (namely, pictures and inkblots) which, according to its nature, leads or determines by itself the individual's reactions as little as possible.[1]

According to the Inkblot test[2] the personalities of Hopi children seem to be characterized on the average by a relatively high complexity on one hand, and the limitation of this complexity within definite boundaries on the other. The variety and range of individuality is rather wide. These children do not appear at all uniform or amorphous. Almost every one of them is a well defined, clearly set world of his own, quite pronounced in his distinguishing characteristics. And most of these multitudinous individual worlds are not, in all their lucidity, gross or simple with regard to the quantity, quality and interrelations of the various traits, but show quite a high degree of differentiation and intricacy within themselves.

At the same time, the children appear deeply disciplined, to an extent which is truly astonishing. We do not find very often an average Hopi child who reveals inclinations towards emotional outbreaks and uncontrolled impulsiveness in his personality structure. On the contrary, from a relatively early age the Hopi children's attitude toward their own emotions and the open expression of them appears predominantly to be one of careful selection, cautious reserve and restraint, which in certain age groups tends even toward their complete avoidance and rejection.

This trend however does not go so far as to make a group of precocious and sullen hermits of the children. The pleasures and attractions of the world are recognized and appreciated and receive their due place, but usually not more. The open and ready emotional responsiveness to impressions from outside which leads to exuberance seems to be toned down. From this point of view Hopi children seem indeed well-behaved and highly socialized in a measured and slightly aloof way.

Do the Hopi children then perhaps use their fullest vitality and their natural energies in an imaginary world of fantasy and dreams? Neither is this usually the case. They have on the average good imaginations. Many of them show the signs of actual or potential creativity, which is often distinguished by a great subtlety of perception. This subtlety, together with a striking gift for clear and convincing organization, as well as very neat and minute elaboration of concepts, seems to be the core of their particular originality. But seldom do we find rich fluidity, liveliness and vivaciousness of imagination. Here again the curious restraint, which has apparently toned down the Hopi children's emotional reactions, reveals itself. The nature of their imagination reminds us somewhat of their drawings of the ka-

chinas. Perfect and complete in their whole figuration and its finely and carefully elaborated details, they evoke, more through their halting attitude than through depicted movements of their limbs, the impression of a live strength which does not seem quiet and relaxed, but accumulated and forcefully controlled.

Thus the Hopi children's inner life of imaginations and thoughts appears under a certain tension. Their inner life is usually well developed and, on the average, the children react somewhat more readily to, and are somewhat more concerned with, the intellectual and imaginative than the emotional aspects of impressions and events. They also seem to know relatively early the consolation which may lie in withdrawal into oneself. But at the same time they apparently do not dare to give themselves freely to the play of their fantasy.

Cautious in general, and particularly in the approach to new situations and tasks, they do not tend to become confused but are rather determined in the acceptance or refusal of what is offered to them. Thus they are apt to appear quite stubborn and unshakeable at times. On the other hand, they seem to pursue what once has been accepted with a tenacity that not rarely takes on features similar to an obsession— not to be satisfied with a reasonable accomplishment but to go on and on in the desire to complete and perfect it even to the smallest details. In such a case the Hopi children's usual sense for order and the actual, striking orderliness of their pursuits seems to become somewhat obscured by an abundance of the unessential.

On the average the children's personalities show a balance which does not appear precarious but relatively well-founded, so well-founded indeed, in comparison to what we usually find in children, that we wonder how and at what expense these adults in miniature are able to keep it up.

In more children than those of most of the other Indian tribes studied, we find anxiety of the kind which, unattached to definite objects of fear, vaguely pervades the mind, especially in the younger Hopi. In many of them, younger and older, there is instead of this anxiety a certain rigidity in their attitudes and reactions which makes them appear over-controlled and lifeless, or overcautiously patterned in their concepts and bare of personal partaking and taking parts. It seems like an exaggeration of the reserve which we have found in general and which, in the majority of children even if they have not become frozen into rigidity, seems to have a more or less limiting effect on their natural spontaneity.

From psychology and psychiatry we know that this rigidity, and avoidance of reacting immediately and openly with emotions and mind, is usually an attitude of defense, adopted either after single bad experiences which are far-reaching and long-lasting in their effect or as an answer to continuous pressure from outside or inside. "Keep quiet, do not move, so that the pain will not hit you again," is the device of security for the person who is tensely, consciously or subconsciously, aware of this pressure. It is quite different from the attitude of one who experiences a sudden attack of fear which arouses all forces of his body and mind into the alertness of quick defense.

In the average Hopi children's lives we find indeed much that may explain and warrant such an attitude. We have only to think of the tales of misfortunes and witches, of the experiences of death and sickness and the lack of food, of the long anticipated shock of punishment from the *kachinas*, of the constant, pressing obligation toward the group which by indirect discipline makes even the small child work and feel responsible, when his natural desires reach out for play and personal amusement.

The price the average Hopi child has to pay for his survival in such an environment of actual and potential dangers seems to be the limitation and frequent frustration of his own desires, emotions and ambitions. Apparently not too seldom deriving from it is the generation of inside pressure which, without adequate outlet, accumulates and arouses a feeling of discomfort or fear. Not knowing that this kind of fear is born from his own overdisciplined self, the child and later the adult is apt to transfer the causes of his fear, together with his resentment, to others and to accuse them in perpetual gossip of petty misdeeds or witchcraft. Thus he himself adds to the already existing, potential sources of fear from the outside. This seems indeed a vicious circle, and apparently not many are able to escape from it.

But at the same time the price does not seem too high, if we keep in mind what is obtained for it. The security which lies in the group and in the family, even if they be sometimes hated and resented, is apparently deep, and the satisfaction and nourishment for the imaginative mind in the ceremonial life sufficient to compensate well for what is painfully missing. To us it is of great significance that the amount of fear, of rigidity, and of signs of maladjustment is not more pronounced than it is. What disturbances there are, are not abnormal in degree and quality. These children are indeed not a group of neurotics and, as has been said before, the balance which they have achieved is well founded. They not only *pretend* not to be aggressive, but in their average basic personality structure, while not submissive or meek, they *are not aggressive*. Whatever we find of aggressive attitudes seems to be essentially based on fear of limitation, and to be comparable to the wild, reactive blows and gestures of a person whom someone tries to strangle, and not to the well aimed blows of the genuine attacker.

When we contemplate a system of defense and its weaknesses and failures, we should also consider its suitability to the situation in which the individual or the group lives and the strength of support which it supplies. In the case of the Hopi, it seems to us that their system of defense is not only an answer to the requirements of the lives which they have to lead, but also in harmony with and suitable for the perpetuation of this same way of life. A Hopi in fear is not in discord with his group. Fear is sanctioned by the religion. A person who suppresses his desires is in closest conformity with the aims of his group, even in the loss of his spontaneity and in his rigidity.

Individual unhappiness alone and the reactive changes in the personality usually do not make a person neurotic so long as there is not added the fact and realization of being an outcast from the group. Until then the support which a system of defense lends will be stronger than its harmful effects. As long as in Hopiland the group functions in its life and doctrines as it still does at present, the individual who is rigid and restrained will be normal and also will feel himself to be normal and will function as a normal social being. Moved to another environment, he might become neurotic. As it is now, the danger of upsetting the balance probably will come not from limitation but from sudden and excessive freedom. In such deep conformity of the individual personalities with the requirements of the group, we may indeed expect real difficulties and disturbances in case the group breaks down.

There is one area in the average basic personality structure of Hopi children which is apparently not affected by the discipline of measured limitation, and that is the area of instinctual urges. They are usually vivid and spontaneous. This fact suggests that the intensity of relationship between person and person may well be affected and reduced by the general restraint imposed from outside and to this the individual may respond by building a wall of defensive seclusion around himself, but at the same time the instinctual desires as such, particularly those of a sexual nature, will probably be satisfied without great restraint. This is understandable when we consider that, by adding new children and new workers, the Hopi adds to the life and strength of the group, while intense emotional relations would deviate his attention to an undesirable extent. Where therefore we find dissatisfaction, this will usually be based not on a suppression of sexual desires as such, but on the inability to establish interpersonal relations of a higher emotional order.

All these considerations apply to Hopi children from both communities. It should, however, be mentioned that the children of First Mesa seem to show more spontaneity than those of Oraibi, for centuries the most isolated Hopi community, which did not experience the attack of Western civilization gradually (as did First Mesa, for example) and which therefore reacted with stronger defense and seclusion.

Looking for confirmation or confutation of what we have found about the basic personality structure of Hopi children by means of the Inkblot test, we find that the Thematic Apperception test, independently and from different material, obtained the following results:[3]

The Hopi children's responses to the test are extremely neat, well regulated and controlled and show an amazing balance in their organization.

Their reactions seem to be firm, clear and determined, and the decisions and judgments which are expressed do not show any alternatives.

The children's attention and interest do not seem to be centralized in themselves or in one specific person, but to be diffused over the members of the group which they happen to visualize in their fantasy.

It is rare to find an expression of personal desire.

The children do not seem to reveal any strong emotional intensity.

Aggression is not directly expressed. What there is of aggression is indirectly expressed and usually tied up with its frustration. In the children's minds aggression, rebellion, and the wish to get ahead of the others will lead to a bad outcome, punishment or submission.

All these data are indeed strikingly consistent not only with those of our other projective test, the Inkblot, but also with the findings of all the tests which relied on direct questioning, and with the evidence of Hopi life and culture which we obtained through observation, reports, and interviews. Again, and this time in the area of fantasy (with which the Thematic Apperception test is directly concerned) we seem to find the powerful influence of the group, which apparently assures and clarifies the children's minds, and simultaneously limits their freedom of expression as such, as well as that of their emotions and personal desires in particular. What from the Inkblot test results we could only define generally as "restrained or reserved imagination," we find confirmed regarding the very content of the children's fantasy. This increases our impression that the influence of the group reaches very deep into the personalities of these children.

If we find indirectly expressed aggression—represented as undesirable or disadvantageous even in the relatively safe area of fantasy—this usually means (as has been noted) that, lying very deep in the subconscious, there exist an insecurity and helpless anxiety which will develop wherever strong personal desires and inclinations are forcefully limited and need an outlet.

But let us point out again—and in fact we cannot emphasize it too much —that as long as individuals or groups are still functioning as the Hopi are, and as long as they do not show serious signs of disorganization or disintegration, we may assume that, although there are areas of dissatisfaction and insecurity, these constitute no more than particular aspects of those reactions which necessarily accompany every process of socialization in its limiting demands on the freedom of the individual. These may very well be called "areas of less resistance" which may endanger the health of a group in a crisis, but if we concentrate our attention on them we may overlook the forces of recuperation which are likely to exist at their very side. Among the Hopi these forces of recuperation seem indeed to be very strong. We may talk about individual fear and insecurity, but let us not forget the equally alive feeling of security which arises out of the family and the group. From the tests we perceive restraint and anxiety, but also perspicacity, clearness, balance, and again strength and assurance which seem by far to outweigh a deeper-lying insecurity. We have noted that if the group should break down in both its limiting and supporting functions, we may anticipate deep disturbances. But even anticipating a catastrophe, we may find ourselves in the position of the doctor who, having given his patient a month to live, meets him ten years later in radiant health.

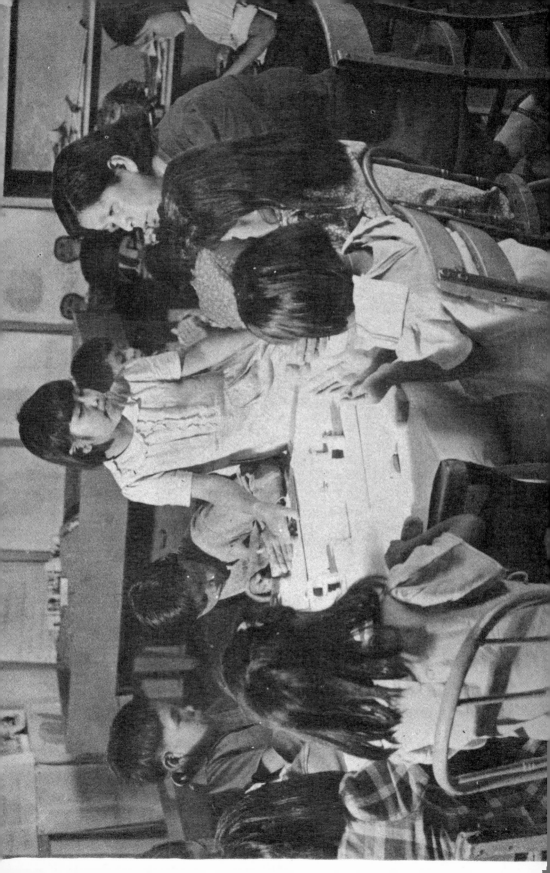

17. REACTIONS TO ROLE

Each group is composed of persons who, besides being individuals and members of the group, have to fulfill specific functions within it. These various functions put them in different categories and usually bring into prominence certain qualities and traits which distinguish them from those belonging to any other category. In the communities we are studying there are children, adults, old people; males and females; prosperous and poor people; ceremonial chiefs and young initiated; farmers and herders, etc. From our test material we can attempt to ascertain the influence which the functions of age and sex seem to have among Hopi children. In this respect, besides the Inkblot test, the Thematic Apperception test is of value. It not only gives us information about the various attitudes and qualities themselves but also, to a certain degree, relates them with the forces which have brought them about.

In Part II we discussed the various roles which boys and girls at different ages are expected to assume in Hopi society. Here we shall try to show their reactions to them.

The younger children who were tested, we observe, appear more relaxed and spontaneous than older children. Already, however, there seems to exist quite a pronounced difference in personality structure and attitudes between boys and girls.

As is natural at about six or seven years of age, boys and girls both are not yet completely disciplined in their reactions, and still show signs of impulsiveness and of inability to master the bewildering abundance of impressions which their environment bestows on them. But in their personality structure the little girls appear to be quite simple, as if set in a firmly established world, which is not problematically

disturbing but also is not very stimulating to them. Their inner lives and their imaginations apparently have not yet developed into consciousness. Unusual contacts and tasks seem to limit their immediate responsiveness to quite a high degree, and the aggressiveness of other people intimidates them apparently as much as it makes them angry.

The boys' personalities appear by contrast more complex. They seem to be much more versatile and mobile than the girls, and they also use their imaginations quite freely and often in an original way. To them apparently the world is already something that they have partly to recreate in their own minds. In this first stage of growing individuality, much of what previously had been self-understood in unquestioned reality, seems to become incomprehensible and disquieting. To a greater extent than the girls, the boys reveal a vague permeating anxiety, in spite of the fact that they seem to be less concerned in new situations and less afraid of being attacked or interfered with by other persons than are the girls.

Learning from our tests that at this age level the girls look mostly on their mothers as the praisers and blamers of their behavior, while for boys the mothers still outweigh everybody else in importance but share much of the boys' attention with other members of the household, with elders and people of the group in general, we think that such findings point at least to some of the causes for the differences in the personality structure between the sexes.

We have seen that the little girls have much less outer mobility than the little boys. The center and the main stage of the girl's life is the home, her main adult company her mother, who not only feeds and protects her but starts early to teach and to prepare her for the role which she herself will later have to assume—the role of a clan mother.

We may assume that this future responsibility of the daughter is constantly in the mother's mind and will be expressed in her attitude, the nature of her affection and attention, as well as in her words, teachings and discipline. Being kept at home more than the boys are, having to learn certain household duties, and taking care of the younger children will thus be presented to the little girl not as deprivation, but as a privilege of which she has to show herself worthy. Early she will be told and will hear that on the girls depends the perpetuating of the clan. This will give her a feeling of her own importance, and a security which during the early pliable years of her life will not be questioned consciously by whatever resentment she may feel about the boys' greater freedom. Neither will it usually be shattered by contrary experiences.

The effect of this kind of training will be twofold. On one hand, it will give the little girl very early a deep outer discipline and a feeling of responsibility, well founded and internalized because, lending her special importance, it will be accepted with comparative eagerness. On the other hand, it will determine from the beginning the direction of her life, will shut her off from much stimulation which lies outside of this line, and will therefore keep back to a certain degree the development of her inner life and her imagination. The transfer from this home atmosphere to the strange school environment will naturally be particularly intimidating.

The little boys have more freedom. Going out with the father to the fields, planting, weeding, building traps for the animals are for the small boys as much exciting and new adventures as they are work. The kind of instruc-

tion the boy receives there, the teachings about ceremonies and myths, the changing impressions from the lives of animals and plants, serve to stimulate his mind. On the other hand, they too aim directly or indirectly towards the responsibilities of manhood, and put him on a definite track in life. The consciously felt difference between the grown-up man and his small son, both working in the fields or practicing in the *kiva*, is much less than that between an engineer working at the railroad and his little boy tinkering at home with a toy train.

The responsibilities and tasks which, for the Hopi boy, are only limiting duties and hard work without much fun, are those which he has to perform at home to help his mother—hauling water and chopping wood. They cannot be connected with play or pleasant fantasies—the water is too easily spilled, the wood not ready for cooking the supper, and there is no escape from immediate scolding and guilty conscience. At the same time he observes and feels, at home, the more or less firmly established authoritative position of his mother, and his father's peripheral significance. He also hears that his sister and not he himself will become the real head of the clan. Thus, while away from home he feels himself as an important and useful assistant to his father and the whole family, while back at his mother's house he has to become the obedient little boy again. And in fact this would not be so unpleasant, considering the warm security of food and bed and the affection given him by his mother, other relatives and friends, if the different position of the males and females were not noticeable in the home atmosphere. This may explain why we find in boys the vague anxiety of bewilderment which the girls show less frequently.

Entering school, the numerous faces are not too strange. Many of them he has met already on trips with his.

father and while playing with other boys away from home. But at school he is suddenly transferred into a third kind of atmosphere. He has to be a small obedient child again, but here he is also a "boy"—somebody who is stronger and more important than the girls, who now as the weaker and "unprotected" sex have to be taken care of. In spite of the fact that most of the White teachers are women, these aspects of our own culture will, openly or unspoken, pervade the classroom. Their effect at first will be quite bewildering, though not immediately so, and we shall deal with it at greater length later.

It is at about the age of eight to ten years that the average Hopi boy and girl seem to show the most natural and the happiest poise of the different forces of their personalities. The children now appear quite disciplined in their emotions, but at the same time open and responsive to impressions from without and relatively free in the use of their fantasy. Just as their attention in regard to matters of detail has increased considerably, they also seem to move in a world of greater reality, a world which is less bewildering and less frightening.

These are the years in the Hopi children's lives when, growing up and becoming stronger, they probably also become more consciously aware of their responsibilties, and of the importance of their roles within the household group. The manifold duties and tasks, which now can be performed with a certain skill, still are less a burden than a means of showing strength and adult-like competence. At this age level, the kind of work which the Hopi children have to do (i. e., for them meaningful and comprehensible work that incorporates them closely into the household group) is in its regulating and assuring effect usually an excellent antidote against the vague anxieties of early childhood. Later, when

work interferes with higher-developed individuality and strong desires for personal independence, it may become an important source or pretext for deep resentment.

School, too, has become a familiar institution where friends are met and where the subjects taught may still seem strange, but not yet problematical or too disquieting on account of their different ideology. Learning another language and reading, writing, and arithmetic does not interfere with the children's beliefs, and the White teacher's way of life is too far removed from their own to be a matter of serious desire or envy.

The influence on the children's behavior exerted by other people of the group, by agemates and teachers, seems now to be increasingly felt by boys as well as girls, while that of the family, though still of greatest importance, has apparently somewhat decreased. The range of outside contacts experienced by boys and girls is now more alike than it was at the younger age level, but still, for reward or blame, the girls look to the household group, and particularly to their mothers, much more than do the boys.

With the widening of the physical horizon the little girls seem to have been aroused from their simple, unquestioned and walled-in existence. From about the age of eight years on they show a rather rapidly increasing development of their imaginative capacities on the conscious level and a growing complexity of their whole average personality structure, which at the age of ten puts them approximately on equal footing with the boys. During this age period the Hopi girl enjoys more personal freedom than before, when dependence on the mother was not only imposed but also desired for protection, and more than during the years to come when, as we have seen, she will be submitted to new restrictions. In comparison with the preceding age period, no new general sources of conflict, have been added. If she has lost certain privileges granted to the small child, she has also gained in importance as a member of the working family group. Her position cannot be compared with that of a girl of the same age in modern urban society who, between the younger and the older sister, often may feel not needed and without scope.

The boys, with regard to their inner development, show about the same picture as on the preceding age level. Their personalities appear somewhat more differentiated, their imaginative capacities are apparently more utilized, but on the whole there are no striking differences.

This seems to us rather interesting as we shall see that the same is partially true for the following age period. The boys have apparently reached very early a level of relatively well differentiated and complex inner development which later, at least until about the age of 18, seems to be rather stabilized in its original direction. Among the many reasons which may account for such findings, the following cultural factor may be of contributory influence.

As we have noted, the first initiation of Hopi children into the ceremonial life takes place between the ages of six and ten years. The little boy of six, even if not yet initiated, will know about the approaching event, and his fantasy will be more or less caught by it. If older boys have not "enlightened" him, he will be vaguely expectant of an important and mysterious revelation which will separate him from the smaller boys and bring him nearer to adulthood. Through a guilty conscience he may also anticipate a hard whipping by the kachinas. If he has been told that the kachinas are not gods but men, he may still be afraid of the actual whipping. He may look forward to the new responsibilities and the active participation in

ceremonial life with vivid emotions. The girls too are initiated, but they are whipped rarely in our villages, and they certainly know that initiation will not change the ways of their actual lives.

For the young children, boys and girls alike, for whom the border between reality and fantasy is still fluid, the revelation that the kachinas are their fathers and uncles may be a shock which suddenly destroys a world of miracles and infinite possibilities, but also a world of fears. However, among those events which on the average happen to all members of the group, for the Hopi boy the first initiation is perhaps the most influential and most· significant during his development from infancy to adulthood, because it introduces him to his role as active participant in the ceremonies. With his first initiation the essential duties and responsibilities which will later determine his life with regard to the group are roughly defined—work and ceremonial performance. They may be elaborated in depth and importance. But for the average Hopi boy the future will hold no other expectancies of an entirely new order as far as they concern his position in the group. The first initiation marks his first complete spiritual and practical delimitation within the boundaries of Hopi life.

For the girl the process of delimitation begins when for the first time she hears and understands about her future role as head of the clan, and it is not concluded until she herself becomes a wife and mother. She is not so abruptly "put in her place" as the boy is.

After the kachina initiation—and we may assume that in both communities studied most of the children are still initiated—the boy takes over the role of apprentice in the theology and ceremonial of his people. This means that, as earlier his physical activities were channelized, now his spiritual life

A Hopi girl
at school

will be more and more so. His fantasy will be tied with rules and laws, his creative capacities directed towards the traditional patterns of the dance, singing, graphic arts and crafts, and while already he has developed, to a certain degree, responsibility as a worker for the family, he will now have to carry also a clearly defined spiritual responsibility for his clan.

That Hopi ceremonial is in its intricacy not only stimulating to the mind but also, within the boundaries of its rules, full of color and exciting rhythm, which may become so many regulated outlets for emotions, and that the ceremonial rules are learned and *personally* executed by the child in active participation, perhaps contributes to the fact that the Hopi boy's personality not only becomes stabilized early but at the same time is rather highly developed and differentiated. It may also partly explain why, during the period of prepuberty from 11 to 13 years, the boys seem to show less pronounced personality changes than the girls. The channelization is apparently strong enough and also sufficiently attractive to give them balance and at least partially to occupy their minds.

In the period of prepuberty boys and girls reveal a tendency towards withdrawal into themselves. Much of the spontaneous responsiveness to outside contacts and impressions, which was present on the previous age level, appears lost. Preoccupation with inner problems and conflicts seems to prevail. We may be dealing here largely with symptoms which are more or less related to the physiological changes of the growing individual. The average personality structure of Hopi children at this age level presents, however, enough specific features differing from those found in children of other Indian tribes to justify the tentative assumption of cultural influences.

The boys still occupy the same roles which they took over earlier. But with growing physical strength, responsibilities grow in weight and now may threaten to become more a burden than a stimulation, because the individual approaching adolescence is usually no longer satisfied with acceptance of orders and imitation of adult behavior, but strives more or less vaguely, subconsciously or consciously, for independence and the creation of a world of his own. The average Hopi boy cannot very well give vent to his half understood or misunderstood drive for independence through emotional outbreaks or continuous small actions of open rebellion against the authority imposed on him. What in our society would be considered a mild case of rowdiness would be a disgrace and danger for family and clan in Hopiland, and independence would have to be gained not only in opposition to a parent or a teacher, but in opposition to the whole group and everything that means Hopi life. The way left will be, on one hand, avoidance and rejection of tempting attractions and contacts and, on the other hand, withdrawal in the attempt to solve problems and conflicts and to reinterpret the Hopi Way in one's own mind.

Thus the average Hopi boy of this age period will show less the boisterous behavior of his White agemate than the sullen, indifferent or ironical attitude of the 17-year-old adolescent in our society. That in spite of the releasing and stimulating functions of the ceremonial role, these reactions are not entirely adequate for the solution of the essential problems of this age group, seems to become evident from the new rise of the vague anxiety or confusion which we found in the six- and seven-year-old boys.[1]

The girls show the symptoms of withdrawal to a clearly higher degree. Our considerations about the greater weight of responsibilities which may be in conflict with a growing desire for independence equally apply to them.

A Hopi man with headband
and necklace of turquoise and shell

While they are free from most ceremonial responsibilities, they are now usually required to show certain more complicated domestic skills, which again will draw them more into the realm of the house and into the companionship of mother, sisters and babies.

Besides, we have noted[2] that at about this age the Hopi girls are usually admonished to keep to their own sex and away from the boys. While the reality of sex and sexual relationships are probably not secrets for Hopi children—parents and children most frequently sleep in the same room and side by side—it seems that the duties, implications, and consequences of the sexual role are now brought into the girls' consciousness by special limitations and perhaps instructions. Actually the now almost complete division of responsibilities segregates girls and boys within their own sex group. There is, however, the difference that the boys, during ceremonial activities and in the kivas, may find a wider range of personal contacts than the girls, who keep to their mothers' houses.

We may assume that in fact the situation of the girls is again noticeably more limited than that of the boys, and also that many of the mitigating factors of such limitation, as the need for protection and warm security at home, have lost much of their value for the girls of this age. Having presumably had a taste of their importance as future heads of the clans from an early age and now approaching maturity, they are, with regard to their position in the group, suspended in expectancy not unlike an heir who, under a restraining discipline, can enjoy the independence of his near inheritance only in his imagination. For the girls, as for the boys, open rebellion would be almost identical with a negation of Hopi life. Thus, it seems understandable that their withdrawal into themselves is very pronounced and that, though sensitivity is increased, spontaneity is greatly reduced and the attractions

from the outside are rejected with a challenging attitude. It appears equally significant that, unlike the boys, in this age period and still in the following one, the girls seem to show a greater awareness of their mothers' disciplinary authority than during the earlier stages.

With puberty this course of development, found in varying degrees in Hopí boys and girls, seems to be interrupted in so far as the one-sided tendency toward introversion of the prepuberty period is now reduced for the sake of an easier acceptance of outside contacts. New in this period and characteristic of it is, however, a remarkable rise in the instinctual urges. It seems that with the attainment of sexual maturity the adolescents have found the one personal outlet for their emotions for which the sanctions of the group are not strong enough to have a truly restraining effect.

As has been said above (page 106-111) the sexual aspects of life are apparently of secondary importance in the Hopi system of moral values. Industriousness and considerate behavior toward the group seem to be more highly valued than chastity; fighting and stealing are matters of much greater concern than sexual indulgence. During prepuberty, while sexual desires are rising into consciousness but still are aimless and vaguely defined, the limitations imposed in their regard by the group will be effective, although they may be potential causes of conflict. The strictly physical symptoms of sexual maturity, however, have probably a greater and more consequential significance among the Hopi than in our society, because they put the adolescents, particularly the girls, within actual reach of a most important aim of the group, the perpetuation of the clan. Presumably this consequence will not be kept from the children's minds, and their attention and interest will be directed toward it.

Thus probably brought into consciousness as a value of propagation without the strong associations of extra-physical love or of sin familiar to us, sexuality cannot be really inhibited as an urge of the personality any longer, by measures of physical limitation in a period when these urges become actually dominant. And this will be the more marked since, in their essential aim, the limitations and instructions used by adults for their adolescent children do not seem to center around sexual relationship as such, but around the selection of an adequate partner, acceptable to the family and particularly the mother. Such limitations will have little hold on the mind of the 14- and 15-year-old and may even be broken without deep feelings of guilt and without great fear of punishment.

Still the limitations imposed upon girls seem to be greater than those designed for boys. A girl roaming around is likely to be followed by her relatives and to be brought home.[3] If she gives her attention to a married man, she may even be spanked violently at the age of 15. The impropriety of being "boy crazy" is discussed at home and is a topic of joking and teasing for agemates. This may partly explain why the girls keep up their attitude of withdrawal to a higher degree than the boys, and also why we now find a moderate number of instances where they lose their previously well-established emotional control. Another influencing factor may be that the girl of this age, who sees the fulfillment of her role as a Hopi woman in the near future, will now become more and more aware, together with the promises of power, also of the hardships and dangers of this role, and will be able to compare consciously the greater freedom granted to her father and brothers with that conceded to her mother and sisters.

The boys' personalities seem now indeed to show their instinctual urges at free play to the disadvantage of their inner maturity. The previously quite remarkable development of their imaginative and original creative capacities is suddenly broken off and reduced to a level of importance comparable to that found in the six- and seven-year-olds. With their growing mastery over their work and their ceremonial duties, they are in fact enjoying a comparatively much greater freedom than the girls, and supervision over them in sexual matters is definitely less. Besides, subconsciously they may follow their instinctual drives not only because this is the main permissible personal outlet for their emotions, but also because it is another balancing factor for their position in a group which gives central importance to the women. It is the conquest of the otherwise unconquerable, and is emotionally balancing as the ceremonial functions are spiritually so.[4]

Since the oldest Hopi examined by our tests were 18 years we can only guess that with further development— with second initiation, marriage, the setting up of a family, etc.—the personalities will probably also show characteristic changes. It would certainly be interesting to know which psychological forces, and which methods of defense help the adult Hopi man and woman to keep up under the burden of their responsibilities, as well as which are the points of strength in their personalities and those of least resistance in the inevitable process of adaptation to our culture which is so foreign to the Hopi way of life.

18. HOPI HOSTILITY

From numerous reports we hear that the adult Hopi are inordinately given to malicious gossip and that they even may accuse their closest relatives of witchcraft. A person in our society who acted in such a way would indeed be ripe for an institution. And with this comparison in mind the Hopi are usually approached by us.

But a person in our society who gossiped to such a degree and who imagined his relatives or friends to be mixers of poison, would show his defective mind in his general behavior, in his work, in his personality structure. The Hopi do not show it, and we shall have first to reconcile these two facts before we may judge them.

Let us stay within our comparison. A person in our society who turns in this way against his friends and relatives has, in order to be able to do this, first to destroy or to convert the whole system of loyalties and all the intensity of loving emotions in which his culture has trained him from earliest childhood. His personality has to become extraordinarily disturbed and disrupted before such thoughts and actions can develop to a high degree. In Hopi society we have seen that the child is less trained in loyalties between person and person than in loyalties to the group, be it the household in its entity, the clan, or the village. Emotions are more diffuse than intense. In order to feel persecuted or to accuse certain members of these groups, no deep loyalties have to be destroyed, and the personality may retain its essential integrity. Ideas of persecution in a Hopi have thus an altogether less and qualitatively different significance than they have among us, and disregard of this fact is the more confusing since, because of their manifest similarity, such ideas among the Hopi have been called and considered a paranoid trend.

From the test results and from the contacts which the author (A. J.) has had with numerous Hopi adults and children, she has found no evidence that there exists on the average any such abnormality of the personality. What appears as such is no more than a culture trait reactive in its nature and well defined, without the deeply destructive and malignant qualities of a neurotic or psychotic condition.

It is, however, probable that the same traits which give rise to interpretations implying the psychopathological nature of the adult Hopi, i. e., excessive gossip, accusations of witchcraft, etc., may correspond to certain patterns of hostility characteristic of and bred by this particular Hopi society. Repeated exposure of a relatively small, town-dwelling group to attack from outside, to the dangers of famine and epidemics, would create a tension which, though useful against a common enemy in a crisis, might under certain circumstances turn against the in-group itself. The human being, trained in alertness toward potential danger, is not necessarily capable of distinction in cases which rouse his anger or his fear. Also, the average person, brought up with constant admonitions to be attentive to and considerate of the other members of the group, will likely dwell not only on their good qualities, but, in immediate reaction, his trained attention will equally be drawn to the observation of their shortcomings. The Hopi group apparently functions, for better or for worse, on the basis that "each person's business is rightly the business of everybody else."

To these general predisposing factors there may be added the previously discussed potential resentment against personal limitations, which may manifest itself defensively in the criticism of specific limiting agents. In this regard we are interested in analyzing our test results as to the average attitudes assumed by Hopi boys and girls toward those exponents of the group who are of main importance in their training and development. We assume that the reactions experienced in childhood are not without relation to and influence on the attitudes found in the adult man and woman.

The tests of Emotional Response and Moral Ideology, as well as the Thematic Apperception, can give us some of the information we need. The following findings seem to us quite significant.

The family occupies by far the highest place in those emotions which in the children's minds are associated with pleasant and enjoyable experiences. (See Table XIII, page 146). Among the representatives of the family, it is the father who seems to be the main source of happiness for children of either sex, though to a considerably higher degree for boys than girls, who in turn receive apparently more satisfaction from the mother than the boys do. Second only to the father's importance are the *kachinas* who seem indeed to be spenders of joy, held in high regard by boys and girls alike. Ranking next are the various, not particularly defined members of the village group. The role of the agemates appears in comparison quite negligible.

The emotions of fear, anger and shame and the "expectations of the worst" show a very different distribution with regard to the persons associated with them. (See Table XIII, again). Here the group i. e., "everybody," and the agemates are for the girls of about equal, for the boys of even greater, importance than the family. The change in the father's role is particularly striking, because he seems rarely to produce unpleasant emotions in boys as well as in girls. The mother, however, is associated in the girls' minds equally with pleasant and unpleasant events, while for the boys she is a somewhat greater source of

anger and shame than of happiness. The supernatural—now not as *kachinas* but as ghosts, witches, the dead—does not evoke anger or shame; its influence is limited to fear, as has been discussed.

On the level of moral standards, of discipline and authority, the tendencies are similar. The family has unquestionably the greatest share in rewarding and praising, the group's function seems to be more one of blaming and punishing the guilty. (See Table XIV, page 146). The difference in the boys' and girls' attitudes is clear-cut. For while the girls appear more family-bound and especially mother-bound in each regard, the boys seem to experience the influences of group and family in close competition, and to them father and mother are equally important.

These findings, together with those of the Thematic Apperception test, which agree essentially with them and in addition reveal subconscious feelings of hostility toward the control exercised over the children, particularly by the mother, seem to point to some potential patterns of hostility involved in the Hopi system of interpersonal relations in regard to children, which may very well have a bearing on the behavior observed in adults.

The quite consistent difference in the attitudes shown by boys and girls, as well as the tendency toward "emotional reservations," i. e., toward connecting distinct persons and agents with specific emotions—the fathers and the *kachina* gods with happiness, the supernatural in other manifestations with fear, etc.—are in themselves significant. We are dealing here with a society in which a rather strict division and distribution of specific roles is started early, always maintained, and directly and continuously enforced by the socioeconomic system superimposed on spontaneous emotional inclinations and affections with which it does not necessarily but may possibly interfere.

The high degree to which the Hopi

are consciously aware of this fact and actually guided by it, may be seen from the information volunteered to the author by a Hopi father who loves his children dearly. "We see to it," he said, "that the father does not pay too much attention to the children. If they loved him too much, they might become sick longing for him. He is so seldom at home." These words express a rationalization and an attitude which are not even distantly comparable with any rationalization and any attitude assumed by the average father in our society. The potential danger implicit in its wisdom is the overlooked possibility that a child may *need* close attachment to a father.

To put it briefly, among the Hopi, not only work and spiritual activities, but even the emotional attachment to the various members of the group, father and mother included, seem to be consciously and practically under the direct, regulating influence of the society. The child who does not submit and tries to form deeper attachments of his own choice will most likely run the risk of finding himself without response from the object of his unruly affection. Repeated disappointments of this sort will usually lead to abandonment first of the open manifestation of such emotions, then of further attempts to establish new attachments. Those relationships which are permissible are, in their proper emotional quality, quite accurately defined and closely connected with the roles which the participants hold as members of the group, and it is astonishing how far, according to our tests, the children respond in fact to this emotional channelization. Its aims and consequences are apparently to arrive at a diffusion of loyalties over the greatest number of people.

The one relationship which seems to be exempt from these tendencies is the attachment to the mother. Deep loyalty toward her is not only permissible but desirable and required, and usually also given. It is interesting in this connection that no report exists of a mother having been accused by her children of witchcraft. But the mother to whom the child's love may go without reservation is at the same time by right and power a foremost representative of Hopi rules and laws and a limiting agent of the first order. Such a combination may become quite a serious handicap for the children's emotional development. This earliest and dominant deep attachment may too often and too easily be exposed to resentment and is on the other hand, by force of its imperative exclusiveness, so strong that it tends to tie the children's emotions for the future as well and to render them still less disposed toward new attachments. The actual life situation, with its segregation of the sexes, gives to the boys more opportunities for secondary emotional relations with various members of their own sex group, while the girls never escape from their mother's direct influence.

The patterns of open hostility arising from such a situation will be characterized by their undefined, diffused nature. The source and original aim of hostile feelings, the mother, who keeps the girls confined to the house and to herself and requires from the boys utmost respect and affection, while demonstrating that the daughter is in a certain sense of greater importance than the son, is unassailable because of her central socioeconomic and moral significance to the group. A perfect symbol of the mother's situation and of the ambivalent attitude toward her is found in Hopi mythology—Spider Woman, one of the most powerful deities, propitious and malevolent at the same time, caught in her own web like the woman in her house, catching others, particularly little boys who venture too far away from home. To struggle against the web of such a goddess is hopeless.

The principle of emotional deviation, which we have seen operating successfully in the directing of fear toward the supernatural, will therefore turn the hostile feelings against various other members of the group toward whom loyalties are circumscribed, bound to the role within the group and of considerably less personal depth. With the one exception of a forbidding sanctuary—the mother—the potential targets of hostility seem to be almost limitless. The resentment against the mother's brother as the executor of discipline, against the widow who attracts husbands (regarding whose faithfulness the wives are often uncertain) are somewhat more distinct crystallizations of this same general tendency, which we notice already in the children's reactions when they associate negative emotions and the functions of blame and punishment so prevalently with the group. Child training,

which rather frequently evokes the spectre of ridicule or other sanctions threatening from the neighbors, reinforces this trend. The moral commandment of "be considerate of your neighbor" is general enough in its formulation to leave room for expressions of hostility as soon as a tolerable justification is at hand.

It is not possible to go into a detailed analysis of all the potential manifestations of Hopi hostilities. They all rest on the same principle which has been discussed, and seem to be, as has been noted, almost limitless. On the other hand, it will be scarcely necessary to point out again the many balancing forces of socio-economic, psychological and moral nature—as e. g., among the latter the law of reciprocity and "good" thoughts—which act against the overgrowth of dissatisfaction and hostile impulses. They have been dealt with at length.

19. OLD VERSUS NEW

How far is a psychological situation like the one we have tried to sketch in a few words, open to the influence of an encroaching alien culture which is based on a very different socio-economic system and engenders very different attitudes?

From an analysis of the results of the Free Drawing test,[1] in which the child is apt to reveal how much of the White material culture he has incorporated in his mind, we find that, among the Indian tribes studied, the Pueblo cultures offer less evidence than the others of White influence, and the Hopi least of all. Furthermore, in their drawings the Hopi children pay very great attention—*which increases with age*—to subjects representative of their own culture.[2]

These findings are quite consistent

with what has been observed concerning the acceptance of modern Western culture by the Hopi. Administrators and missionaries who have worked with them know their tenacious resistance to those innovations which may interfere with native institutions and ideology. The children are sent to school by their parents usually not out of genuine admiration for the values of reading, writing and American history, or because our system of moral education is thought to be truly desirable and superior to their own but, as they openly voice it, because school may provide them with necessary tools for defense —first of all, the knowledge of English —in the fight for their own survival in contact with a physically stronger force.

Considering the fact that the Hopi

children studied are all school children and as such are quite regular school attendants, the interest and the display of emotion connected with school and school authorities in our test results are strikingly low. It seems, however, that the attitude found in girls is of a somewhat more positive nature than that shown by boys, and this agrees with the fact that reports from teachers about pupils who study after school hours at home concern mainly older girls. Our school system, as it is presented to the Hopi children, offers them mainly knowledge and activities built on needs which are based on very different socio-economic conditions. Besides it presupposes, and expresses in simple statements of truth and untruth, an ideology which is different from that held by the Hopi, even as to such basic concepts as space and time.

Groups with little pronounced socio-economic and ideological organization, or those which have become disorganized, may adapt relatively successfully to alien doctrines and ways of life. Their "weakness" may become their greatest chance for survival, if not as a group then as individuals immersed in a larger foreign entity. With the Hopi, however, minute, group-directed organization in practically every sphere of life is a main characteristic. Acceptance of alien values would imply true substitution, that is, destruction of what is still functioning. In order to prevent this—if adaptation be imperative—such a group may react as the Hopi have done toward the White American educational system; they may try to use and to reinterpret it as a means of strict advantage to themselves, without accepting its alien spirit. It is apparently not a coincidence, and not entirely due to defects in our school system of ten years ago, that the Hopi who has gone through the grade school does not show less, but frequently more, resistance to measures taken by the administration than the unschooled Hopi. It is probable that

a highly organized culture which has hold of its members' personalities as thoroughly as that of the Hopi may be touched effectively only at its center.

History has shown that under great pressure from alien cultures (Spanish, Navaho and American) Hopi groups were exterminated, or they segmented, only to reconstitute themselves. Owing to the Hopi social system—a web of relatively independent and at the same time interrelated units, where authority is limited by and inherent in specific roles (no one authoritarian role being in itself indispensable) and where the only universal authority is that of the mothers (who determine physiologically the perpetuation of the clans)—splits and more or less complete reconstitutions are possible without being of fatal consequence to the group. This process is not contradictory to, but rather is inherent in, the kind of thorough organization typical of Hopi society.

We stated that in a group of this character it is probable that adaptation may take place only from the center. This opinion was formed on the basis of actual adaptive processes which may be observed among the Hopi at present. For example, the introduction, acceptance and expansion of herding which, through the shifting of the economic balance toward the men, seems to have effected certain slight alterations in the social and psychological situation, as for example the formation of relatively well functioning cooperatives of cattle breeders at First Mesa, the greater financial independence of the owners of herds which are frequently inherited not by the mother's clan but by the owner's sons, etc. Such a process of adaptation, which reaches to the fundamental socio-economic system, is exceedingly slow and gradual, but it is probably the only kind which may—perhaps—preserve the essential integrity of the society, though in changed form.

Having noted this process, we are

A Hopi woman
wearing a woolen blanket

in a position to understand the Hopi children's attitude toward school. School is only one manifestation of many efforts of Whites to bring about adaptation among the Hopi to modern American concepts and values. The slight difference in the attitude shown by boys and girls is understandable. We have mentioned that the boys find themselves, at school, in an atmosphere which, though implying that they belong to the "stronger" and "more important" sex, on the other hand calls for special protection of, and regard for the weak and helpless girls. This situation will be unacceptable to the boys as long as they feel the women's dominant position in their lives and as long as the school does not provide them with practical proofs of their own greater importance through the creation of a sufficiently large number of occupations and positions which would render them independent.

At present the average Hopi boy knows that, whatever he may be taught at school, he will have to return to the fields of his mother or his future wife if he does not want to leave his home and his people and to live alone in an unfriendly and strange world. The Hopi girls, usually sure of their own importance, will not mind seeing additional regard toward them required from the boys. Furthermore, it may be that certain skills learned in school by the girls, such as dressmaking, canning, etc., are more useful to them at home than those taught to the boys who learn the essentials of farming outside of school. Finally, the functions of school, in providing new contacts and new areas of interest, are of greater importance to the girls in their limited environment than to the boys who have the outlet of ceremonial activities. This social function of the school is perhaps its sphere of easiest and potentially greatest influence. If used wisely, it may, by securing the cooperation of the Hopi women, become of increasing significance in the process of adaptation.

The patterns of hostility, which have been discussed, may constitute so many vulnerable points, particularly exposed to attack by an alien culture. The findings in certain individuals among the Hopi children studied seem to support this opinion. Adaptation based on this kind of dissatisfaction (i. e., on personal resentment and not on the clear recognition and weighing of good or bad conditions) is apt to lead to the disintegration of the group. As may be observed in other minorities, various Indian tribes included, such disintegration finally may lead to a disturbing and disproportionate increase in the number of economically and psychologically maladjusted citizens, who would seem to be too great a price to pay for the comparatively few instances of smooth adaptation and of brilliant individual achievement. Since the physical extermination of minorities is not an aim of democratic ideology, and maladjustment is undesirable in any form of government, it is in our very own interest to find and use ways which do not stimulate the disintegration of self-supporting entities such as the Hopi groups. Guidance toward gradual economic and political adaptation with as little active interference as possible with the native ideology and institutions, so far as they are not seriously harmful to the whole nation of which they are a part and are not in opposition to basic humanitarian principles, seems to be a sound policy toward self-adjustment and the cooperation of a sound stock of people.

Hopi family
at supper

20. THE INDIVIDUAL IN THE GROUP

If the reader will now look again at the sketches of Hopi children presented in Part III, he may find in the individual personalities much of what we have attempted to determine as "characteristic of the Hopi group," in a more dramatic and infinitely more complex form. He will discover that the traits and attitudes which, for the sake of a clearer analysis, we had to treat separately, manifest themselves in the individual in an intimately interwoven pattern and that regarding its composition and structure, this pattern is unique, and though sometimes similar to, it is never identical with that revealed by another person. Different constitutions and different personal experiences alter the reactions to experiences general for the group, from individual to individual and in the same human being from time to time.

Textbook cases are extremely rare, practically nonexistent. An individual may, for example, reveal hostile feelings toward the mother or sister in a more pronounced manner than many others, a boy or a girl may show a particularly one-sided balance of the personality, but obvious domination by one fateful experience, by one drive, by one trait is usually symptomatic of neurotic characters.

To label each of our 11 normal Hopi children as a specific example of this or that reaction would distort the picture of reality for the sake of a clarity which would be purely theoretical. Already the necessity of interpreting the individual personalities in the shortest possible way, of avoiding repetitions and technicalities interesting only to the professional psychologist, has led us to put into relief certain traits and experiences which appeared of particular significance for the personality in question, and to neglect others of less immediate importance. Each child more or less clearly shows *most of the characteristics* which we could establish for the whole group and in addition his own specific reactions which, outside of his group qualities, render him a being of general human interest.

To say that Lawrence is the prototype of the Hopi sheep breeder, Irene that of a widow's daughter, Roger a typical son of a Christianized family would be quite wrong. But the reader, who has ploughed through the interpretations of our test results on the group level, may now see the significance and the interplay of the various influencing factors in a different light than he has seen them before. And it is probable that he will see still more than the interpreter was able to express.

He will see, for instance, that two girls, Irene and Helen, both widows' daughters, show similar reactions, but a very different balance of the personality, which probably is caused not merely by different personal experiences, but also by different constitutions. There are in a group the genuinely cheerful and the genuinely sullen, the phlegmatic and the sanguine, the bright and the dull, etc., whose approach to life may partly derive from the different nature of their physiological reactions. These innumerable variances give to the ·group the multicolored, unpredictable aspect of reality, which in the end defies generalizations and characterizes all human attempts to categorize life as mere approximations to an unachievable aim. The main justification of such attempts lies in the practical consequences of better understanding, even though it be incomplete.

V. IN RETROSPECT

We have now reached the end of our analysis of Hopi personality development in its geographic and cultural setting.   In concluding we shall attempt briefly to highlight and integrate some of our findings and to indicate some implications which seem to us particularly significant.

Every reader who has followed the course of the study must have been impressed by the capacity of the Hopi not only to survive for centuries in an exceedingly limiting and threatening environment, but also to use and develop their natural and human resources ingeniously, albeit without metal tools or a written language, in building up and elaborating a rich and rewarding culture. In fact, it is clear that the very hardships and vicissitudes which were the inescapable physical realities of the Hopi world acted as deeply significant, channelizing agents in the intricate process of culture and personality development.

To appreciate fully the environmental odds against which the Hopi have operated for over a millennium, let us review briefly some points which have been discussed.   It will be remembered that pressure from the external environment has taken two main forms, the influence of the geographic setting and the encroachment of alien groups.

Considering the geography, we note that the chief concern of this sedentary agricultural people has always been the water supply, which is not only meager but also irregular and undependable. Added to this is another major factor, namely that the growing season on the northern Arizona plateau is short and variable, so much so in fact that the main crop, corn, is likely to be injured at either the planting or the harvest season.   We have seen that regardless of how skillful and industrious the Hopi may be, torrential down-pours may wash out the crops, frost kill them or droughts prevent their growth and, if prolonged, even dry up the springs upon which the sedentary desert life of the tribe depends.   Thus although the Hopi perfected their methods of dry farming, stored up food for several years in advance, became expert hunters mindful of the protection of wild life, explored the region exhaustively for useful wild plants, developed craftwork commercially, and even discovered how to use and mine coal—in short, they apparently mastered the physical environment so far as it could be mastered with stone tools—nevertheless there always remained the unmasterable, unpredictable factors of drought, flood and frost.

Turning to the other main type of environmental pressure to which the Hopi were exposed, namely, encroachment by alien groups, we find that the vulnerable position of the Hopi pueblos may be compared to that of sedentary oasis dwellers surrounded by predatory nomads in other parts of the world and throughout history. With the Hopi this pressure has taken two forms at the physical level, namely, sudden and unpredictable raids on crops and herds by nomadic Indian groups, and encroachment by Spaniards, Navaho and Americans on their very land base itself.

127

Against both types of attack the position of the Hopi, attached as they have always been to their land base for support, has necessarily been one of defense rather than offense and, although they developed certain skills of defensive warfare such as remarkable speed and endurance in running and the precise use of their weapons, and they honeycombed their towns on the mesa fastnesses, and although for many years the desert itself afforded them some degree of protection, against Whites if not Indians, nevertheless they remained highly vulnerable.

Thus we see that Hopi culture and character structure developed in an environment which was to a considerable degree actually unmanageable at the physical level, regardless of man's industry, skill, ingenuity or foresight; but without these qualities, cultivated with relentless effort, survival of a sedentary people in Hopiland through the centuries would have been impossible.

Moreover from the Hopi point of view, the external environment, hazardous though it was in the past, has not become any the less a threat in recent years, but on the contrary has become an even more complex one. The proof of vulnerability represented by the Spanish conquest, the nomadic raids and the American regime, has been augmented by the progressive curtailment and concomitant deterioration of the land, represented by the Navaho encirclement and gradual expansion toward the mesas, the extinction of big game, the rapid soil erosion and diminution of plant life, and finally the officially confirmed loss of the use of 75% of the original reservation and the reduction, by almost half, of the livestock. In the context of the traditional Hopi value system with its emphasis on the basic, maternal nature of the land and on the independence and self-sufficiency of the group, these factors have added to

the insecurity and complexity of Hopi life, in spite of the effect that mitigating factors such as government relief, the introduction of new useful plants, techniques and tools, the increase in wage work, and attempts to protect the tribe legally and to develop self government may have brought. Moreover, on account of the interplay of geographic and historic circumstances, the cumulative effect of the environmental threat has been more potent at Oraibi than at First Mesa.

In this precarious setting which, from the Hopi point of view, has become increasingly more complex in its hazards at the same time that it has become spatially more limited, survival has depended on the establishment and maintenance of a delicate and balanced adjustment between the group and the environment, a resilient balance which, if disturbed, could recover itself quickly and completely, a balance which may be compared not to a static equilibrium but to a delicately adjusted vibratory movement within a definitely limited field. This fact has played a major role in the development of Hopi culture. Indeed, so deep and central is it to Hopi life that it seems to have affected the over all structure and dynamics of Hopi society, and to be reflected in manifold aspects of Hopi life and personality.

We have noted, for example, the balanced and resilient character of the social structure in which the kinship system, centering in the women, and the ceremonial system, centering in the men, supplement each other in the organization of the pueblo; and furthermore that the pueblo organization, although highly cohesive through its well integrated control system, in which powerful, diffuse group sanctions are reinforced through their internalization in the individual, is sufficiently flexible so that under exceptional pressures it can segment and completely reconstitute itself.

Turning to the covert aspects of Hopi

Making piki, a ceremonial food, at an open hearth

culture, we find numerous illustrations of the particular type of balance described above. There is, for example, the Hopi conception of the universe as an intricate web of categorized orders of phenomena, held in poised interdependence through the law of reciprocity. The resemblance between the concept of the pendulum-like rhythm of reciprocity eternally vibrating within the known boundaries of the Hopi universe and the above-mentioned balance pattern, is obvious. More concrete and detailed illustrations are found throughout the culture as, for instance, in the relationship between the ceremonial cycle of the Upperworld and that of the Underworld. It will be remembered that the ceremonies being held in the Upperworld are reciprocated in the Underworld and vice versa.

As might be expected, this balance pattern also appears in the Hopi language which, as we know, actively conditions the world view. We have seen that the Hopi are equipped through their language to think in terms of vibratory phenomena and thus to be acutely aware of and to express the type of balance pattern described above. This balance pattern is one which our modern science has discovered to be fundamental in the world of nature. It is difficult for us to grasp and handle, however, because our language does not provide us with adequate tools for its subtle conceptualization and expression.

Although the study of Hopi design has not been included in this investigation, it may be noted in passing that balance of the whole within definite boundaries, often executed with great skill and considerable subtlety, is a marked characteristic especially of pottery designs, and Hopi drawings of *kachinas*, even by children, show the rhythm of the Hopi dance as a highly conventionalized vibratory movement within definite spatial boundaries.

Turning from Hopi culture to Hopi personality as revealed in the analysis,

we find also in this sphere a similar balance. According to the tests, a main characteristic of Hopi personality is its complexity within quite definite boundaries; in other words its sophistication in allowed areas, its originality within limits and without bizarreness, its well-developed but not overdeveloped fantasy, and its deeply disciplined emotions which are channelized into socially approved and socially creative outlets. The balanced character of the Hopi personality structure is clearly revealed, for example, in the complex and well integrated control system. As has been noted, Hopi children show at an early age a highly developed pattern of discipline which is not solely imposed from without but which is to a considerable extent internalized from babyhood. Besides, they use their imaginations creatively without becoming the victims of them. Moreover, they usually control their emotions consciously when these threaten to break out into socially unacceptable forms of behavior. These various personality control mechanisms form an intricate, closely interwoven pattern which is subtly poised.

Having noted one outstanding characteristic of the Hopi nature-culture adjustment, namely, the tendency toward the establishment of a delicate, resilient and strictly confined balance between the group and the external environment, and having found it to be reflected in other aspects of the culture, as well as in the personality structure itself, we shall discuss briefly another equally conspicuous Hopi trait, namely, the tendency toward the organization of complex wholes composed of intricately interrelated and interdependent parts confined within definite limits.

We have seen that the presence of a relatively permanent water supply in the form of springs and a comparatively low run-off after rains differentiated Hopiland from the surrounding desert and made possible the growth of a se-

Old Oraibi pueblo, Third Mesa
Stone houses, with ladder entrance to kiva

dentary agricultural population. These geographic features were instrumental in limiting the mobility of the Hopi and in tending to keep them within certain definite boundaries, and their restricted mobility in turn contributed to their vulnerability to attack. The need for defense still further confined them spatially, until we find that in the early 18th century all the Hopi pueblos had moved to protected but crowded quarters on the mesa tops where they had to expand upward rather than outward. Thus these town dwellers of the desert became still more urban, the entire population of each pueblo inhabiting a single apartment-house-like stone structure built in terraces toward the sky, far above their water supply, crops and herds. These cramped and difficult living conditions, which still prevail in mesa pueblos such as Walpi, Sichomovi and Oraibi, throw a good deal of light on the development of Hopi culture and personality, and particularly on the tendency toward the organization pattern characteristic of the Hopi.

It is not necessary to elaborate the Hopi tendency toward the organization of complex, compact wholes, since it is so marked as to be obvious even to the casual observer. It is revealed strikingly in the complicated Hopi socio-economic structure and the ceremonial cycle. It is very noticeable in the Hopi conception of the universe as a closed system made up of interdependent orders and sub-orders of phenomena interrelated through the law of reciprocity. We would like to call attention also to its appearance even in such details of the culture as the method of creating original pottery designs which, as has been noted, are first conceived as a whole in the mind of the potter and then applied to the surface of the pot within a limited area bounded by black lines without benefit of measuring or guiding devices of any kind. And here again our tests have revealed that the type of organi-

zation pattern described above is an outstanding characteristic of the personality structure.

In fact, acording to our analysis, the Hopi show marked capacity not only for organization of wholes in intricate detail, but also for solving problems of the puzzle and maze type, a development which brings immediately to mind the baffling, indeed the well-nigh overwhelming problems presented by their changing external environment and their steadily contracting and relatively inelastic physical boundaries, and upon the more or less adequate solution of which the very existence of the tribe depends.

These factors are also obviously interrelated with their characteristic playing-down of physical aggression and playing-up of interdependence and cooperation in all aspects of life.

We have noted, however, that problem-solving at the physical level, no matter how ingenious, has not brought to the Hopi a mastery of the environment. In this particular desert setting, where the possibilities of development on the material side of life are strictly limited, especially without the use of metal tools, and where even with the utmost industry, patience, skill, foresight and organizing ability, nature still defies man's efforts at control, the Hopi have turned to the cultivation also of the non-material aspects of life, and have elaborated religion and rite in an attempt to eliminate or reduce the hazards and to give security and abundance to the individual and the group.

In spite of its complexity and law-boundedness, however, Hopi ceremonialism has never become stereotyped, and has never degenerated into mere formalism. It emphasizes control of the universe not only by means of the supernatural or magic, but also through the mind or will. The Hopi conception of man as differentiated, in the universal system of mutual interdependency, through his role as an active rather than a passive agent in the fulfillment of the law, compels the active participation of the individual in the ceremonial at not only the physical but also the ideational and emotional level and imposes on him a high degree of personal responsibility for the success of the whole and not just for one small part of it. This in turn operates as an important influence in bringing about the internalization of the law and its apprehension as a whole and in its parts, which is very different from the sort of participation which following one's little part by rote without responsibility or need for concerning one's self with the whole at the ideational and emotional level would give.

The Hopi interest in the immaterial aspects of life is reflected not only in their elaborate ceremonial and their conception of the universe, but also in their capacity for abstract thinking as revealed in the analysis. This, as well as their capacity for organization and their problem-solving ability, in the context of Hopi culture and environment viewed in historical perspective, give a clue to their high intelligence, as revealed in tests of both the performance and the projective types, in comparison to the other Indian tribes studied and also to the White Americans and Europeans on whom the tests were standardized. Whether or not hereditary factors have played a role in this connection we do not know, but in view of the circumstances of Hopi life, the selective character of the environment, and the millennium-long isolation of the group, it would seem reasonable to assume that, if hereditary factors play a part at all in the determination of group intelligence, they may be operating in this case. On the other hand the Hopi pattern of personality development, in the context of the nature-culture configuration, seems in itself sufficient if not entirely to explain, at least to throw a good deal of light on these findings.

In analyzing thus briefly the relationship between the external environment and the Hopi configuration of culture, it becomes clear that the particular adjustment which the Hopi have developed through the centuries and the differences in adjustment between the two communities studied are the result of the interplay of multitudinous factors—the changing geographic environment, the pressure of outgroups for water and land, the socioreligious organization, the world view and symbol system, and also the group personality structure—each of which has had its effect on the dynamic totality; and it is only in the context of that totality that any one aspect—whether it be, for example, the emphasis on peace, the high Hopi I. Q., the closeness of fit between the expected and the actual patterns of behavior, or the astonishing survival value and resistance to encroachment from without—may be understood. Moreover, we see that between these factors is operating not a simple linear or two-way cause-and-effect relationship but a complex multidimensional one, in which the parts are continuously affecting each other as well as the whole, and the whole in turn continuously acting upon the parts. In fact, while it appears that the physical environment plays a limiting and conditioning rather than an actively determining role in the process, factors of environment, culture and personality are apparently continuously interacting through time to create, maintain and recreate a finely balanced adjustment between the individual, the society and the total environment.

Contemplating the complex and dynamic character of the Hopi nature-culture-personality configuration, we are arrested by its essential consistency. In fact, no detail as revealed in our findings, whether of ecology, social organization, religion, symbolism or personality—fails to fit into the general scheme. And this consistency applies not only to its structure but also to its dynamics. The over all configuration

—in which the intricately structured and definitely bounded whole is made up of many parts and subparts interrelated by means of a system of mutual dependency and nicely balanced through the dynamics of reciprocity— we can trace in greater or less complexity not only in the kinship system, the economy, the secret societies and the pueblo theocracy, but also in the world view, the ceremonial system, the mythology, the language, even in the children's games and the craftwork designs, and finally deep down into the personality structure itself. Our findings substantiate the hypothesis that a direct, functional dependency relationship tends to establish itself with the passage of time between the manifold aspects of culture and its expression in group and individual personality, as well as between these and the natural environment.

To what extent such a relationship is also present in the physiological adjustment of the human organisms in the group we do not know, but on the basis of dietary, health and intelligence data we believe that a study of this aspect of the problem would be highly illuminating, particularly since the Hopi, with their millennium-long experience in an unusually limiting geographic environment and their great resistance to outside influences, provide a rare instance of biological isolation for such study.

The discovery and documentation of a relationship of functional dependency in the Hopi socio-psychological configuration has not only important theoretical implications but far-reaching practical ones as well. Besides increasing our understanding, particularly of the covert aspects of the culture and its expression at the depth psychology level, it also anticipates the development of the power to predict on a scientific basis by means of completing or filling in the details or the gaps in our knowledge of the configuration as we observe it changing in time, on the basis of internal evidence. That is, if we can establish for the group a regular pattern of culture and personality change through time within certain environmental conditions, then we may be able to sharpen this tool for use in anticipating the effects of change within certain conditions in the future. We are, in other words, one step nearer to the goal of effective social planning—for only when our understanding of a culture is so complete as to have prediction value, shall we be able to depend on the scientific method rather than that of trial and error in administration. And until we develop a science of administration which takes into account the psychological as well as the socio-cultural factors in interrelationship with the total environmental setting, we shall have little hope of laying firm foundations for enduring peace.

Moreover, our study, in focusing on the Hopi nature-culture-personality problems as a whole, besides adding by means of objective techniques to our knowledge of Hopi personality, integrates the wealth of data that has already accumulated regarding numerous details of Hopi life and focuses them in a new perspective. In this process our conception of Hopi culture becomes clearer and more objective, and certain aspects which have been misunderstood, neglected or obscured stand out as significant. For instance, we are far more impressed with the remarkable cohesive and centripetal aspects of Hopi organization than with the non-cohesive (splitting) or centrifugal ones so often stressed in the literature. And we find that rather than being loose, amorphous or weak in character, the Hopi's in-group cohesion and control system is remarkably strong and resilient, with the power to hold the group together with a minimum of physical coercion through centuries and also under certain conditions to enable it to segment and reconstitute itself completely. We discover that a distinctive system of internal control, built up in the personality of each individual, integrated with a system of diffuse social sanctions operating within the group, plus pressure from the external environment in the form of droughts, epidemics and alien encroachments, functions effectively to hold the group together with a minimum of physically coercive sanctions, and has been able to do so effectively over many centuries.

In analyzing this arresting system of control, which successfully channelizes practically all the creative energies of the individual toward group responsibility and group ends not by means of physical coercion but by a sort of covert group persuasion, which requires him to develop and exercise a certain free-will-within-the-law and thus to internalize much of the social code in the form of an individual conscience, we discover that we are getting to the very heart of the problem of how a society may function when oriented toward peace rather than war, and how the individuals within such a society may develop personalities which, as we have seen, are not openly aggressive.

Moreover, we become acutely aware of the price of peace which the Hopi pay, a price paid at the level of individual personality in a certain repression of spontaneity and a tendency toward rigidity, which in some individuals may become even somewhat obsessive, and also in the generation of a certain amount of hostility which finds expression in gossip, jealousy and accusations of witchcraft.

The adjustment of the Hopi is, however, obviously an extreme one, growing out of unusually difficult conditions which to a considerable extent are quite beyond their control. Our analysis brings to mind the hypothesis that while a certain amount of external pressure may have a stimulating and creative effect, too much is detrimental to the fullest development of rich and liberated personality.

Nevertheless we conclude that for the Hopi the price paid is well worth the security it gives the individual and that, as far as the group is concerned, is a crucial factor not only in successful survival in spite of an exceedingly vulnerable position in a highly hazardous environment, but also in the development of a culture so rich and rewarding, so exciting and absorbing, that the outside world offers no adequate substitute.

The full significance of these findings in relation to modern world problems will appear only in comparison with similar studies of other groups, as for instance those of the other Indian tribes to be presented in the Indian Education Research series. And a fair, over all evaluation of the method and findings of the research can be made only in the context of its total results, including their practical application to administrative problems, the ultimate goal toward which this study and the forthcoming tribal analyses, are oriented.

APPENDIX

1. FOOTNOTES

Introduction

1. Technically the Hopi environment is classified as semi-arid

2. In the Hopi language the word *hopi* means "peaceful, good, that which leads to happiness and life," while the word *ka'hopi* means "not peaceful, bad, that which leads to death"

3. The Hopi village of Moencopi, located some 40 miles to the northwest, is not included in this study

4. The Hopi speak a Shoshonean language, while the inhabitants of Hano speak both Tewa, a Tanoan language, and Hopi. Moreover, practically all Hopi and Tewa between school age and 45 years and many older ones speak some English. Many Hopi also speak Navaho and some speak Spanish

5. Since descent among the Tewa of Hano, as among the Hopi, is reckoned through the mother's line, one can be seven-eighths Hopi in blood but still be "Tewa." During the last two and a half centuries the Tewans have merged with the Hopi, so that today they do not differ markedly from them from the standpoint of race or breed. (See Fewkes, 1894-a). Apparently they do differ in character structure, but this problem has not been investigated

6. In this work the Oraibi pueblo will be referred to as both "Oraibi" and "Old Oraibi"

7. In this work Kyakotsmovi will be referred to as "New Oraibi"

8. Hargrave, 1932, p. 1

9. This is about 12% of the total number of Hopi children aged 6-18 years. (See United States Office of Indian Affairs, Annual Reports of the Commissioner of Indian Affairs, Statistical Summary, 1942, pp. 16-17)

10. For example, one mentally deficient child was omitted

11. It should be remembered that this is a sociological, rather than a racial distinction

12. For a description of the tests used, see pp. 91 and 92.

13. Dr. Joseph was trained in the administration, scoring, analyzing and interpretation of the Rorschach test by Dr. Bruno Klopfer, Director of the Rorschach Institute

Chapter 1

1. Stephen, 1936, pp. 30, f. p. 38, 62

2. Forty miles farther to the northwest across the Navaho country lies Moencopi, another colony of Oraibi, and the only Hopi village with an abundant water supply

3. See Hack, 1942, p. 58

4. The growing season in Hopi country is about 130-140 days (Hack, 1942, p. 20; Superintendent, Hopi Agency, Correspondence, 1944)

5. At First Mesa, where the old custom is still observed to a certain extent, there is a series of nine ceremonial plantings, each planting day bearing a name. Observations are made by both the Hopi and the Tewa Sun Chiefs but there is no announcement from the housetops. (See Parsons, 1925, pp. 74-75; Stephen, 1936, pp. 389-90, 1038; Beaglehole, E., 1937, p. 38; Eggan, F., 1933, p. 146; Forde, 1931). At Oraibi 12 named points on the eastern horizon mark planting dates. Observations are made by the Water House (Patki) chief, Sun Watcher for the first half of the year. There is no formal announcement or ceremony when a planting point is reached. The Sun Watcher merely tells a few neighbors and the word spreads. Individuals are not compelled to observe these dates in the actual planting of their fields, and here, but still more at New Oraibi, the custom is falling into disuse. (See Titiev, 1938; Eggan, 1933, p. 143)

6. The Second Mesa village of Shipaulovi claims to have an inadequate land base. (See Forde, 1931, p. 367). The Agency Reports indicate that 7,130 acres were cultivated in 1943. (Superintendent, Hopi Agency, Correspondence, 1944)

7. For information concerning attempts to introduce the allotment system to the Hopi tribe, see pp. 29 and 31.

8. Information concerning Hopi seeds and their sources is from Whiting, 1937

9. Hack, 1942, p. 71

10. Ibid., pp. 70-71

11. United States Soil Conservation Service Report, 1937

12. Ibid.

13. This whole garden complex may have been introduced by the Spaniards. (Hack, 1942, p. 37)

14. Whiting, 1936, p. 13

15. Watson, 1942, pp. 72-73

16. Whiting, 1939, p. 52

17. The total net agricultural income of the Hopi for 1941 was estimated at $143,823 (United States Office of Indian Affairs, Annual Extension Division Reports, Hopi Agency, 1942)

18. The following discussion of Hopi flora is based on Whiting, 1939. In 1943, it was estimated that 5,000 pounds of pinyon nuts were gathered by the Hopi. (Superintendent, Hopi

Agency, Correspondence, 1944)

19. For a detailed account of such a journey which took place in 1912, see Titiev, 1937. The Hopi of First Mesa obtained salt from a salt lake south of Zuni, which is the nearest non-Hopi pueblo, located about 200 miles to the southeast. (Beaglehole, E., 1937, pp. 52-56) These journeys for salt have been discontinued as salt is now purchased from the traders

20. See Brew and Hack, 1939. Some of the ancient drifts have been reopened recently and some Hopi are again mining coal in small quantities for household purposes. (Colton, H. S., 1936). Mines are also being worked by the Agency. (Eggan, F., Personal correspondence). Coal is gradually taking the place of wood as fuel because of the difficulty in obtaining wood

21. Chapple and Coon, 1942, pp. 63-64

22. Colton, M. R. F., 1938. In this connection it is interesting to note that an incomplete list of products manufactured in Hopi pueblos, prepared by the Museum of Northern Arizona, contains 58 items

23. Whiting, 1942

24. See Bunzel, 1929, pp. 56-60, Hubert, 1937

25. Ibid.

26. The estimated income of all Hopi weavers for the year 1941-42 was $7,855, of which Walpi and Sichomovi received $545 and the two Oraibis, $515. (Whiting, 1942)

27. Ibid.

28. Whiting's estimate of the Hopi annual trade in arts and crafts for 1941-42 is as follows:

Total sales to Whites......$5,200- 6,800
Total sales to other Indians.. 1,600- 2,200
Total sales and use—Hopi.. 1,500- 2,000
      Grand Total $8,300-11,000

29. Ibid; Parsons, 1939, pp. 34-37

30. Ibid.

31. For an account of Hopi hunting and hunting ritual, see Beaglehole, E., 1936

32. Until recently unlimited grazing was encouraged by the Government. (See United States Office of Indian Affairs, Annual Reports of the Commissioner of Indian Affairs). In 1943 livestock grazing on the Hopi Jurisdiction (624,064 acres of grazing land) was as follows: sheep, 18,917; cattle, 2,288; horses, mules and burros, 1,222; goats, 1,305. (Superintendent, Hopi Agency, Correspondence, 1944)

33. There are about 575 recorded Hopi owners of livestock. This figure is probably less than the actual number of owners

34. Beaglehole, E., 1937, pp. 49-50

35. The Hopi have three cooperative stock associations, established through Government credit: 1. the Hopi Stockmen's Union, organized in 1940, with 21 members, 15 bulls operated cooperatively and 808 individually owned cattle; 2. the Polacca Stockgrowers' Association, organized in 1941, with 11 members, 8 bulls operated collectively and 274 cattle owned individually; 3. the Hopi Tribal Ram Enterprise, organized in 1942, with 274 members owning 20,820 sheep individually and 100 rams cooperatively. (United States Office of

Indian Affairs, Annual Extension Division Reports, Hopi Agency, 1942)

36. United States Office of Indian Affairs, Annual Extension Division Reports, Hopi Agency, 1942

37. The stock reduction estimates (1943), reckoned in sheep units (S. U.), were as follows:

First Mesa

Total Rangeland............240,567 acres
Carrying Capacity .... 10,193 S. U.
Stock .... 12,757 S. U.
Necessary Reduction .... 2,564 S. U.
Livestock Owners............ 192

Second Mesa

Total Rangeland............179,506 acres
Carrying Capacity .... 6,561 S. U.
Stock .... 8,421 S. U.
Necessary Reduction .... 1,860 S. U.
Livestock Owners........... 175

Third Mesa

Total Rangeland ....196,781 acres
Carrying Capacity .... 6,139 S. U.
Stock .... 10,685 S. U.
Necessary Reduction .... 4,546 S. U.
Livestock Owners........... 177

Total

Total Rangeland ....616,854 acres
Carrying Capacity .... 22,893 S. U.
Stock .... 31,863 S. U.
Necessary Reduction .... 8,970 S. U.
Livestock Owners............ 544

Chapter 2

1. Et seq., from Colton and Baxter, 1932; Hargrave, 1931-a; 1931-b; 1932; 1935

2. Hargrave, 1937, p. 6; Parsons, 1939, p. 861; Brew, 1939

3. Et seq., from Bartlett, 1934; Fewkes, 1894-b, pp. 394-96; Brew, 1939

4. Et seq., from Parsons, 1939, pp. 18-19 1064-65; Brew, 1939

5. The Hopi say that Shipaulovi was founded by Shungopovians as a safeguard for ritual tradition in case the Spaniards should destroy Shungopovi

6. Et seq., from Bartlett, 1934; Hargrave, 1931-a; 1931-b

7. The Tewans of Hano, originally refugees from Spanish oppression, are traditionally considered to be the guardians of the Hopi of First Mesa. (See United States Office of Indian Affairs, Indian Reorganization File 9603 C 1936-057)

8. This drought occurred in 1777-79

9. About 30 families are reported to have left Hopiland at this time. (Bartlett, 1934, p. 59) and the population was further reduced by starvation and disease (Parsons, 1939, f. p. 863). The estimated Hopi population for 1780 (798) is about 80% less than that of 1775 (7494). See Donaldson, 1893, p. 15

10. Donaldson, 1893, p. 1

11. Data in this and the two subsequent paragraphs are taken from Bartlett, 1937; Donaldson, 1893

12. The Hopi population of 1861, estimated by the United States Indian Agent, Ward,

was 2500, about 60% less than that of 1853, prior to the smallpox epidemic, estimated by Leroux (See Donaldson, 1893, pp. 14-15, 35)

13. The pueblo of Sichomovi, abandoned on account of the smallpox epidemic, was resettled, partially at least, by Zuni people, according to both Hopi and Zuni tradition. (Fewkes, 1903, p. 26; Hargrave, 1931-a, p.6)

14. The first contact of the Hopi with Americans (1834) was when a party of fur trappers plundered their gardens and killed 15 to 20 persons. With this exception early contacts were peaceful. The United States Government attempted to aid the Hopi by sending supplies to them (1864-65), but was not able to control the Navaho raids for some years. (Bartlett, 1937)

15. Parsons, 1939, p. 862

16. Et seq., from Cushing, Fewkes, Parsons, 1922; Bartlett, 1937; Donaldson, 1893; Titiev, 1944, chap. 6

17. This was called the Moqui School. Buildings formerly used as a trading post were purchased from T. V. Keams. The School had a capacity of about 50 children. By June 1890, the enrollment was 45, and the staff consisted of eight Whites and five Indians at a cost per child of $36.16 yearly. The session lasted ten months. Twenty-five acres of land were allotted to the school. (Donaldson, 1893, p. 36). Fewkes gives 1889 as the date of the founding of the school. (Cushing, Fewkes, Parsons, 1922, p. 273)

18. Attempts to introduce the allotment system on the Hopi Reservation, made between 1892 and 1910, were abandoned in 1911. Some allotments, however, were made on the public domain in the vicinity of Moencopi between 1899 and 1905

19. Et seq., from Cushing, Fewkes, Parsons, 1922, pp. 268-83

20. For a description of the architecture of Oraibi and First Mesa in 1887, see Mindeleff, 1891, pp. 61-66, 76-77

21. According to the Indian Bureau Census (1890), the "Moqui" pueblos had a population of 2200 (United States Office of Indian Affairs, Annual Reports of the Commissioner of Indian Affairs, 1891)

22. For further information concerning the hostility of Oraibi, not only to Whites but also to other Hopi pueblos, see Titiev, 1944, chap. 6

23. Fewkes, 1894-a; 1894-b. The total population of Walpi-Sichomovi was 440

24. The Mennonite mission was started by the Rev. H. R. Voth who in 1901 built a church (destroyed by lightning in 1942), the ruins of which may be seen at Oraibi. Voth recorded many Hopi traditions and ceremonies. The Rev. C. P. Coe organized the Baptist mission which was expanded to Second Mesa almost immediately. (Board of Indian Commissioners, Report, 1927, p. 29). Parsons and Titiev report that a Mennonite mission was established at Oraibi between 1870 and 1880. (Parsons, 1939, p. 862; Titiev, 1944, chap. 6.)

25. The Polacca Day School had a capacity for 50 pupils, the Toreva School for 75, and the Oraibi School for 160. The Chimopovy (Shungopovi) Day School was established in 1910 and the Bacabi (Bakabi) Day School in 1912, and was changed to the Hotevilla-Bacabi School in 1916. (See United States Office of Indian Affairs, Annual Reports of the Commissioner of Indian Affairs; Education Division Reports)

26. These were distributed free of charge at first, but later (1904-1917) put on a work-pay basis (Watson and Pijoan, 1943, p. 27)

27. At this time the Reservation was quarantined and measures were taken by the Government to disinfect it

28. Cushing reported that in 1883 Oraibi was already divided into a conservative and a progressive faction and at this time the conservatives were the stronger (Cushing, Fewkes, Parsons, 1922, pp. 258-268) and Parsons wrote that as early as 1700 there were two parties in the pueblo, "a conciliatory one... and a stiff-necked one..." (Parsons, 1939, f. p. 862)

29. For a detailed account of the split of Oraibi, see Titiev, 1944, chap. 6. Titiev reports that at the time of the "push" the "Friendlies" line-up, augmented by relatives from Moencopi, numbered 324, while the "Hostiles" numbered 298

30. United States Office of Indian Affairs, Annual Reports of the Commissioner of Indian Affairs, 1907, pp. 84-89

31. The following statistics represent the total population of the Hopi tribe according to official censuses and estimates. (Statistics for the years 1890-1933 are from the United States Office of Indian Affairs, Annual Reports of the Commissioner of Indian Affairs; for the years 1940 and 1943 from the United States Office of Indian Affairs, Annual Reports of the Commissioner of Indian Affairs, Statistical Summaries):

1890	2200
1900	2182
1910	2112
1920	2515
1930	2842
1933	2920
1940	3444
1943	3558

32. The excess of males over females in Hopiland apparently increases with age, and is most apparent among the adults. (See also Beaglehole, P., 1935, p. 41)

33. It is noteworthy that the unbreakable resistance of the Third Mesa group to allotment finally in 1911 persuaded the authorities to desist. In the years 1907-1911, it was the announced purpose of the Government to allot all the reservations of the Southwest. The Hopi's resistance appears to have had the historical effect of saving the other Pueblos and the Navaho, the Mescalero, White River and San Carlos Apache, and the Papago from allotment and its disastrous consequences

34. The Hopi Constitution and By-laws were drawn up by a committee of Hopi leaders and Indian Service personnel with legal and anthropological training. One of the latter spent three months in the field working on this problem. In working out the Constitution the advice of anthropologists who had specialized

in Hopi culture was sought and given, but was not accepted

35. The Hopi High School was established at New Oraibi in 1939. Although school attendance is officially non-obligatory, the Hopi leaders themselves urge the people to send their children to school and practically all Hopi children attend school for a few years at least. The present enrollment of Hopi Reservation Schools (1944) totals 768, of which 112 at Keams Canyon are Navaho children. It is distributed as follows:

Keams Canyon Boarding School	152
Polacca Day School	112
Toreva Day School	80
Shungopovi Day School	50
Hopi High School	186
Hotevilla Day School	93
Moencopi Day School	95
Total	768

In addition there are approximately 80 Hopi students in non-reservation Indian Schools and approximately 40 in public schools. (Superintendent, Hopi Agency, Correspondence, 1944)

36. The hospital now has 38 beds. (United States Office of Indian Affairs, Annual Reports of the Commissioner of Indian Affairs, Statistical Summary, 1942, p. 23)

37. This grazing unit, called Land Management Unit 6, is one of 18 such units into which the Navaho and Hopi Reservations have been divided for purposes of soil conservation and range control

38. At the present time there are 16 licensed traders on the Hopi Jurisdiction. Three are operated by White and 13 by Hopi traders. The volume of business is as follows: less than $500 per year, four traders; $500-$3000 per year, five traders; $3000 per year, seven traders. The trade is about 50% with Hopi and 50% with Navaho. (Superintendent, Hopi Agency, Correspondence, 1944)

39. There are now six mission churches for Hopi located on the Hopi Jurisdiction: three Baptist missions, (Polacca, Second Mesa, Keams Canyon); two Mennonite missions, (New Oraibi, Bakabi); and an independent mission (Sichomovi) established by a native missionary, who also conducts a Navaho mission at Tolahogan Canyon. There is a Catholic mission at Keams Canyon, but it is devoted entirely to the Navaho of the area. Since they began their work over 50 years ago, the Protestant missionaries have succeeded in converting only a very small percentage of the tribe. It is estimated that there are about 30 converts, mostly to the Baptist church. (Superintendent, Hopi Agency, Correspondence, 1944)

40. Also at Moencopi, especially in the upper section of the village

41. Exclusive of Alaska, which has a native population of 32,750. Of these 15,716 are Eskimo; 11,385, Indian; 5,649, Aleut

Chapter 3

1. In attempting, on the basis of the literature, to present in this and subsequent chapters thus briefly an over all view of the complex Hopi social structure and religion, many details of which are not yet completely understood, we are aware of the danger of erring, especially on the side of oversimplification. If, however, we succeed in giving a clear picture of the whole within the limits of the available data and space, we shall have attained our object. The following summary is based on Eggan, F., 1933, 1936; Titiev, 1944; Parsons, 1925, 1939; Lowie, 1929

2. By the term "empathy" we mean that quality of being able to put one's self in the place of another and to identify with him to the extent that one is able to begin, at least, to see the world and its values as he sees it

3. Titiev, 1944, chap. 4

4. See Ibid.; Eggan, F., 1933, pp. 18 et seq., 96 et seq.

5. See p. 20

6. Springs, gardens and farm land are thought of as belonging to the clan, but are usually associated through usufruct with the households, except at the Third Mesa where land belongs to the user irrespective of clan affiliations. (Forde, 1931; Eggan, F., 1933)

7. Ibid., p. 172

8. Colton, H. S., 1934, p. 23; Watson, 1942

9. See Parsons, 1921, p. 98

10. The phratry groups are ideally tribe-wide, but not all phratries are found in each village or on each mesa. For example, on Third Mesa (the Oraibi group prior to the split) there are nine phratries which include 29 clans, exclusive of those that are extinct. (See Titiev, 1944, chap. 4). At Walpi-Sichomovi, on the other hand, there are ten phratries (which Parsons called "clans"). The number of living clans in these phratries is not entirely clear. (Parsons, 1925, p. 10; 1939; Stephen, 1936, pp. XXXI, 1068-1073)

11. For a complete list of Hopi kinship terms, see Stephen, 1936, pp. 1043-1045

12. Parallel-cousins are cousins who belong to the same clan. The Hopi, as well as many other tribes with a similar classificatory kinship system, distinguish parallel-cousins from cross-cousins, that is, cousins who belong to different clans

13. For a complete description of Hopi kinship, see Eggan, F., 1936; Titiev, 1944

14. See Parsons, 1936, pp. 229-231; 1939, p. 1153; Kroeber, 1928. This mother-house-fetish complex is also considered to provide a clue to the historic development of Hopi society. For the importance of the "house" concept in the Hopi world view see p. 39

Chapter 4

1. The Hopi world view, never explicitly stated, is part of the covert culture which is expressed by implication in the ceremonial and the mythology. In the following brief and obviously incomplete exposition we have attempted to give a simplified version of our interpretation of it, as well as some of its explicit expressions in behavior patterns, on the basis of the literature; especially, Eggan, F., 1933;

Fewkes, 1903; Kennard, 1937; Parsons, 1925, 1939; Stephen, 1936; Titiev, 1944; Voth, 1905; Whorf, 1940, 1941

2. Note the importance of "willing" (na'-wakna) in ceremonial life (Kennard, 1937, pp. 492-496)

3. An investigation of the language from this point of view would doubtless be illuminating. The system of classification of the Zuni is apparently clearer than, and similar to, that of the Hopi. (See Durkheim and Mauss, 1903, pp. 34-44)

4. Eggan, F., 1933, pp. 107-120

5. The following myth is taken from Voth, 1905, pp. 36-38

6. The Hopi add two more directions, "above" and "below," to the four cardinal points we distinguish.

7. See Eggan, F., 1933, pp. 150-153

8. A study of Hopi ceremonial from this point of view would undoubtedly throw light on the world view and other covert aspects of the culture

9. See Parsons, 1925, f. p. 37

10. Colton in Whiting, 1939, p. 7

11. Note the expression of this concept in the "road line" of the pottery design, p. 22

12. Viewed from another angle, the house, the kiva and the Underworld apparently symbolize the womb

13. See Parsons, 1939, vol. 1, pp. 1-3

14. See Voth, 1905, p. 1

15. The following description of the Hopi sense of time is based on Whorf, 1936, 1940, 1941

16. Ibid., 1936, p. 131

17. Ibid., 1941, p. 79

18. Ibid., 1941, p. 84. While the Hopi do not objectify time and give it dimensions in space (in fact, they do not use spatial terms except actually to express objective, spatial concepts) they do have an extraordinarily rich vocabulary to express durations, intensities and tendencies with exactitude. Whereas such concepts are expressed by us mainly through the use of metaphors involving spatial extension—that is, since we have very few non-metaphorical terms in this field like "early, late, soon, lasting, intense," we express duration by "long, short, great," etc., intensity by "large, great, much, heavy," etc., tendency by "more, increase, grow," etc.—the Hopi have an abundant means of expressing duration, intensity and tendency as such, without the use of analogies for imaginary space, and hence they are able to make manifold fine distinctions in this field, quite impossible through the medium of our language

19. Ibid.

20. See Kennard, 1937, p. 492

21. See Parsons, 1939

22. See Titiev, 1943; Beaglehole, E. and P., 1935, pp. 5-11; Parsons, 1939, pp. 62-63

23. Ibid., p. 549. It is interesting to note that the malevolent aspects of the Spider Woman are stressed on Third Mesa. (Eggan, F., Personal communication)

24. Except the Snake-Antelope and Flute ceremonies which are performed on alternate years in some villages

25. For details of the Hopi Calendar, see Stephen, 1936, app. 1; Eggan, F., 1933, pp. 143-149; Titiev, 1944, app.

26. For a list of the kachinas of First Mesa, see Stephen, 1936, pp. 1137-1152

27. Each main ceremony is held twice yearly, once in a major and once in a minor form. When the major form of a ceremony is being held in the Upperworld, a corresponding minor rite is held by the spirits of the Underworld. During the other half of the year the abbreviated ceremony is held in the Upperworld. It is reciprocated by the major form of that ceremony then being held in the Underworld. For instance, in regard to the Snake Dance, a minor ceremony is held for one night in January which is supposed to correspond to the main Snake Dance in the Underworld. The main 17-day Snake Dance ceremony of the Hopi is held in August, and at this time it is believed that a correlative minor ceremony is being held in the Underworld. (Note the emphasis on acts of a preparatory nature in this arrangement)

28. See Titiev, 1944, chap. 8

29. There are five kivas in Walpi, two in Sichomovi, and 14 in Oraibi. (Parsons, 1925, p. 12; 1939, p. 865; Eggan, F., 1933, pp. 156-157)

30. For detailed accounts of the ceremonies, see Stephen, 1935

31. See Lowie, 1925

32. See p. 46

33. See also Parsons, 1925 p. 17, f. p. 20

Chapter 5

1. Titiev, 1944, chap. 8

2. Thus the Marau Society at Walpi lapsed with the conversion of its chief priestess in 1903, and the Horn Society at Oraibi became defunct when under missionary influence its chief priest burned the Society's ceremonial paraphernalia in 1922

3. See Stephen, 1936, p. XXXVIII

4. Authorities differ as to the exact membership of the kiva group. (See Titiev, 1944, Chap. 8; Eggan, F., 1933, pp. 154-159; Parsons, 1925, p. 12; 1939, p. 865)

5. See Ibid. 1939, pp. 866-870

6. Ibid., p. 869

7. See Titiev, 1944, chap. 8

8. There are no curing societies at Oraibi at present, according to Eggan, F., 1933, p. 137

9. See Titiev, 1944 chap. 11. This council is not held at New Oraibi or Upper Moencopi and is held irregularly at Oraibi

10. See Titiev, 1944, chap. 5; Eggan, F., 1933, pp. 162-168; Parsons, 1925, f. p. 26; 1939, p. 864

11. This custom is no longer observed at Oraibi

12. Other village officials have similar insignia

13. See Titiev, 1944, chap. 5; Sutton; Cushing, Fewkes, Parsons, 1922. The Hotevilla village chief has a similar stone which he has exhibited to Indian Bureau officials on occasion. (United States Office of Indian Affairs, Indian Reorganization File 9603, 1936-066)

14. Titiev, 1944, chap. 5

15. See especially Eggan, D., 1943; Titiev, 1944, chap. 5. This petty strife is more conspicuous among the women than the men

16. Cushing, Fewkes, Parsons, 1922, p. 283

17. It is interesting to note in this connection, however, that both Sikyatki and Awatobi are considered by some scholars to have been Keresan rather than Hopi in language and culture. (Parsons, 1936-a; Hargrave, 1937, p. 66)

18. See Titiev, app. 8, for a report of such a meeting

19. These units are as follows: .The two ceremonial units on First Mesa (namely, Walpi-Sichomovi and Hano) form with Polacca one voting district; the three ceremonial units on Second Mesa (namely, Shungopovi, Shipaulovi and Mishongnovi) form three corresponding voting districts; and the three ceremonial units of Third Mesa (namely, Oraibi-Lower-Moencopi, Hotevilla and Bakabi) form with New Oraibi and Upper Moencopi, five voting districts, namely, Oraibi, Hotevilla, Bakabi, New Oraibi, Upper Moencopi and Lower Moencopi. (La Farge, 1936)

20. Ibid.

Chapter 6

1. Eggan, F., 1933, p. 66; see also Parsons, 1939, pp. 17-18

2. For a discussion of "ideal patterns of behavior," see Kluckhohn, C., 1941, 1943

3. See p. 40

4. See Eggan, F., 1933, p. 186

5. See Parsons, 1939, p. 45; Beaglehole, E. and P., 1935, p. 29; United States Office of Indian Affairs, Indian Reorganization File 9603-A, 1936

6. Dennis, 1940-b, p. 29

7. Barrett, 1937, p. 563

8. Beaglehole, E. and P., 1935, p. 31

9. This custom is observed in all Hopi villages with the exception of New Oraibi and Upper Moencopi where it has been abandoned in some families. For a description of Hopi cradling customs, see Dennis and Dennis, 1940; Beaglehole, E. and P., 1935, p. 32

10. First Mesa cradles are usually made of wicker, a type which was apparently formerly used on all the Hopi mesas

11. See Leighton and Kluckhohn, Part II, for the effects of cradling on the Navaho child

12. Dennis, 1940-a; Dennis and Dennis, 1940

13. Beaglehole, E. and P., 1935. p, 5

14. Dennis, 1940-b, p. 34

15. Ibid., p. 84

16. Beaglehole, E and P., 1935, p. 40

17. See Dennis, 1940-b, pp. 179-185

18. See Parsons, 1921; Fewkes, 1903, pls. X, XII, XIII; Earle and Kennard, 1938, pls. X, XI

19. See Birdwhistell, pp. 8, 19

20. Dennis, 1940-b, pp. 170-185

21. See Birdwhistell, p. 25

22. Beaglehole, E. and P., 1935, p. 65

23. These factor probably account to a certain extent for the expectancy that women will be "meaner" and more prone to gossip than men. They also throw light on the recent upsurgence of creativity among the women of

First Mesa with the introduction of what to them was a new and highly stimulating art medium

24. Simmons, 1942, pp. 47-50

25. See p. 41

26. Sutton

27. Et seq., Dennis, 1940-b, pp. 48-52; Beaglehole, E. and P., 1935, p. 43

28. Et seq., Parsons, 1925, f. p. 60; 1939, p. 48

29. Formerly the first initiation ceremony took place at about the age of 10 to 12 years. (Eggan, F., 1933, p. 64; Titiev, 1944, chap. 2)

Chapter 7

1. The godfather and aunt are selected from a clan which is not affiliated with either the child's phratry or that of his father. (Titiev, 1944, chap. 1)

2. Apparently a boy may also join any society whose chief priest or priestess belongs to his own clan. (Eggan, F., 1933, p. 68)

3. For details of the whipping rite, see Eggan, F., 1933; Titiev, 1944, chap. 9

4. Eggan, F., 1933, p. 67

5. Titiev states that the girl's mother decides which of the societies her daughter is to join. (Titiev, 1944, chap. 2)

6. Eggan, F., 1933, p. 68

7. Beaglehole, E., 1936, pp. 14-15; Parsons, 1925, p. 24

8. Parsons, 1925, p. 16

9. "A strong man always gets his wish and is able to set aside trouble and concentrate upon following his road in life to the end." (Kennard, 1937, p. 493)

10. This point is clarified by the following advice from a Hopi father to his son:

"My child, tomorrow morning you will go for a bath. Just as the sun comes out you will pray (na'wakna) that your life shall be good. Then the sun will come out and give you good life. And you shall live happily. Here you happily will work for me and I'll eat those good things. With them I will grow strong. I shall continue to live well, I won't be sick. Going on (my road) I shall always be happy. And these people having something to live by will think (only) of continuing their good lives. And having made the good life for them, don't ever be mean (angry). Whoever is not mean will live long. Whoever is mean will surely die. Therefore anyone who is happy always sings. And so go take your bath. If you do that you will be strong, and your mothers and fathers (clouds, kachinas, the dead) will be happy when you work for them. They will be parents to your plants. One who lives thinking this way has a peaceful (hopi) life and is always happy." (Kennard, 1937, p. 493)

11. Dennis, 1940-b, p. 49

12. Ibid., pp. 59-60

13. Ibid., p. 53

14. Ibid.

15. Ibid., p. 64

16. Ibid., p. 58

17. See Asch

18. Watson and Pijoan, 1943, p. 33

19. See Birdwhistell, pp. 40-43

20. Dennis, 1940-b, p. 84
21. Beaglehole, E. and P., 1935, p. 44
22. Dennis, 1940-b, pp. 84-85
23. Hopi girls who go to boarding school have another brief period of freedom, at least from home duties, somewhat comparable though more restrained than the earlier one, before they marry and settle down to the responsibilities and privileges of a Hopi woman who has attained full adult status
24. See p. 22
25. Dennis, 1940-b, p. 85
26. The menses are not considered to be dangerous or unclean
27. Et seq., Beaglehole, E. and P., 1935; p. 45; Stephen, 1936, pp. XXVIII, 139-143; Parsons, 1939, f. p. 58. The girls' adolescent rite is apparently no longer observed on Second Mesa (Nequatewa and Colton, 1933, p. 42) and on Third Mesa (Titiev, 1944, chap. 2, part III)
28. Titiev, 1944, chaps. 3, 10
29. The rules of exogamy in regard to ego's father's phratry and even his clan are less rigidly enforced than those in regard to ego's own clan and phratry. (See Titiev, 1944, chap. 3)
30. Titiev, 1944, chap. 3; Beaglehole, E. and P., 1935, p. 62
31. See Beaglehole, P., 1935
32. Beaglehole, E. and P., 1935, p. 46
33. Titiev, chap. 3

Chapter 8

1. The rite has not been held at Old Oraibi, however, since 1912. (Titiev, 1944, chap. 10)
2. For descriptions of the tribal initiation, see Ibid., Stephen, 1936, pp. 957-992; Parsons, 1939, pp. 866
3. Parsons, 1933, p. 51; Titiev, 1944, chap. 10
4. Titiev, 1937, p. 244
5. Et seq., Beaglehole, E. and P., 1935, pp. 23-24. The warrior initiation was "like a woman having a baby," according to one informant
6. See Titiev, 1944, chap. 3; Beaglehole, P., 1935, p. 50
7. See Titiev, 1944, chap. 3
8. See p. 60
9. Beaglehole, P., 1935, p. 47; Parsons, 1925, pp. 21-22
10. See Titiev, 1944, chap. 3; Parsons, 1925, pp. 34, 71
11. See Titiev, 1944, chap. 2
12. Ibid., chap. 3
13. See Ibid., chap. 2
14. Beaglehole, P., 1935, pp. 45-46
15. The wife helps in building the house and is considered to be the owner. Upon her death it is inherited by her female heirs. (Titiev, 1944, chap. 2)
16. It is obvious that conversion to Christianity holds more attractions for a Hopi woman than for a Hopi man
17. See Beaglehole, P., 1935, pp. 45-46
18. Eggan, F., Personal communication
19. As has been noted, these two villages are New Oraibi and Upper Moencopi

20. Eggan, F., 1933, p. 66
21. It is interesting to note in this connection that suicide is very rare among Hopi. (Parsons, 1925, p. 75; Titiev, chap. 2; Beaglehole, E. and P., 1935, p. 18)
22. Kennard, 1937, p. 494
23. The paternal aunt attends the corpse only on First and Second Mesas. (Beaglehole, E. and P., 1935, p. 11)
24. Eggan, F., 1933, pp. 83-84

Chapter 9

1. For obvious reasons, pseudonyms have been used in these portraits

Chapter 11

1. All tests were administered by employees of the Indian Service: tests II to VI by teachers; test I by the Reservation Principal, Hopi Agency, and the Principal of Polacca Day School, trained in the administration of the Grace Arthur test; tests VII and VIII by the author of this chapter (A. J.)
2. See Arthur, 1933
3. See Goodenough, 1926
4. This test was suggested by Kilton R. Stewart who devised it for work with Negritos and other non-literate groups
5. See Bavelas, 1942
6. See Piaget, 1929; Lerner, 1937; Russell and Dennis, 1939; Dennis, 1943
7. See Mordy; Rannells. This test was suggested to us by Dr. Trude Schmidl-Waehner
8. See Murray, 1943; Henry, 1944-b
9. See Klopfer and Kelly, 1942

Chapter 12

1. Orr and Gilks, Medical Research Council, Special Report No. 155, London, 1931. Cited from Best and Taylor, 1940
2. Taken from Watson and Pijoan, 1943
3. Ibid.
4. We wish to point out again that under "vitamin deficiencies," listed cases comprehend only those which showed mild symptoms of deficiency, as for instance in vitamin B deficiency skin lesions, in vitamin C deficiency changes in the gums, in vitamin D deficiency more or less slight rosary formation. No manifest cases of advanced scurvy, pellagra, or of crippling and disfiguring bone changes in rickets were found. Except for one case of suspicious nicotinic acid deficiency, vitamin B deficiency denotes here riboflavin deficiency. Under vitamin D deficiency dental changes alone have not been listed as symptomatic. The absence of biochemical examinations and the restriction in time, which forbade the search for possible occurrence of hemeralopia (night-blindness), are the reasons why vitamin A deficiency has not been listed at all. This does not mean that it may not be present among Hopi children, but certain existing disturbances of the eyes and a susceptibility to infections could not justify the diagnosis
5. Eggan, F., Personal communication

Chapter 13

1. See p. 91
2. For detailed data on the two intelligence tests and the exact results obtained from the other tribes, see Havighurst and Hilkevitch, 1944; Havighurst, Korol and Pratt

Chapter 14

1. For details, see Havighurst, Comparison of American Indian Children and White Children by Means of the Emotional Response Test
2. Three hundred sixty-eight school children from an industrial Midwestern town were given the Emotional Response test
3. See Asch
4. See Eggan, D.

Chapter 15

1. See Havighurst, The Moral Ideology of Indian Children of the Southwest and Sioux
2. See Piaget
3. For details on the test and exact data, see Havighurst, Belief in Immanent Justice and Animism among Indian Children of the Southwest and Sioux

Chapter 16

1. For a brief description of the theory of projective techniques, see Frank, 1939

2. Detailed results of the Rorschach test will be published elsewhere. See also Joseph, 1943
3. Henry, 1944-a

Chapter 17

1. The relatively few evidences of sexual anxiety found in this age group are not directly comparable with similar findings in White children
2. See pp. 59; also, Dennis, W., 1940-b
3. Ibid.
4. E. W. Rannells, in an analysis of the free drawings which we obtained from the Oraibi children, came independently to the conclusion that "the drawings reveal a sharp division of interest between Hopi boys and girls, i. e., an early acceptance of sex roles." (Rannells, p. 12)

Chapter 19

1. See Mordy
2. See also Rannells, p. 11, "The peak of realism . . . is reached very early, at the ages of 12-14, but already at 12 the boys are drawing *kachinas* and the transition to abstract line is beginning"

2. BIBLIOGRAPHY

Arthur, M. G.
   1933 A Point Scale of Performance Tests, 2
         vols., New York
Asch, S. T.
         Personality Development of Hopi Chil-
         dren (ms)
Barrett, S. A.
   1937 An Observation on Hopi Child Burial,
         AA, n.s., vol. 39, pp. 562-4
Bartlett, K.
   1934 Spanish Contacts with the Hopi,
         MNMNA, vol. 6, pp. 55-9
   1937 Hopi History, II: The Navajo Wars,
         MNMNA, vol. 8, pp. 33-7
Bavelas, A.
   1942 A Method of Investigating Individual
         and Group Ideology, Sociometry, vol.
         5, pp. 371-77
Beaglehole, E.
   1936 Hopi Hunting and Hunting Ritual,
         YUPA, vol. 4, pp. 1-26
   1937 Notes on Hopi Economic Life, YUPA,
         vol. 15, pp. 1-88
Beaglehole, E. and P.
   1935 Hopi of the Second Mesa, MAAA, vol.
         44, pp. 1-65
Beaglehole, P.
   1935 Census Data from Two Hopi Villages,
         AA, n.s., vol. 37, pp. 41-54
Best and Taylor
   1940 Physiological Basis of Medical Prac-
         tice, Baltimore
Birdwhistell, R.
   1944 The Hopi Life Cycle (ms) Indian Edu-
         cation Research, Committee on Hu-
         man Development, University of Chi-
         cago
Board of Indian Commissioners
   1927 Christian Missions among the Ameri-
         can Indians, (mimeographed pamphlet)
         Bull. 280, United States Department
         of the Interior
Brew, J. O.
   1939 Preliminary Report of the Peabody
         Museum Awatovi Expedition of 1937,
         American Antiquity, vol. 5, pp. 103-15
Brew, J. O. and Hack, J. T.
   1939 Prehistoric Use of Coal by Indians of
         Northern Arizona, Plateau, vol. 12,
         no. 1
Bunzel, R. L.
   1929 The Pueblo Potter, CUCA, vol. 8,
         pp. 1-134
Chapple, E. D. and Coon, C. S.
   1942 Principles of Anthropology, New York

Colton, H. S.
   1934 A Brief Survey of Hopi Common Law,
         MNMNA, vol. 7, pp. 21-4
   1936 Hopi Coal Mines, MNMNA, vol. 8,
         pp. 59-61
Colton, H. S. and Baxter, F. C.
   1932 Days in the Painted Desert and the
         San Francisco Mountains, Northern
         Arizona Society of Science and Art,
         Bull. 2, Flagstaff
Colton, M. R. F.
   1938 The Arts and Crafts of the Hopi In-
         dians, MNMNA, vol. 11, pp. 1-24
Cushing, F. H., Fewkes, J. W., and Parsons,
   E. C.
   1922 Contributions to Hopi History, AA,
         n.s., vol. 24, pp. 253-98
Dennis, W.
   1940-a Does Culture Appreciably Affect Pat-
         terns of Infant Behavior? Journal of
         Social Psychology, vol. 12, pp. 305-17
   1940-b The Hopi Child, New York
   1943 Animism and Related Tendencies in
         Hopi Children, JASP, vol. 38, pp.
         21-36
Dennis, W. and Dennis, M. G.
   1940 Pueblo Cradles and Cradling Customs,
         AA, vol, 42, pp. 107-15
   1940 The Effect of Cradling Practices upon
         the Onset of Walking in Hopi Children,
         JGP, vol. 56, pp. 77-86
Donaldson, T.
   1893 Moqui Indians of Arizona and Pueblo
         Indians of New Mexico, United States
         Census Office, Eleventh Census, Extra
         Census Bulletin, Washington, pp.
         1-136
Durkheim, E. and Mauss, M.
   1903 De Quelques Formes Primitives de
         Classification, L'Année Sociologique,
         1901-02, pp. 1-72
Earle, E. and Kennard, E. A.
   1938 Hopi Kachinas, New York
Eggan, D.
   1943 The General Problem of Hopi Ad-
         justment, AA, n.s., vol. 45, pp. 357-74
Eggan, F.
   1933 Social Organization of the Western
         Pueblos (ms), Thesis, University of
         Chicago.
   1936 The Kinship System of the Hopi In-
         dians, Chicago
Fewkes, J. W.
   1894-a The Kinship of a Tanoan-speaking
         Community in Tusayan, AA, vol. 7,
         pp. 162-67

1894-b The Kinship of the Tusayan Villagers, AA, vol. 7, pp. 394-417

1903 Hopi Katchinas, ARBAE, vol. 21, pp. 3-126

Forde, C. D.
1931 Hopi Agriculture and Land Ownership, Journal of the Anthropological Institute of Great Britain and Ireland, vol. 61, pp. 357-405

Frank, L. K.
1939 Projective Techniques for the Study of Personality, Journal of Psychology, vol. 8, pp. 389-413

Goodenough, F. L.
1926 Measurements of Intelligence by Drawings, New York

Hack, J. T.
1942 The Changing Physical Environment of the Hopi Indians, Cambridge

Hargrave, L. L.
1931-a First Mesa, MNMNA, vol. 3, pp. 1-4
1931-b Shungopovi, MNMNA, vol. 2, pp. 1-4
1932 Oraibi, MNMNA, vol. 4, no. 7, pp. 1-8
1935 The Jeddito Valley and the First Pueblo Towns in Arizona to be Visited by Europeans, MNMNA, vol. 8, pp. 17-32
1937 Sikyatki, MNMNA, vol. 9, pp. 63-66

Havighurst, R. J.
Belief in Immanent Justice and Animism among Indian Children of the Southwest and Sioux, Indian Education Research, Committee on Human Development, University of Chicago (in preparation)
Comparison of American Indian Children and White Children by Means of the Emotional Response Test, Indian Education Research, Committee on Human Development, University of Chicago (in preparation)
The Comparison of Indian Children and White Children by Means of the Moral Ideology Test, Indian Education Research, Committee on Human Development, University of Chicago (in preparation)

Havighurst, R. J. and Hilkevitch, R. R.
1944 The Intelligence of Indian Children as Measured by a Performance Scale, JASP, (in press)

Havighurst, R. J., Korol, M. and Pratt, I. E.
The Performance of Indian Children on the Draw-a-Man Test, Indian Education Research, Committee on Human Development, University of Chicago (in preparation)

Henry, W. E.
1944-a Hopi Thematic Apperception Cultural Analysis (ms), Indian Education Research, Committee on Human Development, University of Chicago
1944-b The Use of the Thematic Apperception Technique in the Study of Personality-Culture Relations, Thesis, University of Chicago

Hubert, V.
1937 An Introduction to Hopi Pottery Design, MNMNA, vol. 10, no. 1, pp. 1-4

Joseph, A.
1943 First Report of the Rorschach Study— Hopi, (ms) Indian Education Research. Committee on Human Development, University of Chicago

Kennard, E. A.
1937 Hopi Reactions to Death, AA, n.s., vol. 39, pp. 491-6

Klopfer, B. and Kelley, D. McG.
1942 The Rorschach Technique, New York

Kluckhohn, C.
1941 Patterning as Exemplified in Navaho Culture, in Language, Culture and Personality, Menasha, pp. 109-30
1943 Covert Culture and Administrative Problems, AA, vol. 45, pp. 213-27

Kroeber, A. L.
1928 Native Culture of the Southwest, University of California Publications in American Archaeology and Ethnology, vol. 23, pp. 375-98

La Farge, O.
1936 Notes for Hopi Administrators (ms), United States Office of Indian Affairs

Leighton, D. C. and Kluckhohn, C.
1944 The People and Their Children, Monograph, Indian Education Research Series (in preparation)

Lerner, E.
1937 Constraint Areas and the Moral Judgment of Children, Kenosha

Lowie, R. H.
1925 A Woman's Ceremony among the Hopi, Natural History, vol. 25, pp. 178-84
1929 Hopi Kinship, Anthropological Papers of the American Museum of Natural History, vol. 30, pp. 361-88

Mindeleff, V.
1891 A Study of Pueblo Architecture, Tusayan and Cibola, ARBAE, vol. 8, pp. 13-234

Mordy, B.
1944 Content Analysis of Indian Children's Drawings: A Method for Comparing Culture and Degree of Material Acculturation (ms), Indian Education Research, Committee on Human Development, University of Chicago

Murray, H. A.
1943 Thematic Apperception Test Manual, Cambridge

Nequatewa, E. and Colton, M. R. F.
1933 Hopi Courtship and Marriage, MNMNA, vol. 5, pp. 41-54

Parsons, E. C.
1921 Hopi Mothers and Children, Man, vol. 21, pp. 98-104
1925 A Pueblo Indian Journal, MAAA, vol. 32, pp. 1-123
1936-a Early Relations between Hopi and Keres, AA, n.s., vol. 38, pp. 554-60
1936-b The House-clan Complex of the Pueblos, Essays in Anthropology presented to A. L. Kroeber, Berkeley, pp. 229-31
1939 Pueblo Indian Religion, 2V, Chicago

Piaget, J.
1929 The Moral Judgment of the Child, New York

Rannells, E. W.
Drawings by Hopi Children (ms), Department of Education, University of Chicago

Russell, R. W. and Dennis W.
1939 Studies in Animism:
1. A Standardized Procedure for the Investigation of Animism, JGP, vol. 55, pp. 382-400

Simmons, L. W. (ed.)
1942 Sun Chief, New Haven

Stephen, A. M.
1936 Hopi Journal, ed. E. C. Parsons, CUCA, vol. 38

Superintendent, Hopi Agency
1944 Correspondence

Sutton, E. V.
Dwellers on the Mesa; A Saga of the Snake Dance People (ms)

Titiev, M.
1937 A Hopi Salt Expedition, AA, n.s., vol. 39, pp. 244-58
1938 Dates on Planting at the Hopi Indian Pueblo of Oraibi, MNMNA, vol. II, pp. 39-42
1943 Notes on Hopi Witchcraft, Papers of the Michigan Academy of Science, Arts and Letters, vol. 28, pp. 549-57
1944 Old Oraibi: A Study of the Hopi Indians of Third Mesa, Cambridge

United States Office of Indian Affairs
Annual Reports of the Commissioner of Indian Affairs
Annual Extension Division Reports, Hopi Agency
Indian Reorganization File, Hopi Agency

United States Soil Conservation Service
1937 Report, Hopi Agency

Voth, H. R.
1901 The Oraibi Powamu Ceremony, FMAS, vol. 3
1905 The Traditions of the Hopi, FMAS, vol. 8, pp. 1-319

Watson, J. B.
1942 Hopi Foodways, A Study in the Cultural, Nutritional and Environmental Factors in the Diet of the Hopi People (ms), United States Office of Indian Affairs

Watson, J. B. and Pijoan, M.
1943 A Casual Inquiry into Hopi Foodways (ms), United States Office of Indian Affairs

Whiting, A. F.
1939-1937 Hopi Indian Agriculture, MNMNA, vol. 8, pp. 51-53; vol. 10 pp. 13-16
1939 Ethnobotany of the Hopi, Bull. of the Museum of Northern Arizona, vol. 15, pp. 1-120
1942 Report on Hopi Arts and Crafts (ms), Arts and Crafts Board, United States Office of Indian Affairs

Whorf, B. L.
1936 The Punctual and Segmentative Aspects of Verbs in Hopi, Language, vol. 12, pp. 127-31
1940 Science and Linguistics, Technology Review, vol. 42, pp. 3-7
1941 The Relation of Habitual Thought and Behavior to Language, in Language, Culture and Personality, Essays in Memory of Edward Sapir, Menasha, pp. 75-94

KEY TO ABBREVIATIONS

AA	American Anthropologist
ARBAE	Annual Reports of the Bureau of American Ethnology
CUCA	Columbia University Contributions to Anthropology
FMAS	Field Museum of Natural History, Anthropological Series
JASP	Journal of Abnormal and Social Psychology
JGP	Journal of Genetic Psychology
MAAA	Memoirs of the American Anthropological Association
MNMNA	Museum Notes of the Museum of Northern Arizona
YUPA	Yale University Publications in Anthropology

3. TABLES

Table 1 will be found on page 96

TABLE II

Age	Hopi Boys (Percent)				Hopi Girls (Percent)			
	5-7	8-10	11-13	14-18	5-7	8-10	11-13	14-18
Good Health	7.1	14.3	13.3	7.7	7.1	14.3	26.7	28.0
Good Nutrition	28.6	33.3	27.7	30.8	35.7	66.7	70.0	80.0
Fair Nutrition	21.4	38.1	40.0	46.1	21.4	13.3	13.3	16.0
Poor Nutrition	50.0	28.6	33.3	23.1	42.8	23.8	16.7	4.0
Malnutrition	28.6	14.3	46.7	76.9	21.4	38.1	43.3	44.0
Vitamin B Deficiency	21.4	9.5	46.7	30.8		28.6	23.3	12.0
Vitamin C Deficiency		4.8		61.5			4.8	40.0
Vitamin D Deficiency	14.3				21.4	9.5	3.3	
Impaired Vision	21.4	33.3	20.0	7.7	42.8	52.4	43.3	56.0
Conjunctivitis	14.3	14.3	6.7		7.1	9.5	13.3	8.0
Trachoma		4.8		15.4	7.1	14.3	3.3	4.0
Irregular Teeth	57.1	47.6	26.7	30.8	50.0	47.6	26.7	24.0
Decayed Teeth	64.3	42.9	13.3		78.6	61.9	20.0	7.7
Enlarged Tonsils	35.7	42.9	33.3	15.4	50.0	19.0	16.7	16.0
Removed Tonsils	21.4	23.8	20.0	53.8	7.1	38.1	53.3	36.0
Swollen Lymph Glands	35.7	33.3	26.7		35.7	9.5	20.0	8.0
Suspicious Tuberculosis of the Lungs		23.8	13.3	30.8	7.1	19.0	23.3	24.0
Colds	28.6	14.3		7.7	21.4	4.8	6.7	12.0

Table III will be found on page 101

TABLE IV

In presenting this kind of table, which from our abundant documentary material offers only a few items for illustrative purposes, we wish to point out again that interpretative conclusions are not based on the quantitative results of one test alone, but on the correlation of all test results, together with qualitative and cultural considerations.

Happiness (Emotional Response test)

	Hopi	Midwest
Amusements (ceremonies and holidays excluded)	14.9%	16.5%
Individual achievement	2.5%	9.9%
Work	4.8%	2.3%

TABLE V

Best Thing (Emotional Response test)

	Hopi	Midwest
Personal achievement	18.0%	26.0%
Meeting social expectations	13.9%	4.0%

Some examples of answers obtained: "Maybe I might go on to school and become a teacher and that would be nice." "Go some place and work." "Raise good crops." "Help my mother."

TABLE VI

Sadness (Emotional Response test)

	Hopi	Midwest
Death	24.0%	25.7%
Sickness	24.6%	17.1%
Discipline	11.2%	2.6%
Aggression	13.2%	1.9%
Personal disappointments	5.7%	36.9%

TABLE VII

Worst Thing (Emotional Response test)

	Hopi	Midwest
Death	14.3%	9.0%
Sickness	32.3%	8.8%
Discipline	17.8%	2.5%
Aggression	3.9%	2.2%
Inadequacy	1.3%	18.3%
Bad Behavior	10.9%	4.6%

A few examples of answers: "Don't want my mother to die." "To die." "When I see the dentist I run away because he pull our teeth. If he catch me it would be the worst thing." "Be angry." "Get mad." "Fight." "If I not go to field."

TABLE VIII

Anger (Emotional Response test)

	Hopi	Midwest
Restraint on personal desires	10.5%	15.4%
Authority	12.1%	7.4%
Aggression	23.9%	21.3%
Inconsiderateness of others	13.2%	21.0%
Inadequacy	2.7%	5.4%

A few examples: "When my father did not let us go to the Fourth." "Cross at my old grandfather. I didn't want to press his shirt when he was going to a dance and the irons weren't hot and I said I wasn't going to press his shirt." "When they talk about me." "When some kids tease you all the time."

TABLE IX

Shame (Emotional Response test)

	Hopi	Midwest
Embarrassment	24.3%	1.6%
Bad Behavior	29.7%	48.0%
Discipline	8.0%	3.6%
Aggression	10.4%	2.1%
Failure and inadequacy	8.5%	21.3%

Table X

Fear (Emotional Response test)

	Hopi	Midwest
Supernatural	25.4%	1.0%
Subjective danger	20.3%	14.3%
Objective danger	18.6%	51.0%
Discipline	4.1%	2.1%
Aggression	7.3%	8.6%

We termed "subjective danger" that fear of the non-concrete which is based on the individual's own mind, his beliefs, imaginings, etc. Some examples of the fear of the supernatural: "One time some of the kachinas chased us at Second Mesa—chased us up on top. We got away." "When the kachina whip me in kiva. Last year I initiated."

Subjective danger: "I went to Old Oraibi in the winter time. We went to see a dance and walked through some graves."

Objective danger: "When I was six years old a goat scared me and I almost died."

TABLE XI

Moral Ideology test

	Hopi	Midwest
Amusements	1.6%	5.5%
Work	31.9%	10.0%
Thoughtfulness	12.0%	11.1%
Aggression	9.4%	2.6%
Stealing	13.9%	2.0%
Drinking	.2%	1.6%

TABLE XII

Immanent Justice

Piaget's Swiss children:

Age:	6	7-8	9-10	11-12
	86	73	54	39

Lerner's American children:

Age:	6-7	8-9	10-11
	82	70	31

Hopi children of our study:

Age:	6-8	9-11	12-18
Oraibi	77	88	90
First Mesa	43	79	84

Note: Figures indicate the percentages of children who showed a belief in immanent justice.

Animism

Hopi children of our study:

Age:	6-8	9-11	12-18
Oraibi	67	76	66
First Mesa	76	47	30

Note: Figures indicate the percentages of children who showed a belief in animism.

TABLE XIII

Persons involved (Emotional Response test)

	Happiness and Best Thing		Fear	
	Boys	Girls	Boys	Girls
Family	52.9%	53.1%	25.7%	19.3%
Father	31.4%	16.7%	8.6%	3.2%
Mother	4.3%	10.4%	5.7%	6.5%
Supernatural	18.6%	18.7%	8.6%	22.6%
Everybody	15.7%	14.5%	31.4%	32.2%
Agemates	4.3%	5.2%	14.3%	14.5%
Teacher		2.1%	2.9%	3.2%

Fear, Anger, Shame, Worst Thing

	Boys	Girls
Family	22.1%	33.3%
Father	7.2%	4.9%
Mother	6.6%	10.3%
Supernatural	3.0%	4.9%
Everybody	28.1%	30.9%
Agemates	29.3%	18.4%
Teacher	3.0%	1.7%

TABLE XIV

Persons involved (Moral Ideology test)

	Praisers		Blamers	
	Boys	Girls	Boys	Girls
Family	60.9%	58.8%	34.0%	48.5%
Father	16.2%	5.1%	10.5%	3.6%
Mother	21.4%	30.1%	8.9%	29.8%
Group (Hopi)	26.1%	24.0%	37.6%	31.3%
Teacher	4.8%	6.3%	6.8%	5.5%

4. INDEX

A

Abstract thinking, 80, 101, 131
Achievement, 68 ff., 71, 73 ff., 77, 84, 87,
Adoption, ceremonial, 36
Adjustment, 70 ff., 75, 81 ff., 85 ff., 88, 129
Adolescent, 61, 73, 76, 80, 118
Adulthood, 61 ff.
Affection, 76 ff., 79, 81, 121 ff.
After-birth, 51
Agave Society, 61
Agemates, 68, 69, 74, 121
Aggression, 74, 82, 84, 91, 104 ff., 106 ff.,
    110, 112 ff., 130
Agriculture, 17, 20
Alimony, 85
Allotment, 20, 29, 31, 136
Animals of death, 105
Animism, 106 ff., 141
Antelope, 24
Antelope Mesa, 16, 19, 27
Anxiety, 68 ff., 80 ff., 86, 110, 112 ff., 141
Archaeology, 20, 47
Archery, 57
Arizona, 18, 30, 75, 127
Arrows, 53, 57
Arthritis, 93
Arts and crafts, 24, 32, 54, 57, 59, 84, 117,
    135
Asch, Solomon, 58
Association, ceremonial, 34
Attachment to mother, 122
Attitudes, 90, 92, 101, 103, 121, 124
Authority, 48, 64, 70, 74, 106, 114, 118, 121
Automobiles, 32
Awatobi, 19, 27 ff., 48, 139

B

Bakabi, 16, 19, 30, 46
Balance, 44, 78, 98, 110, 112, 129
Balanced:
    adjustment, 128
    development, 86
    order, 101
    pattern, 129
    personality, 101, 109, 126, 129
    social structure, 128
    whole, 22
Balancing:
    factor, 79
    forces, 123
Baptist mission, 16, 29
Baseball, 58
Basketball, 57
Basket-carrier tabu, 60 ff., 62
Basketmaker III, 26, 27
Basketry, 22, 24, 26, 33, 34, 59
Bavelas Test, 92, 102, 121
Bean Dance, 42, 55, 60
Beans, 26, 55
Bear, 24
Bear Clan, 16, 38, 42, 46
Beatty, Willard, 14
Behavior, 50, 62, 65, 71, 77, 87 ff., 101 ff.,
    104, 106, 108
Birth, 50 ff., 53, 55, 85
Birth rate, 31
Birthdays, 102
Black Mesa, 16, 19, 22
Blankets, 24, 124

Bone:
    changes, 95
    formation, 98
Boundaries, 18 ff., 108, 116 ff., 129, 130
Bow, 24, 51, 54, 102
Buffalo Dance, 44, 55, 82
Burros, 27
Butterfly Dance, 44, 82

C

Calendar, 16, 42
Caloric intake, 94
Capacity:
    creative, 119
    imaginative, 115
    intellectual, 75 ff.
    for organization, 130 ff.
Carbohydrates, 94
Carding, 57, 62
Catholic mission, 27 ff.
Cattle, 24 ff., 27, 73, 75
Centripetal movement, 58, 132
Ceremonial, 17, 29, 32 ff., 44, 49, 55, 58,
    68 ff., 70 ff., 78, 83, 96, 116 ff., 130
    aunt, 45
    calendar, 42
    career, 55
    cycle, 42, 44, 129 ff.
    father, 45
    organization, 47 ff., 58, 64
    regalia, 35
    system, 36 ff., 40, 44, 61
Ceremonies, 42 ff., 50, 56, 59, 61, 64 ff., 73,
    83, 102, 105, 107, 114
Character structure, 67, 128
Chastity, 118
Chief:
    Crier, 43
    Priest 42 ff., 139
    Village, 30, 46, 48, 64
    War, 47
Chiefs' Talk, 46
Chieftainship, ceremonial, 64
Child training, 40, 55, 101, 103, 114
Childhood diseases, 97
Christian, 63 ff., 72, 74, 85 ff., 106
Christianity, 30, 33, 45, 85, 140
Christianized, 74, 126
Citizenship, 32
Clan, 35 ff., 37 ff., 43 ff., 50, 58, 60, 63, 68,
    75, 78, 82 ff., 101, 118, 137
    head, 34, 45, 64, 114
    Mother, 34, 45
    names, 35
Clan, Child of the, 50
Cleanliness training, 52
Clowns, 43, 82, 104
Coal mining, 22, 127, 135
Co-education, 58
Collier, John, 5, 14
Committee on Human Development, 5, 12 ff.
Configuration, 33, 36, 49, 131
Conflict, 72, 116, 118
Conscience, 65, 104 ff., 107, 116
Conservation:
    of game, 24
    of resources, 26
Constipation, 52
Constitution, Hopi, 31, 136 ff.
Continence, 43, 63

147